In letters, there is nothing like *Golden Handcuffs*, and nothing better.

—*Harry Mathews*

Golden Handcuffs is among the handful of truly important contemporary literary magazines. It fights the good fight for work that would otherwise want for a champion, and for this reason I read each issue with great enthusiasm.

—*Rick Moody*

WOW!

—*David Antin*

to Linda Gerrard, Walter Parsons,
Jack Hodge—Northwestern icons

GREAT WRITERS OCCUPY

Golden Handcuffs Review

Anthology of the New

edited by Lou Rowan

Golden Handcuffs Review Publications
Seattle, Washington

Golden Handcuffs Review Publications

We are a 501(c)(3) non-profit supported by readers, donors, foundations, subscribers, and tasteful advertisers.

Editor

Lou Rowan

Contributing Editors

David Antin
Andrea Augé
Brian Evenson
Bernard Hœpffner
Harry Mathews
Rick Moody
Toby Olson
Jerome Rothenberg

LAYOUT & PRINT MANAGEMENT BY PURE ENERGY PUBLISHING, SEATTLE

This anthology is our 20th book, *completing the* Volume I *series.*

Information about subscriptions, donations, advertising at:
www.goldenhandcuffsreview.com

Or write to: Editor, Golden Handcuffs Review Publications
1825 NE 58th Street
Seattle, WA 98105-2440

Contents

THE WORK

ART

POETRY

FICTION

ESSAY

AUTOBIOGRAPHY

THE ARTS OF TRANSLATION

RESPONSE

Preface
"unable"

Joseph Donahue

One page of the facsimile edition of the letters of Emily Dickinson shows a letter by Emily Dickinson, written to Sue Dickinson, completely blacked out. Even for one familiar with the back-story to such radical textual interventions in the Dickinson archive, the effect is dramatic; so, too, the sheer paradox of its presence.

So much effort was expended on this particular page to assure it could not be read, and yet the blacked out letter is there, as if the negation of the letter needed to be preserved, as if that was what also must live forever amid the poet's words. If the written page was the true medium of the poetry, I felt compelled to ask in the spirit of letters and their relation to the spirit, was this act of blacking out also a work of art?*

If so, then for all its darkness, how brilliantly rendered the censure is; the unsigned artist has chosen to obliterate not simply a letter of Dickinson's, but a letter that is also a poem, not simply any poem, but THE poem, it seemed to me then and now, in which, Dickinson's defining idiom arises, in the breach, still preserved here, that separates stanza 4 from stanza 5. Further, this poem is doubly notable, and so the censure doubly effective, since the discovery of

---

*See Martha Nell Smith's essay on "unable" (p. 282 below) for images of these "interventions."

the style is associated with the naming of the poets beloved, Sue, forever more. In this letter/poem, the beloved is explicitly linked to the order of the cosmos. She is a star chosen from amid many "from out the wide night's numbers," by the beginning poet. So, not just the poet but the intervening artist is cosmologically minded. If the poem calls the universe to be around the name of the beloved, the artist adds the act of negation as a part of the world making ambition of poetic utterance. And yet we do know the page, the poem, which the artist doesn't want us to know. As initiates into the Dickinson work we know both the poem and its deletion.

Who was this anonymous artist? The editor of the letters thinks its Austin, but there are others who take it to be Mabel. What we do know is that this artist has struck out not merely the name of the poet's beloved, but the whole poem, not just the whole poem but the entire tradition of what was once famously called love in the western world, which Dickinson inherits and passes on, from Petrarch and Dante to Sydney, to Shakespeare, to Tennyson, the Pre-Raphaelites and the Brownings, to Dickinson's contemporary, Mallarme. We may take this darkening as a simple obliteration, or we might, given the shrewd mastery of her materials that our artist demonstrates, be forgiven for entertaining the suggestion as hers that the entire love lyric tradition might carry within it such a blinding *coup de foudre.* As this tradition of poetry is innately theological in that it involves both gods coming to earth, and the divination of the beloved through the devotions and consecrations of the lover, in Dickinson's term, the idolater, we might well understand out artist to be saying that a part of Love's agony is precisely to experience within the act of desiring such a negation as the blackening out of the letter enacts.

In approaching this cancelled love letter, this abstraction in the place of a name, I have been especially influenced by the work of Barton St Levi, especially in regard to his reading of Dickinson's relation to the 19th century American Sentimental Love Religion, a religion which on the evidence of their letters can claim Mabel and Austin among its most enthusiastic practitioners. In this religion, which I seriously take to be such, writing is an act of deification. The beloved is raised up and set amid the stars. I tend to see this love religion as a part of the vast imaginative effort to make what Catherine Albanese has recently traced in her extraordinary work, *A Republic of Mind and Spirit: a Cultural History of American Metaphysical Religion.* Albanese work allows us to see more distinctly the cosmological implications of Dickinson's lyrics, and to see in what Dickinson wrote and how she wrote it the practice of her own combinatory spirituality. This spirituality draws upon a magical world-view, both from the culture coming to be around her, and from the English folk past. Indeed Robert Duncan in the recently posted recordings of his 1981 seminar on Dickinson is emphatic on this. For him, Dickinson is not just a fully self-conscious "pagan," she is an initiate of the hidden religion; her poems and letters are spells and hexes. And one of her predominate poetic form is the Valentine.

What I will read tonight is a suite of poems that are a part of a multi-volume ongoing poem called *Terra Lucida.* *Terra Lucida* touches in a number of places upon 19th century art, thought, and culture, most especially the Hudson River School and Luminist painters. With "unable" I presume to intuit Dickinson's world, to find there, in a phrase than has long been key to my understanding of poetics, "an adjoining zone." I begin with a response to Mabel Todd's Manichean gesture, and move out from the letter to the world both Dickinson's world and our own, and my own. My title comes from lines of Dickinson, lines she sent to Sue on the occasion of the death of Sue's sister:

> *Unable are the loved to die*
> *For love is immortality*
>
> *Nay*
> *Deity.*

unable

Black diagonal waves
across the sky of

the page,
in the

rush of, the
surge and rip of,

a censorious
wind, raising up

stipples of
negation

black slashes
tilting right

where were
words . . .

*

Must be
underneath,

an unfolding of
thought and feeling,

must be
a love letter

from deep within the
century before last,

underneath all the
xes, loops, squiggles and

horizontal
strikes

must be
an incantation

a lyric, calling into
being a paradisal

homestead
an Eden made

anew, of
summer fields,

birds, flowers,
an orchard,

the rising sun,
the wonder of love,

the gleam
of bees,

the miracle
of honey.

*

Must be
the scratch of

a skilled a hand
a hand that puts gold leaf

to ceramic cups, that
can paint flowers

on silk, so that
no syllable of the letter

sent does not
dissolve in the stir of

a rich black ink,
as if

bearing its own
obliterative

witness in
the church of

"hermetic memory"
where all is transformed

by the touch of
this inky spell,

even the avowed
rarities of the earth,

never to be
struck

from the
living record

of you, my preceptor,
the gems, pearls out of

the depths, the deep mines
in distant continents,

the jungles
and deserts the age

was itself
dazzled by,

opal twilight, the sun
at midpoint,

possibly
over Ecuador.

*

Must be
an anti-script of

pure lightlessness
pouring forth from the hand of

care, envy, rage, grief
in a letter, across

a letter perhaps
to no ultimate point beyond

assuring scholars
this letter was

in some sense
answered.

*

Must be
this page is the

creation, and the black of the
cancelling hand,

the flourish
of a Manichean.

     *

Must be
this annihilating

post-script is malevolent
tendency rising from the singing of

the name of the
beloved.

     *

Must be
an anti-logos

there before any
word, before even the paper itself

the blackness
before the page was,

soaking through from behind
pulled into visibility

with a
pen stroke.

*

So, before ink or pen or paper
came to be there was

an immense and
inaugural passion

Love's name,
cried out,

a star was chosen
from amid the many

in the night within which
birdsong gathers.

*

So, not anti-logos,
                    anti-valentine.

*

So, there will come further elisions.
As well as, now and then,

the scissoring
to shreds of the

name of the
beloved.

*

So, which of
                any of

our passions will
not be blotted out, which

love not swallowed in a storm of black,
a welling of final sky

a rescission
of all starlight

a redaction of
our every delight,

our celebrations will be our Calvary
as through our deepest

joy falls
a black dash,

a few loops,
a curlicue or two.

*

Nonetheless
who among you has not

written out the name of your secret love
at least once, so that it might, if only for a moment,

shine before your eyes
like an offering?

      *

Who,
in love

- and literate -
has not written out

if only on a scrap of
tallied

numbers, or in
the snow, or deep inside

a textbook
so to

almost touch,
almost enter

the rendering
of the sound of

the one
name

unuttered yet
sounded

in the hollows
of an overwhelming

devotion
it secretly

rises into being
and then sinks away,

in illegibility,
in scribble.

*

Cloud of ink
ink of unknowing.

*

So, feel a flow through the
fingertips of that which light

ultimately illumines,
the presence of the dark,

the shape of the beautiful loops of,
the dark beneath the dark

now flowing
over the white page

the valleys and peaks
Love's world coming to be

within the black fire and wind
blowing sideways the tips of

each lick of flame, tilting
toward where the wind

says say the name the
single vibration that

has been the object of
your long idolatry,

feel the name of your love
pass onto the page, into the page

drowning within the page
the wave of the name

pulled under
by the successive

cross-currents
of its own dissipation.

*

So, where the pen lifts from the page
and flies above it, then settling

hear Mabel Todd saying:
I am ready for more. I am

ready to do the work of death again
to be the scythe Longfellow sang of

and lay this field of love on its side
and plant the new black crop

that so abundantly
fills this field.

00

northwest passage

So, sister, could you risk the
glaciers, blocked channels, step past

the remnants of encampments
the frozen flags and

diaries in the ice,
that we might meet in

the yet to be claimed transit
blending one ocean and another

mixing twilight and dawn
eternity and immortality

grandeur and grief?
Sister, it may be the case

that my last note to you
may have scuttled in the

Arctic sea between
our two houses,

black depth rising
up through love's vessel.

Sister, if you love me,
could you set to sea yourself,

could you complete,
in secret, a crossing

so enticing to propose
and treacherous to pursue,

as Lord Franklin, much to
his dismay, found out?

Sister, I am here amid
the polar uproar

in less an outpost
than a long shadow

without my soul, my second,
my Sue, abandoned amid

the distances that make
all passage possible.

Sister, find me in
such a northwest

that opens itself to
no other expeditions.

00

Drink till the time be at hand
to say however softly

and in strictest solitude
love's name aloud,

employ such a fervor
that the name will be nothing

less than a place the mirror
of the place where you

both will meet,
an arctic waste

or a garden where the
a love, unweddable

in this life, waits in
immense joy

for the world
to end.

                    *

Drink till an apocalypse
comes each hour of the day

let the face of the Beloved
be the veil of an altar

love of a lover
love of God

impossible proximity
delirious distance

a Persian passion
has entered Amherst

Saddi approaches
Hafiz is here

voice of the beloved
voice of the peerless one

peerless one the
taverner's daughter.

*

Drink till you return from afar.
But were you to see me

here in the church
during services,

among the others
even you could not doubt

the orthodoxy
of my belief.

Within me, however,
all is different.

I pray only to you,
my absent beloved.

My idolatrous heart
is a shrine to you.

Heretical passion
enflames me.

*

Drink till the turbans are all unbound
Drink till the house like the world turns round

*

Drink till a sip will be sufficient.
Drink till the whisper of a sip

will be too much, should one
be born into being with eyes

the color of sherry
in the glass

after the
guests depart.

00

So, a concession was made to the pagan world
hidden within the legend of the saint so that in

let us say even a Catholic schoolroom in New England
in the 1960s among the paper flurry might be sent secret,

unsigned valentines, the venerations of undisclosed
devotees, and the recipients awaiting a relation

which may never arrive, a love far more fabulous
than any forthright request for surrender of self.

To be loved by one of whom one is ignorant, a guess is
possible but fraught, claiming to know could be

humiliating, or at least humbling and exalting, better
to simply be one at whose feet figurative flowers are set,

and feel kissed, if only from an immense distance,
to know only that the unknown itself has chosen you,

owns you, made you a slave, the sign of which is
an envelope that has found its way to you, slipped

into your pack, your pocket, your desk, your lunch.
In the depths of Christianity another god was at work.

I love you greater than Jesus loved men might be
a way to put it, fold it, send it in a cream-colored

or deep red envelope, heart of flower, the cry be mine,
be adored, so might first be felt the ache of being ached for,

before hand was ever held, before the first heat of
a slow dance at a mixer, nuns pulling the too

passionate apart, should such a secret valentine arrive,
a message from spring at the onset of Lent in which

an apparently less dire agony announces itself.
In some small way you might feel invisible arms

around you, feel grasped by a naked and minor deity,
feel an invisible arm slip itself around you and hold you,

as if you were cut from green marble, as if you were
placed on a mantle, a gift from a wedding of which

the bride remarks: "Some ice-cream, and it was over."
Of which the groom says later, and to his mistress,

he had felt he was going to his execution. And so,
in the palace of Amherst, Christianity fell out of fashion.

The pagan world returned, night after night,
throughout all seasons, Eros found Psyche.

00

my Sue

So that no delight
in writing, in reading,

could ever exceed that which
came from the writing and reading of

our love-notes, those left
so furtively, and so retrieved,

from under a loose brick
in the long stair up

to the front door while
hoping the only one

to catch me in my
devotion would be Sue,

up there, in the white
wave of the curtains;

her notes only
read around the

corner, behind
a tree, facing away

from the street, in
an ecstasy; all those

words, folded,
unfolded, all

our writing,
our wooing . . .

00

a song

Lips, at a cup
bee amid my petals

(I can't sip till
you've tasted first)

sweetness
is near, is near

hover without
touching

lips to the
infinite

lips, at a cup,
bee amid my petals

hover without
touching

(I can't sip till
you've tasted first)

is near but
not yet

lips to the
infinite

sweetness,
lips, at a cup

00

Such would be the long death throes
of the transcendental

the arrow of the
transcendental

is lodged in my heart.
Duncan says later

we'll get to the agony
but the seminar recordings

never return to it,
that agony,

yet it seems to be
greater than that of

Christ or Eros,
or at least

to precede theirs,
to be the source of theirs,

and of all true song
as Dickinson

makes so clear.
The arrow of the

transcendental
hurts me all the time.

The arrow cuts deep.
I don't understand

this agony
which deepens

with each new hope
of elucidation.

       *

          song

Such would be to have
the heart of the sun

the heart of a daisy
the heart of a woman

the heart of a gun
such would be to have

the heart of a woman
the heart of a daisy

the heart of a woman
such would be to have

the heart of the sun
the heart of the sun

       *

Such would be
but my tutor is dead

as well, years gone, now
only a noble ghost.

He went to the garage
and turned on his car

and sat inside it
and breathed.

Often he came
to me in dreams,

but not for a while now,
not for many years.

My tutor, who
gave me your

lexicon, the garden,
the orchard, the hills,

the infinite, where
amber turns to

violet, gold
to opal.

                *

There was a while when
a camera could bring back the dead

There was a while when a new pigment
added to oil paints could make the beauties of

the world more ravishing
made paradise appear on earth

as clouds, mountains, and streams
as the light that fell on all

there was a while when science
confirmed the flights of the soul across

oceans and continents
to gardens on other planets

and received instruction
in a new morality

there was a while
when phantasms of the spirit

appeared in a far away twilight
at the exact moment of death

dying in India, appearing on a porch
amid blue shadows in England

there was a while
when theologies arose

from romance novels, when
illicit desire was the sign of election

there was a while when
perfection was possible and

higher orders of being emerged
there was a while when

the dead were happy
and puzzled by our grief

there was a while
when a moment of terror

might bring forth an heretofore
entirely hidden personality

there was a while
when anomalies were

evidence and gathered up
from all over the earth; accounts of

visitations, and sightings
and powerful dreams

were studied, and held to be
revelatory of what is.

*

There was a while
when men and women

could be divine be
alive, be loved, through

love be divine, be worshipped;
by a window, a hedge, a gate

a back road, a carriage,
a staircase, a study,

at twilight, these
could be the stations

of an absolute devotion.
And so, for example,

Mabel Todd might be
a holy emanation, might be

Beatrice and Layla
might be Christ; and Sue

might be lifted up
and placed in the night sky

might be Stella, Astella,
chosen, studied, addressed

be a light in the night or not
a star hidden in a pure black sky

a boat of light in the inundating dark
worshipped, cursed,

proclaimed a star yet
blotted from the sky

and the proclamation
itself also blotted

words are hiding in the dark
are the presence of light in the dark

Sue the overwhelming dark
that alerts us to the barest light

the words that bring the star to be
by a poet who seems at times almost Roman

in a world where citizens
might become gods

a Mediterranean world
a north African world of

stations and shrines
idolaters and idols

where a beloved might be told
slay me and my soul

shall rise to paradise
still thine.

00

Come back, Jesus,
and set a man

against his father,
a daughter against her

mother, and even a daughter-in-law
against her mother-in-law . . .

Come back to river valleys,
to farmland and towns

in New England
and New York

decade after decade.
Come back Jesus and make

enemies within
households

sister against a sister
brother against a sister

Come back Jesus, just to set
a bachelor against his fiancé,

come to colleges
amid religious

revivals so that
at an assembly

at a call to the saved
some will stand

and some
will not.

     *

The Jesus
Christ you

love remarks he
does not know me . . .

     *

Come back Jesus, start an argument
about where and when

heaven is, decade after
decade, and over centuries,

let each soul at some point
in the disputation chose

if heaven is to die
or is to be born.

Decade after decade
within each generation

let the argument end
and start again

        (if only so one friend
        might write another:

We differ often lately,
And this must be the last.)

    *

Jesus, let each believe
differently, so that

each will die differently;
let deathbed décor be

by turns lavish or spare,
the final horror ringed

by an unpredictable
mix of accouterments.

    *

Jesus, in the emerging ideology of style
as the world of commerce

emerges from that
of the churches

let last words be
either revelatory

or irrelevant, either
a spellbinding,

heaven-disclosing
dénouement, or

psychologism, sedation,
a pill, a sip, a shot, a dose.

*

Jesus, let the last
gasp take on a new timbre

whether in the mouth of the dying
or in the ears of those there

in keeping with whatever
each believes

breathy, dry, wet,
raw or withered

one generation to the next,
or even among members of the

same generation
ringing the bedside

or when children hear
their parents die

or when parents have
the misfortune to

live to see
a child die.

00

to Emily Dickinson

Last words, secret words,
the last words said to me,

bitter words, maternal, heard
by me alone, heard, never

written out, never told,
preceptor, you might be

the one at last to savor
their desolation.

00

Of all the agonies left
unaddressed by Duncan of

surpassing interest
would be the fate of

Emily Dickinson
in the afterlife,

called, I presume,
to see Love's

name
lacerated.

*

See, from deep within
an adjoining zone

a living hand
rewriting her lines

until they would seem
in their very disappearance

to be all beauty, hauled off,
now, and buried

under black
shrubs.

*

What moved this
intervening

nub cannot be spite,
hate, envy as these are earthly

motives
and this occulting

was a heavenly gift,
this seeming rescission

of all passion in the name of
eternity, a name struck

from the roles of the
once real world.

*

Duncan may have speculated
about an intimacy in the beyond

face to face, amid angels.
But first, for her, there is

a consummate hopelessness,
dark spilling ink across the light.

She must see the star
she chose go dark.

*

unable are
the loved to die . . .

    *

       ditto copies

Sweet air of
paper and ink and

alcohol, as if
a blossom

came to
rest on each desk

so would begin
a lifetime of the love of

paper and ink
and alcohol,

and light, and shade,
and of course words

a hint of all that
is to come

but amid such multi-
part intoxication

how can we deduce
what our fate will be

from nothing more that
a sheet fresh from

a ditto machine, also
known as, though

we did not know this then
a "spirit replicator"

summoning forth
your words

in lavender and alcohol
words wet as a fresh pearl

that first, truest
drunkenness

we were all
bees hovering

above purple blossoms
dew-glazed field

wobbling in
wonderment as

from your earlier moment in
the history of print technology,

before wax coated pages
and spinning drums

honeyed fumes
twilight colored letters

your words came to you, came to be,
and in mimetic magic

as I read I became an "I"
that had read your words

at that instant
in autumn,

in New England,
deep violet words

rising in waves from the page
felt then the truth about light and

shade and the future and the
falling sun, the first of it,

first scent of
that flower of

poetry, handed out to each
in a small classroom

waft of a word never
known before, what

did it mean,
Presentiment?

*

*unable are
the loved to die . . .*

*

The black of this ink
is the black of daylight

during which a zealous
astronomer might dream of

photographing the moon
turned utterly black

might gather his best lenses
and travel to California

or Texas, or Japan
pack his plates

and spend weeks
heading towards the

sighting that would make his name,
lift it, as it were, to the stars,

obliterated though they be
at the moment of

totality, that might establish
for him, on earth, and among

the scientists of his day.
a place of eminence

The stream of black his
wife spreads across the page

is what the death of the sun should be,
the corona given off by

the rays of original script
as if these whorls were a ritual

assuring the cloudlessness
of the day which fills

for several minutes
in 1878, 1887, 1886, 1900,

1905, 1914, 1918, 1919, in
Tripoli, Russia, Florida, and Brazil

with all the famously
terrifying metaphysical

silences of the night sky
as if the light of the earth

must be extinguished
as well, so to join

the sun and moon
in lightlessness save for

and this astrological darkness
must begin with a shadow of a hand

falling across a love letter,
all their coquetry and loss

and wit and twists of thought
all verbal instances of the

reign of Venus on earth;
whose transit back into the sun

is complete, is photographed,
was photographed, by

David Todd
in 1882

and now the sun
is filled with ink.

00

Let the sky of
the page be full of

haloes and waves
shadow bands, rose-

colored prominences
red eruptions and

for a moment
or two, a corona.

00

song for little Gib

unable they that
love to die

the garden is Eden
    the garden is grief

unable they that
love to die

unable they that
love to die

the garden is Eden
    the garden is grief

Welling, Replenishing

Richard Berengarten

---

water *over wood*

Consultation of the diagrams

> *Consultation*
> *of the diagrams*
> *is helpful*
>
> *in the construction*
> *of hypotheses, buildings*
> *and voyages,*
>
> *in the precise*
> *locating of wells, mines,*
> *bridges, towers, mirrors,*
>
> *in alleviating*
> *insomnia and fears*
> *of death,*
>
> *in the correct*
> *turning of antennae*
> *towards origins*
>
> *and in all forms of*
> *measurement and modes*
> *of harmonising.*

---

self-replenishing *inexhaustible*

1. who drinks from an old well?

Our well has dried
up. Not even birds
circle or settle here.

Our clerks have been
corrupted by one regime
after another. Even

lawyers and judges
have sold out. Kept in
pay of ministers

and landlords, they
collude in repression
and persecution.

Young and old alike
abandon houses, pack
bags, emigrate. Can

we find a dowser
with forked hazel
or willow branch?

---

buckets come up empty   *or half full of sediment*

2. Sometimes they answer

Sometimes they answer
even though I've asked
no question.

Sometimes they say
nothing, and appear to
smile and look away.

Or else they stare, like
the dead, through me,
towards infallible sky

as quietly they pick
out question behind
question, before even

any thought lurking under
images and their nuances
or timbres has arisen

let alone right words
to articulate thought have
discovered me and opened.

catching   *fish*

3. From underground streams

We clambered down ladders
and ropes. Workmates at the
top let down shovels, sieves,

buckets, poles, mallets.
We dredged up a mountain
of mud and waste fallen

in and mulched down
there over years. Hauled out
rich stinking vegetable stuff

and rotten wood. Separated
it from clay to fertilise fields.
Hammered in new

stepping brackets and
handles as we relined walls.
Deepened and widened

entire cavity to hold more
water pooled from underground
streams than ever before.

dredging   _the well_

4. *I Ching*

Fifty years my
friend, companion
and spirit-guide

always trustworthy,
never diffident
never irrelevant

solid yet flowing
firm yet yielding
radiating images

self-replenishing
inexhaustible
fathomless

ever-fresh well –
in plumbing you
I soar

feet still
grounded rooted
in *this here now.*

5. I lower my question

I lower my
question on a rope
of thought.

I draw up
water-wisdom. It
flows everywhere.

I drink from a fund
of deep light. Could
wine be sweeter?

If its taste is bitter
then I swallow it. Its
bitterness is me.

Is it sweet? Then
I'm thankful – but
keep aloof from

drugs coiled in
sweetness. These ways
I come and go.

6. Well, inexhaustible

Self-replenishing
and inexhaustible
well, generous

secret, open face
of Underworld, with
rounded mouth

and level gaze –
polished mirror and
porthole of night,

silvery cord
and vertical pipe
invisibly joining

heaven and earth's
skin and core,
beneath these eyes

in your reflection
on the sky's forehead –
a star.

Plot
and Five *from* Graphic Novella: Collage and Gloss*

🌿

Rachel Blau DuPlessis

Plot

Is time crystallized inside things? If one could enter things again and find it and re-saturate? It seems against the laws of physics. But then why collect--that rock, that shell to decorate your house?

At least water flows through these pipes and is not cut off by armies. Not betrayed by industry and smart-mouthed by legalese.

The mourning doves sit and fluff out, adjusting themselves comfortably under our outside table, a place that protects them from hawks.

A friend said to a tourist, trying to wise her up, "You know Americans are not that well liked here right now." She wrote him later in an email: "I hope you are dealing with your anger."

And, by the way, "heavenly hurt" does not mean it is a "more soothing" hurt than that which is achieved on earth.

Well, the student said, it was just an educative guess.

---

* "Collage and Gloss" begins on the next page.

Five *from* **Graphic Novella: Collage and Gloss**

~~Every assumption is false. Every word is hand-wringing. Apologies,~~
~~minoritizing stances, helpful helplessness, insistence on convention,~~
~~the novel is some apogee, one wants a mirror, popularity, "I have a~~
~~story, tell my story," June wanted George to write a best seller, like~~
~~Mailer, and these are readable, can poetry be "read"? Can poetry~~
~~"say the same"? "SEY" the same?~~

Or

"sey" is another action? Writing into unknowable
design, a set of probes and pulls on a difficult terrain.

Look, we know there's material. Too much of it. Material--the
random pulsing substances of being, feeling, living, the oddities,
outrage and sadness--"she" clearly already had her regrets. Passes
the responsibility over to "you." "You" can do it; "she" can't. She has
already mourned her own inadequacy. Is resigned. But she does want
to help. The little units may be too neatened and squared. Black
blocks only. Yet empathize, for the yearning is patent.

But for what?
The word used is "a novel." This contains the word "new" but only
etymologically. Something formed, something fashion-able (it can
be made, the tools can still be found- write down my story!). And-
-inevitably--fantasies of the fashionable (it can succeed in the terms
we know: reviews, interviews, yr. photo here, success, arty clothes, a
starry nova). She (like many) seems to wobble between these points.
Does she want the knowledge of telling? or does she want renown for
the tale?

Refuse! To get something from all this, it all must be overturned and
picked through differently. The only "convention" (conversation?)
(invention?), the only foreseeable "genre" (juncture?) (generalization?)
will be loose ends. You are the amateur, tinkering, but with a wicked
connoisseurship. Unsecured mess is a necessary outcome. This
statement is not "the" story, "the" plot, or any such thing. This is not
telling, it is talus, it is tailings. This is random; this is splay and the
interstitial; this is scrubland, scatter and swerve. This is refuse.

\#
She noticed, "Oh, you wrote that down."

She said "you should."

Said "if only I could write."

Said "Just listen to this, you'll have plenty of material

if you ever want to write a novel."

The studio is empty.

The watch ticks. It dials itself up. It seems to have cost a lot.

The screen shot gives us 10:10. The word "alphabet" is visible.
Then there are more words. What happened to the specific letters?
Are words meant to stand for letters? Well, they can't. There aren't
enough. P and S repeat too much. Plus E occurs several times. N, L
and W do also. Cardinal points, with a few extras? Something is
drastically incomplete, ill-thought out.

Perhaps these words, the list you see, might be only substitute words,
not the necessary words. Screen words, concealments. Perhaps they
are "studio words," before the clearing and the emptiness of which
we dream (we think we dream). Perhaps they are shadows saying-
-nothing is ever fully empty. There is always "nakedness"; there is
"portal" mixed with "partial." There is "evidence"--it's that detective
story yet again.

There is always a before. No space is clear. The point is to live inside
of saturation. Yet to filter for priorities. Even origins have agendas.
This means you and this means yours.

Every act is an act in the poetics of yearning.

ALPHABET

nothing

letter

poetry

space

phoneme

WORD

phrase

sentence

whatever

teller

error

paper

time

erasure

evidence

Even origins have agendas.

Remove from the studio
all earlier works.
Result:
an empty studio.

partial or portal

smart-ass

nakedness

dream

title

bumps

lenses

wrinkles

Can we represent what is actually happening? happening to the
world at large? happening to us? Can we even imagine it? Look at
the scale.

language is a secret maze we can barely fathom
nor that it contains an infinitude
of openings and potential passages
along an irregular line
of understanding.
So I'm writing on a light filled screen
from moments of darkening, making pixels
of flickering dark,
(and the screen is connected!
it sends me "updates"--do I
"want" them?)
and all this smudges the question of

"including history."
A poem cannot "include" this
(like a pick and choose),
it is flooded out already and drags itself to shore
swamped
sometimes
sickened

Both the labor that produces the object
and the waste from its production and consumption
are suppressed

except in the nausea of the drowning discard.

In the mean time, I admired her aphorisms.

"They just sent down the administrative flavor of the month."

"If you are not in the system, we can't help until you are."

For example.
But I couldn't believe that I was not already in the system.

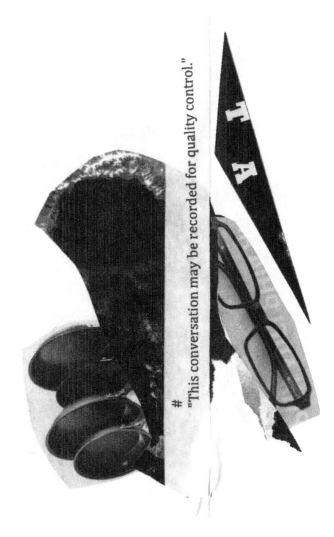

"This conversation may be recorded for quality control."

More plots. They just bubble up, unstoppable.

Well, accept that plethora. You cannot reject these stories totally-
-they will return with a vengeance, the well-known operatic
vengeance of the spurned lover. They will return because the
patterns are lurking, because they are palpable, because they are
palatable, satisfying, because we are trained by years of tales and
turns, precisely to respond to these plots. How to break into this
circle of feelings? Not by fiat, not by force. Is it by erosion? Slight
shifts? Variation? Confrontation? Encirclement? Examination?
Extension? Selective erasure? Doubling? Substitute pleasures? At
least by these. Do you tap into the ethos, the "in the air" or does
the ethos tap into you. Which comes first, the artist or the chicken.
Therefore let the plots, the characters, the myths happen and wander
here and there, among all these looser, less pinned-down visitants.
Yes, include the revenants and the rejects. Invite them, gather them,
let them talk and drink, and then rattle them like dice. You are not
going to be limited to only one throw, one chance, one number (was
it 707 after all?). But you won't get an infinite number, either.

Anyway, we were also noticing plots--as cover-ups, secrecy, as the
weird narratives of political pay-off and economic complicity, the
creation and maintenance of heavy inequality by its tear-jerking
Cinderella stories of make-over and random elevation (the lottery,
perhaps)--we need to understand all the cover-story narratives so we
can identify and resist all this.

A field of thorn bushes, could get stuck on any one.
Just let me get in here, or out of here, or through and through
without too many scratches.

#
the the. The the. The The. The THE
description.
poignant stories.
scene setting.
repression.

#
Paragraph one, a few people, bushes, scrap land
maybe they are hunters. Lovers.
Maybe just stepped from the car.
Odd place.
Paragraph two, more brush, a hill, someone skids
down a mood tersely.
Badly met--discontent. Boredom.
An old story, strike a match
for cigarette.

Paragraph three, premonitory
abruptness and confusion.
Some shock. Gasp? Hushed.
Loud is repressed.
A rustle in the underbrush?
something broken? tripping over--
what's that?
what just happened?

Talk about the matrix--what can be collected and examined, what can generate open spaces, what force is allowing, and how to refuse to censor this odd, odd business when it turns even odder.

Why attempt a labyrinth? So sealed, so frightening, so centered on the fraught and monstrous center, and then on the anxious escape. Isn't a random journey better? Well, at least it's un-centered. If the poem is always its poetics, what have we here? An undriven, loopy *dérive*? A casting around for alternatives? A net with rips? A dewy web wasted by noon?

Is my skein of yarn long enough to reach ... what? The question is off. For if there is no labyrinth, there is no declared secret. Nothing lurking. (No discovery?) And there is no declared path. No need for extra thread to mark the way. Just hold a odd-sized piece of string, not very long. Like the divining rod for water, but softer.

It says simply try "sorts" --a sortilege, a reading of lots, of plots as they fall. That solves the question of family narratives, of the ambivalent "mother," of gothic rooms with scintillations of concealment.

Most people writing journal-like material eventually get allegorical. I really mean this as flatness. A folder almost without binding. You could make your own pages. Here's your blank name tag. But don't feel obliged. Just loop in and out wherever you want with your own soft piece of string.

Tuesday: Me," etc. Funny. Very. But he missed the
Then "Tuesday: Tuesday."
It should be "Monday: Monday."
rary diary began "Monday. Me;

#
The
ba

#
This is
a whi
the pe
be n
bu al
ar o
Spea

#
Caught flat within the narrow slot of
attempting a labyrinth
cannot answer the question
how crossing into language
sometimes makes
distances uncrossable,
portals, stopped; ideas, cement.

#
Story is a mother of Sorts
a punning on choices.
Or types arranged by kind.

Story is a mother out of Sorts
restless and wishing
that even the dust were different.
Fed up with the parasites
she nourishes
and has nourished.

is a strip of plas
n the ground h
block of sidewalk curb
the asphalt road

tic

ke a blue jay

2 Poems

❦

Jesse Glass

Apophenia Song

   Visual problem, casanova's trip
of "otherness"
      has performed
      an illegal operation
        (Diana
        Labia)
   Visual problem, casanova's trip
of "otherness"
      Reduced to ashes
      Suspended from 14 chains
      Over a flower bed
PHOTOGRAPH IT. FAX IT.

NOW OX STEPS IN THIS CIRCLE,
   Same circle twice
NOW OX STEPS IN THIS CIRCLE,
   Same circle twice.

I am a friend of the dead
      Whether they like it or not.
            Come join them for
A midsummer barbeque:
Talk all day about fire
        w/out burning
              yr. mouth.
To tear spiritual flesh
      Strike a gong, or
          Better yet—
slide brass cymbals together.

     Visual problem, casanova's trip
of "otherness"
    Viz:

         Frankfurt bell
         Smashed in fall
         A lizard climbed
         A sunlit wall

         Giant crucified
         Head down
         In a block of salt
         Sez:

         Madame I'm adam
         Madame I'm adam
         Madame I'm adam

         It's the future
         One line
         At a time

   & will be shut down.

Écorché

They dragged me up from my crouch with block & tackle
& hook through socket & they went away beyond the plains; feet
took them over the rolling hills the King grinning crazy among
them wrapped in a bedsheet/ rolled him in a wheeled basket to the
mountaintops where they made him weep & suck his thumb & shit in
a handkerchief. They asked me to be his monument and I said Why,
yes.

They taught me to sing sans lips tongue jowls: a hollow and
a brow ridge left finally of me. They gutted me, dears, & left me
behind with pendulum arms & rocking jaw attempting to explain
to the sky why the earth is fat with ruined walls and eternal day.
Naked as a harpsichord, the wind thridding my wires, my muscles
sag like shucked mollusks weeping brine on the all-absorbing dust. I
steal the resonances of stone and struck steel while tethered to this
spot.

How long will I stand here? Until I can lift one arm of my
own volition, or levitate a robin's egg, or grow a leather orchid in my
chest, & the King returns from the strappado, thumbscrews loosened,
broken bones reset, marrow repacked through the soles of his
trotters. Then I'll caper with tabor & harp in long dance & round
dance move deosil then widdershins before any jukebox you choose
& step on flayed heels beyond humiliation beyond silence & an Old
Man will draw me, and a Young Man will engrave all the Old Man's
mistakes, and a Woman will drag paper & brayer down the copper
plates & pass my image along the soup lines the unemployment
compensation lines the free clinic disposable syringe lines. Then the
people will take one look at me with their tired doped and dazed
eyes, and they'll add 0 to 0 with a ground-down purple pencil find
that it makes 0 and crumble me up and say So What and throw me
away, because the Universe is very large & we are very very small,
say the King's men through digital teeth.

For, I know THE PEOPLE are the collective SKIN I lack,
the multitudinous TONGUE that was bitten away by kestrels,
the GLANDS of Springtime, the ENDOCRINE CAPSULES
I donated to the destitute, the many EYES that once filled my skull with light.
The PEOPLE can make STONES OVULATE if they concentrate and set
THE ASTROLABE OF STATE on its proper axes if they stop to consider

how strong they really are. The PEOPLE with arms in synchronous motion
can stack dust into UNAGING MONUMENTS OF INTELLECT, comfort the lonely,
bring tears to the eyes of painted Madonnas. And the PEOPLE will welcome
the return of the King once he has been modified to their specifications. Yes
when the King returns, supported by his generals, he'll force his hand down
my throat and pluck the leather orchid growing there. Then he'll hold it
above his head to the PEOPLE'S great applause, aim it at the sun as they cheer,
while I dance so subtly in his honor it will appear that I am merely dead.

Tracks

(for Margo Lockwood)

Fanny Howe

1.

Mixed in sunset colors, the snow
Seen closer is a pox of pebbles.
And that wind across the brick
Spun the bird's nest over
Until it became a tunnel
Of straw and dangling string.

2.

Why did the names of seasons depress me that year?
It was near the end but not there
So I could have been a lot happier if I had not said "summer"
When I was talking to a friend.
If I were deaf, the flowers would tremble
And the sky would laugh by opening its feathers
Onto the blue of Massachusetts Bay.
It smiled at me for being clever but I couldn't return the favor

I was so stricken at the word summer.
I should go to Quincy and return to
A place not a season.
Increasingly names are saddening.

3.

Back Bay Station is waiting for you to return.
Two terrible times: one without a kiss of greeting
And one with her running to give you the bad news.
The bad news of failure and public humiliation.
Back Bay Station is waiting for you to turn and give the blessing
Now all trace is gone.

4.

I don't know where everyone went.
We were at an oblong table
Ending with poppy seed cake
And sweet German wine.
It was fifty years after the extermination
And we were laughing
and speaking of life-spans .
What a perfect sight but none of the actual
Places remain.
I did feel there was always someone else
Everywhere I went, even
On nights unparalleled.

Third Circle

(from *Excess - The Factory*)

❦

Leslie Kaplan

(translated by Julie Carr and Jennifer Pap)

You stand at the assembly line, it's an assembly line for crackers.
The workshop is next to the oven, it is very hot. You pick up a row
of crackers, you place them in a bag. The line moves on. You fill the
bag. Your fingers are raw from the grain.

The line moves on. The bags are foiled paper. The crackers are very
hard.

In the courtyard, before you come in, you already smell the flour.
When you are in the courtyard, you're not in the workshop.

There's a machine to close the bags.

⊖

You are standing at the line of crackers.
Workshop next to the oven, it is very hot.
The crackers go by quickly.
You have your head in a scarf.

From the line you see a corner with piled up boards and sheet metal. You look and look. Boards and sheet metal and the three lines of the corner. There are also rags.

Under the boards and sheet metal there is cement. The boards and sheet metal go in all directions.

The rags are weak.

The boards are thicker than the sheet metal.
Sheet metal, smooth. The little lines go in all directions.
The cement is on the ground.
There is oil on the rags.

Infinity is here. You look.
You are on a stool, above the ground, tense.
The assembly line is a little high.

All around, columns of air. Little waves curving.
Endlessly space folds and unfolds.
You are not supported, there is nothing between the lines.

The space folds open. Walls and partitions, corners, cement. Sheet metal, understand.
Soft and fat. Boards and wood.
Cement and screws. The cement is on the ground.
The little lines go in all directions.
You don't know, you can't know.

You go outside, in the café music is playing.
Images stand out.

You go shopping. The grocery store, it's all the same.

⊖

Upstairs, the room waits.

You go there. In a sense, the room is always too big.

You eat without hunger. Where is the taste?
You bite the teeth of the other.

You look at a fingernail, an elbow, an eye.
You look and look.

You are immobile. You circulate between walls of flesh, little blood-
rivers. The body works and falls. You go nowhere, pleasure is hard,
transparent.

You sleep in a nightmare. You slip from room to dream, the
substance is the same.

The room is a room. You pay the rent.
You live, you die, each instant.

⊖

The suburb, it's all the same. Space, space kills.

You stand at the bus stop. You wait for the bus. Sky and telephone
poles all around. The sky is full of wires.

The sky is immense. There are these wires. You wait for the bus.
The road is there.

The buildings are erected in the middle of fields. The bus stops in
front of some buildings, it doesn't stop in front of others.

At the café, music. It's nothing.

You stand at the bus stop, you look at the buildings, over there.
You think of the alleys between buildings.

The alleys are open.

Here and now, there and elsewhere, you wait for the bus. The stop is by the café. You smell the dust. The sky is very blue. The air floats. All these wires.

Road is there.

You are outside. You got off the train, you wait for the bus. The buildings come and go. The air breathes, breathes in and out. Doors open, doors open everywhere, you pass, you pass.

from N27 and N30

❦

Hank Lazer

4/1/14

i have written a wisdom book ;
lost in a larger book ;
hidden from myself if i
would find it i
must do as you
would do i must
read it again ;
listen to what it
is saying ; then
shall we
extract it
or simply let it
remain hidden

that place before name where being

consciousness in

share

of for

the singular the invisibly bends

8/28/14

mourning
dove balancing
& bobbing
in the trapeze
platform
bird
feeder
early morning
after
meditation
the bird
& its motions
this is
the complete
story
of a mind
at work
or a mind
at play
cracking
open
the necessary
sun
flower
seeds

light &
shadow
from the pine
tree.
a trace
of incense
what can
be
said
of the simultaneity
of being
hummingbird
coming to
the white
crepe
myrtle
blossom
beside
my study
window
what do

you
mean by
"real
time"?
is it
the male
cardinal
displacing
the mourning
dove
at the
bird
feeder?

"the thing can never be separated from someone who perceives it; nor can it ever actually be in itself because its articulations are the very ones of our existence, and because it is posited at the end of a gaze or at the conclusion of a sensory exploration that invests it with humanity. To this extent, every perception is a communication or a communion ... the achievement by us of an alien intention or inversely the accomplishment ... beyond our perceptual powers and so of ... the synchronizing ... of things." 1334 7

mourning

dove balancing

& bobbing

in the trapeze

platform

bird

feeder

early morning

after

meditation

the bird

& its motions

this is

the complete

story

of a mind

at work

or a mind

at play

cracking

open

the necessary

sun

flower

seeds

light &

shadow

from the pine

tree

a trace

of incense

what can

be

said

of the simultaneity

of being

hummingbird

coming to

  the white

crepe

myrtle

blossom

beside

my study

window

what do

you

mean by

"real

time"?

is it

the male

cardinal

displacing

the mourning

dove

at the

bird

feeder?

"The thing can never be
separated from someone
who perceives it; nor
can it ever actually be
in itself because its
articulations are the very
ones of our existence,
and because it is posited
at the end of a gaze
or at the conclusion of
a sensory exploration
that invests it with
humanity. To this
extent, every perception
is a communication or a
communion, the taking
up or the achievement
by us of an alien
intention or inversely the
accomplishment beyond
our perceptual powers
and as a coupling of
our body with things."
<334>

(Merleau-Ponty,
Phenomenology of
Perception)

8/29/14

as parents
are a perpetual
voice-over
whether living
or dead
i could not
draw you
a picture
of time
or
for that matter
of being
as my mother
whose own
mother
is invisible
still speaks
in a way
designed
to justify
to her mother
what she
does
& especially
what she
wants
the picture
of being

is only present
in these
words
if you
say them
but it all
boils down
to a matter
of need &
to live
makes no
requirement
that you think
about
being ext. LXXiii?
time
though
is another
story
my mind
is
a dark sky

"Although creative vision and expression are visible only in the depths of the body becomes visible and others in a single

perhaps brought to perfection in permanence living expression is it is a 'continuous force' in the sense that when what was form or verse or

as parents
are a perpetual
voice-over
whether living
or dead
i could not
draw you
a picture
of time
or
for that matter
of being
as my mother
whose own
mother
is invisible
still speaks
in a way
designed
to justify
to her mother
what she
does
& especially
what she
wants
the picture
of being

is only present
in these
words
if you
say them
but it all
boils down
to a matter
of need &
to live
makes no
requirement
that you think
about
being
time
though
is another
story
my mind
is
a dark sky

*"Although creative
vision and expression
are perhaps brought to
perfection in painting, all
living expression is, as
Merleau-Ponty puts it, a
'continuous birth,' in the
sense that a man is born
when what was visible
only in the depths of the
maternal body becomes
visible to itself and others
in a single act."* <xxii>

Richard McCleary,
translator's preface to
Merleau-Ponty's *Signs*

9/2/14

same task
as any
day
to see it
or
to think it
ę the thinking
with its
subsequent
life
inevitable
ę unknowable
as the invisible
orbital
of an imagined
election
but the thinking
wants to know
what
happens next
well beyond
the lifetime
of this body
if what have we
become

"appeared on the scene." <3>

"The philosophers road

the long moment to me! far from

of some that road has

points a way for those

"It is as

may be hard, but we from it float to rise of

unmanifestation passing away

some running To come." <3>

same task

as any

day

to see it

or

to think it

& the thinking

with its

subsequent

life

inevitable

& unknowable

as the invisible

orbital

of an imagined

electron

but the thinking

want to know

what

happens next

well beyond

the lifetime

of this body

what have we

become

"It is as if some cunning mechanism whisked events away at just the moment they appeared on the scene." <3>

"The philosopher's road may be hard, but we can at least be sure that each stop points a way for those to come." <3>

Merleau-Ponty, *Signs*

vertical flood

Marthe Reed

I floated in a station, slowing sorrow's ruddy geraniums, sound of voices like blue shirt-tails flying, almost gentle. Here beside the bed, cars and scenes replicate, a faint smear of something. Emotion, clean shirts. Little coarse stones that thaw the lake. Or might. I feel an old-fashioned corridor, entirely accidental, and travel north. Riding would be easier, a river car, a mechanical fetch. There are no blue sheep. Another time, abruptly, I feel very slow. Hugging the empty museum, its gold finger-bones a gentle initiation we don't know. Old mechanical contrivances drawn on watch-cases and green air.

⊖

I lost a sense of excess, the most splendid meat. What matters gestures without spectacle, that familiar-looking ghost, sparrows on a lump of dung. Father knows how to cry. Cocked chin, head, and sleep. I saw a petal crowd, tall white bodies stretched on the ground. I seemed to be caught: a metal strap, its vanished yellow creosote stuck to my skin. I regretted the snake-bone woman, the buzzing wire. I headed into that vertical flood, a dress of nested pockets and bottle-cap emotion. Amorphous anger, like animals in beautiful suits, the panoramic view. A liar. And as I, I landed rimmed by no sound, I was within the lemur-nothing, the paler mother-nothing. I sat down, tiny and burning, there amid its extinct rocks and hills.

I entered the weather, splendid, mute and feral. I felt the way children do, flattened against the meadow. Wobbly-legged, I panicked, a contradictory space, red leatherette venuses similarly extensible. Little dreams, lush and weightless—a bishop's gardenia, a continuum of corpses—murkier when the sky is misshapen. I approached the crest of the hills, thick-lensed daughter already a soldier. I could see nothing in boyish trappings, all the objects of petty commerce, emerald with silk emotions. I felt love, a little of the old charm, small white carnations, out of focus, coin purses. I was returned to the landscape of the body, estranged from the world. Copper women beneath the Vatican amplifier dark.

from "MoonFields" *Suite of Twenty Drawings graphite sticks, etching needle, and pink pearl eraser**

◊

Arie A. Galles

*The entire suite, and information about the Galles-Rothenberg collaboration may be found at http://www.ariegalles.com/writings.html

Arie A. Galles, MoonFields XIV, 18 ¼ " x 12", 2011, Graphite

Arie A. Galles, MoonFields X, 18 ¼ " x 12", 2011, Graphite

Graffite: Three Suites after Images by Arie Galles

Jerome Rothenberg

Twenty Moon Fields

> *"I was on the terrace, wrestling with the Moon"*
> – F.G. Lorca

1
a knife falls
in the water
grows a second knife

& over each knife
looms an eye –
my second eye trails off

2
life has spirit, death
has only chalk

with chalk a word
is written

but not by you

3
end it here,
the man says
as he puts his thumb on it

the thumb is raw,
behold,
the man is even now alone

4
easy sleep
easy rest

easier to be an animal
than not

5
after Nerval

like inserting two pictures
in a single viewer

(he writes)

then moving my hand as if
sketching my signature

6
DIRECTIONS

rub this side of the chain
against that side

how many years before
the chain rubs out?

7
death has a taste
after we hear of it

a man's taste
or a woman's

a child's taste
or a cat's

8
someone slips below the sod

the grass grows over him

as if someone has died,
but no one stops to ask

9
A FUTURE POETICS

with inspiration vanished
respiration took its place

is expiration next?

10
there is something
we like to hide

if not our tongues,
our eyes

if not our immortal souls,
our daily vices

11
easy sleep
easy rest

easier to be an animal
than not

12
go inside
look around you
come back out again

13

a rabbit sneezes with the desperation of a man
a knife drops inward with the sound of water

14
everything is possible
meaning nothing

and if nothing is possible
everything is too

15
clap hands together

never forget
the lessons taught you

the value of a song

16
the place of resistance
has moved away from us

so that we're running to keep up
& stumble

17
as many people
will be murdered this year

as were murdered
the year before

18
there is a constant
at the heart of things

that serves to keep
the universe in motion

19
the resistance is all the moon that's left to us

20
the spirit of the dead
means nothing

The Pepper Trees

"They are gone, the pepper trees"
- F.G. Lorca

1
the more a man's arms
stretch
to reach the woman's

& the branches
can no longer bear
their weight

2
moss is foremost
if the mind will entertain
matters of fact

a tactile splendor

3
ferns & rind
the black a distance
deeper than a star

4
heavy as a heave
the layered cork & wood
cry out to you

or is it only
something furtive
hidden

in your heart?

5
at the side a shadow
like a child
beside the fallen bodies

the last chance
for sleep

6
serpentine
a limb athwart
coiled branches

forest dreams
& shiny shadows

7
is there a black hole
here on earth?

a place so deep
that even leaves
turn black

8
spiny dust
over the swollen
bark

the hairy wood
is like a man's flesh
or a woman's

9
a memory of where

we lived & swung –
our place in nature

10
to seat yourself
inside it
ache of trees
& ache of majesty

he who falls
recovers grace
only a little

11
the ferns take over
& the question
rattles our minds

where have the bodies
gone   where
in the world is love

12
plain in our sight
the black hole
carved into the center
limbs askew

more what the woman gives
a field of light
below her

down where the world
takes root

13
they dance together
taut arms rising
from dark trunk

in front of which
the dancer
leaves her shadow*   * her meadow

eager to draw him back

14
that which is lost
leaves only a wound
behind

the mystery of light
more than the mystery
of something lost

the memory of where
we were
guarded by snow

a scar that will not heal

15
between an island
& the main
blind spring arrives

the strange allure
of black on white

drives color from the brain
refraction from the eye

16
is every image that we see
seen from a height

& every block of wood
as stiff as stone*   *as bone

receivers & believers
we let the shadows go

17
counting by threes
is learnt by rote
nohow forgotten

more as a number known
by comrades
than by a bride & groom

the tallest tree of all
no taller than
those that surround him

the way that every count
leaves space & air
between

18
brought back to earth
the sadness
of mute nature

waiting for the dead
to rise & shine

19
like stony ridges
schist & caulk*   * chalk
no sign of verdure

but the layers
stacked   each one
atop the next

offers a broken wall
a perch for demons

20
eggs dropped
along the way
or hanging from
the rotted bark

a bed laid bare
the rank turd
lies within
firm in its nest

eggs & turds
the rest is barely
bark & sunlight

traces of a life
long gone

Twenty Cloud Poems

But none of them paused,
none of them wanted to be a cloud
- F.G. Lorca

CLOUD POEM (1)

among the clouds
one face appears

a world of babes
& shadows

wrapped in its caul

CLOUD POEM (2)

stretched out in coils
the bodies of the lost
lie dormant

babes as fair
as paradise
who sleep their dreams

so hard to lend an eye to
& to look inside
to see the earth below

more like the sky
when turning softly over
the blue above

goes grey

CLOUD POEM (3)

inside the grey world
black eyes open

black lips
lie in wait

ready to suck down
the lights

the white
an opening more real

than morning
a limpid hole

CLOUD POEM (4)

the dead return

the nearly dead
lie sleeping

keeping a line
between them

hungry, mutilated
faces lost

ghosts wrapped
in gauze

& set in rows
like sleepers

CLOUD POEM (5)

land breaking through
at last   at sunset

at the breaking down
& folding up

of borrowed
time

CLOUD POEM (6)

to be a cloud
face up
against the other
brighter cloud

more like an animal
a life gone by
who would not
rather be?

CLOUD POEM (7)

denial
where the winds rush
lifting bodies
like false clouds

from darkness
into light
& back
to darkness

CLOUD POEM (8)

a god is easy
sighting

easy body
of a man
or woman

easy dreams
of power

from the side
where light
fades out

the face of night
is lurking

CLOUD POEM (9)

in flying
& the fear
of flying

stars pop up
then hide
their brilliance

in the shadow
little lives
fly by

& vanish

CLOUD POEM (10)

a wound first
or a slit
in time, in sex

a pool or lake

an island
flying past

a smaller body
& a larger

open jaws

CLOUD POEM (11)

look down
& see
what
to the eye
are only
clouds

the earth below
forgotten
(almost)
in the mind
is only
earth

CLOUD POEM (12)

lost habitat
through which
a fish

or snake
breaks loose
a vestige

blown across
the sea
& sky

the wish for life
nearly
unmans him

before he dies

CLOUD POEM (13)

the lines
across the earth
escape us

at the center
where the clouds accrue

a white Dot
calld a Center   (W. Blake)

CLOUD POEM (14)

a fracture
like a mouth

a gash
in space & time

unstable
changing

mouth on mouth

CLOUD POEM (15)

to drift away
a cloud
no longer

lighting up
the sky
in triplicates

they vanish
where the night
begins

a smearage
smeared by hand
& darkened

CLOUD POEM (16)

to drown
& to be gone
forever

swallowed
by the tufts
of smoke

a hateful
morning
half alive

I do not want it

CLOUD POEM (17)

beauty so great
the fear awakens
& breaks through

the lights
that should bring joy
bring terror

bodies
bumps in time
& space

all that they write
turns back on them
erased

CLOUD POEM (18)

now dark
the fingers of
one hand
glow past their time

an alphabet of sound
before all sound
goes black   condensing
colorless & cold

the ships leave harbor
in a flight
so bountiful
the night drifts by

CLOUD POEM (19)

peninsulas like clouds
& clouds
like phantom fingers

freed from touch
the lines dissolve again
& now again

the gaps appear
like holes in time
ever anew

CLOUD POEM (20)

the cloud as metaphor
makes me recoil
gliding above them

fearing a ledge
that will not hold
but succors me

only for now
this tender moment
vagabond

a paradise of clouds
that shrouds
the hell within*   *the life within

from Memory Cards: Dogen Series

Susan M. Schultz

Although mountains belong to the nation, mountains belong to people who love them. Mountains lean like mothers; at night they're what isn't lit, can't be felt save as assumption based on fact. If memory writes fact, we are tattooed skin, nerve, synapse. We know the mountain exists because our brain has been altered by it. Cajal's mountains and waterfalls, gravity's nerves shuttling in rock pools. To assume means to think you know, gain power from that knowing. We assume what memory offers, until it stutters, runner caught between first and second, wagering his vacillations against another runner's sprint. There's no clock in baseball, but it's still all time. The mountain has its rain delays, days we time the water's flowing stops to arrive at clarity. Shama thrushes and Miles Davis: sun and spotify. It's "nation" that sets boundaries, as a mountain does. What is the mountain's quantum of river blood, its signature on the rolls? Where is the place of my hand, index lanced, red dot bubbling?

--1 June 2014

Look then / Where the father of all things swims in a mist of atoms /
Electrons and energies, quantums and relativities. The poet's ashes were
set in concrete; my mother's in a plastic bag, box. What there is to
describe is gray, particulate, post-blood quantum. Blood dissolves
as dust. The "moron" or "fool" deserts his mountain camp at night.
POW of the near-beyond, man in an attic drawing girls with penises,
pansies. Who breaks our rules is broken like a thrush's song by civil
defense. Thirty three states have laws against feeding the homeless.
They are pigeons to us. Think outside the box, when box is house,
estate, contains nothing for sale. The man beneath the bridge beside
the creek has tarp and bike, abode. Behind him is lo`i, mountain,
before him road crew directing traffic. He's the scholar in a scroll
painting, or he is bulk refuse. We see him push his bike to the road,
heading for He`eia. The little hills of the ahupua`a were formed from
the hanged body of a woman grieving.

--3 June 2014

Is there not a sufficient quantum of distress and misfortune? The door
opens to a room of fluttering post-its: lines of Proust, grocery lists,
small maps of a house, inspirational blurts. My card would say: *I am*
white; I am not here for you. "We're not the same race," my son says to
me. I am not bird to his bird, but bear, sheepdog, meerkat. Merchant
of origins, time's your tarp, cover-up. Find faces in the leaves, death's
graft in green. Pinned like butterflies on cork, my son's eyes look out
at me. Last night he browsed headphones on amazon, read the 3-star
reviews. I tell my student to use the past tense, personal pronoun.
Love of origins breeds sentiment: not these leaves in resin, post-it
notes. A fan sweeps back & forth; the Black guard thinks he knows
me. Short white English professor, woman.

--5 June 2014

The old plum tree is boundless. / A hard cold rubs the nostrils. Attend
the breath; it is film, banyan, mosaic. Four empty squares grow in
Kuan Yin's Waikiki mural. A construction worker in green shirt
and white helmet stands on a scaffold to pull her down, tile by blue

tile. Make space for Saks, for Christian Dior. Hongly encountered
Khmer Rouge soldiers after the war, one of whom was sick. Asked to
take the man to hospital, he drove a wooden cart miles down jungle
roads. *Nine of my family members died in that "hospital,"* Hongly said,
outside a blue building in Battambang. And then we ate lunch. You
cannot see Kuan Yin for her shopping cart, her wall eyes. They're
meeting in secret now, sending emails without her address. She
called the ambulance when she found a man dying in the bushes.
So many maggots, the ambulance driver wouldn't take him in.
When asked, Nico Schultz, of Taubman Co., LLC, responded: "We
recognize, respect and appreciate the protection and prosperity
Buddha and the goddess Quanying have bestowed on the property
through their mural for the last 30 years." Toward the end of his life,
my father grew more deaf. A maid in Waikiki brought cold water in
a bucket for his burned feet. They assure us the old banyan tree will
be protected.

--7 June 2014

When memory arises of memory arising. Because my memories
scared me, I stayed home. It was a kind of "memory care," that self-
dementia, lacking care's burden. She wasn't speaking the language of
idiocy, but of modernism. That was when I learned the meaning of
"moderation," stuck between two scholars arguing. It's the function
of leaves to grow, not entomb, yet the dead seem to blossom there.
One character born at adult height grew down, until his feet took
their place in rusted molds. The mountains walk forward and back;
in heavy rains waterfalls fall upward. In the Swiss woods, my father
and I saw a young deer. Imagine that someone would take a gun and
kill it, he said. *I could just be with him, without speaking. He was so self-
contained.* His voice a trellis. His garden shoes, 7.5D, sat beside the
laundry room door.

--9 June 2014

A painting of a rice cake does not satisfy hunger. Nor a painting of the
mountain the desire to see from its summit. The ocean view is a

cheat, he says, you can see the telephoto effect. My son remembers his past by way of what he ate. In the mirror I saw his cheeks full, fists clenched. My memory of that meal does not satisfy his hunger, or mine. We remember best what we write in our own hand. How do blind people know where the bumps are? he asks. Words are mountains. We hike up Diamond Head, then eat malasadas. Increasingly, spikes are put on sidewalks, so the homeless cannot sleep there. *But words will never hurt me.*

--11 June 2014

A small twig is the everywhere of old twigs. The former athlete lives in section 8. He's 36. He can't walk except with hands held to the wall, suffers lack of muscle memory, spasms. Can't hold his trumpet, or his kids. Drinks whiskey & pepto bismol. Eidetic means "what we see," John says. What is visible is marked. Think of what inhabits your losses now: count them like beads, call them out. A neurologist sighed. The man who walks Ku`i the tortoise on Lulani Dr. directs him with lettuce, flower petals. Ku`i means to stitch or to pound, to churn, to seam, to boom, to crush, to clash. To care is to manage, to assist living. To cut the sentence whole cloth. Use a straight edge & a knife, my husband says.

--12 June 2014

It is the work of mountains. To cleave is to join and to rip apart. We live with sunrise and water, the mountain's teeth flashing when it rains. Remainders were the best part, for they suggested left-overs. Last breaths remind us to count, where accumulation lessens. As I poured water in the cup, a brown gecko leaped out, landed on the red fire extinguisher by the sink. He climbs the knife-holder, the pill bottles, drinks from our cups. The mountain erodes like anger, trees at odd angles, an unrazored chin. The space between desire & fact is too often violence. "Do you really want a bat on your wedding cake?" she asked. "It's a weapon." No, I said, think of it as violin.

--13 June 2014

Do you want me to be a nice person? My son bargains; he's designing a house, while his friend finds food. The next phrase begins with if. Comma, then. At school, they're painting monsters on a desk, stick figure jedi. Has to do with being individual, like or unlike others. Monsters are easier to paint than people. One resembles a rabbit; a jedi hangs on a long strand of hair. I remember the day she started to grow hers, not the day it was cut. Memory's all if. Our deaf cat no longer jumps; his legs twitch when he naps. *You can also visit a land of mushrooms if it sounds more like your cup of tea.*

--14 June 2014

The path of water is not noticed by water, but is realized by water. The dammed river knows itself, unrealized. The first time I saw the Mekong, son in arms. She sits with her daughter on the plot where her husband wasn't buried, wondering how it would feel to him. Something about time in the poem, one woman noted; it's not there, except for "April or May." Suspickit, my daughter said. At the cash register I turned to look at my son in the stroller. Saw instead my father, white-haired, his liquid eyes. His cleft re-sewn at 20. Mine stitched at one. We don't think to stitch the mountain's clefts; waterfalls do that when it rains.

--Father's Day, 15 June 2014

stanzas

Mark Scroggins

Timeless isn't right—without time,
sans the density, ghosts and moving
shadows, invisible lines but palpable
of ruined and overbuilt buildings;
air empty of everything but
humidness, funk and fume
of currency and machines. Shall
I build me a history, brick myself
into a country house of leaves
and bindings? bind me, dark-hair.

⊖

We don't see the towns fly by
when we're on the pavement—a canal
away it's a different tax structure,
and they do things differently, maybe
don't speak the language. Can't say
I talk it much, anymore. Married
fifty years without a trace

of dissatisfaction, if you believe
the stories. I'd like to. Don't believe
much of anything these days.

⊖

Writing up against love, as the anaesthetic
wears off, pushing up against love
like the growth in her belly, against
its wall. Penstrokes not enough,
scalpel-strokes. Philosophy in the
bed, awakening to the dialectic
in the semi-private room. Enlightenment
as x-rays. No time for puns.
No time at all. Pen pushing against
time, against cancer, against love.

⊖

What's that again? my hearing's
not what it used to be.
Neither is my eyesight, smell
or touch. Taste as questionable
as ever. Once it was as lithe
and flexible as an eel, that
tender prehensile organ of my
mind— Fooling myself again:
the songs are the best, change
that station right away.

⊖

The sky goes dark in the way
a computer-generated sky
does, the fires burn down, and
the lights dim. A breathless moment,
then the doors hiss open on a room
of palpable blue-black
darkness, the plaster casts

of the dead huddled, scattered,
petrified in moving, motionless
agony. The pet pig made her weep.

Two Poems

Maurice Scully

TAP DANCE

Artists
in their
factories
are

working
hard now
filling in
steel

boxloads
of grant
application
forms

on an
ongoing
shift
basis

through the
generations
beyond
making.

Life is
good.

There is
breathing
space.
The

galleries
are show
ing the
normal.

Formal.
The avant
garde. The
pig in a

   poke.

Elderly ladies
eyes closed
heads lifted
listen to

   mell
   if
   luous

poetry
& no
body's
bitter.

   .

Dips from
its pergola
touching yr
head as you

pass a rose by
way of caress
on a chill bright
winter morning

turning on its
stem pale
cream along a
black path

into the
park

sometimes
the slits
of an owl's
lids open

to watch a
drop

falling from a
horn of lime
hanging from the

underarch
of a bridge.

.

O
come dance
with me
ye

prety maidens
& hark the foulys
song along an
avenue

of Boojum where
huge pyramids of
crystal new-fangled
interwoven

logics laugh at
the little people
tiny down there
among the

latest splashes
of the
hyper-baroque.

It's good
to be
dead.

Past the
pastoral fascists
& gallery
thugs.

Pluck that
string. It
really feels
like this ...

cycles
within
cycles.

And a dog
out there in
the dark going
Art! Art-Art!

Art!

MUGAPU

My first enounter with Mugapu was at a staff meeting
of the village school. He came in and sat down among
us at the table. Only a little more ragged than the rest of
us and accepted by all, I thought he was another member
of staff.

Mugapu, as it turned out, had one word of English: *was*.
When he got excited he would string a lot of *was's* together
like this: *was-a-dee-was-a-dee-was*. He was speaking English,
according to himself. And in a sense, he was.

Ntate Bosa was reading the minutes. Indeed he was reading
the minutes from what seemed a blank page, his head tilted
to one side and his eyes closed. Suddenly Mugapu started
speaking English.

There was a pause, then ntate Bosa, smiling slowly, moving
his head a little and resting his eyes gently on Mugapu, began
to recite a strange litany. It was the names of all the little
villages along the route to the far-away town.

This had a powerfully calming effect. Mugapu, it seems,
now in his child's mind, was speeding along the yellow
dust-track in some beaten-up jalopy towards town: *ga goloi*
in his own language. This was his great passion in life.

Now, how many times have I used the word 'was' so far here?
In other words, how much of this might interest Mugapu?
Wherever he is now, I wish him well. Or perhaps, and more
likely, he is long dead. He had special privileges in his community,
coming and going from household to household, compound to
compound, never hungry, never short of a little change for
loose tobacco which he stuffed into the empty cartridge of a
plastic biro and smoked, somehow, riding the buses hither and
thither for free on their precipitous journeys over the mountains
and joining the women in the fields and children in the dust to play.

Was-a-dee-was-a-dee-was-a-dee-was.

Stone VI
from Dictator

❦

Philip Terry

Cut i

He wash | the dirt | out of | he hair | … and | clean he | ~~behind~~
he shake | out the | lock of | he hair | over | he back
he throw | off he | old shirt | … and | he put | on a | clean one
he put | on a | jacket | ~~fix the~~ | button
DICTA | TOR put | on he | hat of | gold + + +

To beau | tiful | DICTA | TOR the | woman | sex god | turn an
| eye …
"Come DIC | TATOR | give I | the fruit | of you | body!
Give I | the taste | of you | perfect | skin…
~~Be I | husband | and I | will be | you wife!~~
I will | give you | a gold | sport car
With gold | wheel and | a sun | roof …
You will | drive a | fast road | machine | a hot | mother!
Enter | this house | smell the | sweet air
When you | enter | the house
the ho | ly man | will kiss | you foot | + + + as | they do | in the
| city | of gold

Minis | ter may | or and | gener | al will | bow down | in front |
of you …
Mountain | and land | will bring | + + + fruit | to you
You an | imal | will have | many | off spring
You po | tato | will grow | deep you | corn will | grow high
You horse | will win | the big | race …
You cow | will pro | duce fine | + + + cheese"

DICTA | TOR make | of he | mouth a | shape and | move he |
tongue ...
He say | to the | woman | sex god
"What can | I give | you if | I take | you for | a wife?
Will I | give you | oil for | the bo | dy … | and cloth | of gold?
Will I | give you | bread and | + + + cheese?
you who | eat the | food of | the god
you who | drink wine | fit for | a dip | lomat?
[For you] | they pour | out + + + | [holy | water]
[you dress | in cloth] | of gold
[what] a | distance | between | [you and | DICTA | TOR] if | I
take | you for | a wife!

You be | a camp | fire that | go out | in the | rain …
a back | door that | shut out | neither | wind + + + | or storm
a base | camp that | kill the | young boy | that de | fend it
a car | with a | door that | fall off
a bomb | that ex | plode in | the hand
a bot | tle that | leak … | over | the one | who drink | from it
stone that | break up | in the | … ci | ty wall
a spy | that go | over | to a | foreign | power
a shoe | that bite | the foot!

Who that | you love | do you | love for | ever?
Which of | you par | ty boy | please you | for long?
Come I | will name | all you | love boy | for you"

Cut ii

....
....
....
....
... + + + + + + + +
+ + + + + + + + + + + +
+ + + + + + + + + + + +
+ + + + + +
+ +
+ + + + + + + + + + +
+ + + + +
+ + + + +
* * *

"... the | god of | the ~~cow~~ | ~~man~~ you | love once
you send | he to | visit | the un | der world
Year af | ter year | the peo | ple cry | for he
You love | the dark | ~~cow bird~~
you seize | he and | + + + break | he wing
He stand | in the | forest | and cry | 'Come back | wing! Come |
back wing!'
You love | the big | cat ... | ~~full of~~ | ~~strength~~
you dig | for he | seven | hole and | seven | hole* in | the ground
                                        *many
You love | the war | horse + + + | strong in | battle
you give | he the | bomb + + + | and the | bullet
because | of you | ... he | ~~run for~~ | the hill
because | of you | ... he | hate the | water | he drink
because | of you | he moth | er cry
You love | the cow | man who | work in | the field
who give | you fruit | and bread | to eat
who ev | ery day | kill a | young cow | for you
You strike | he and | turn he | in to | a + + + | wild dog
He own | boy drive | he + + + | a way
and he | own dog | ~~tear and~~ | ... ~~tear~~ | ~~he skin~~

You love | as well | he who | look af | ter you | father | garden
who for | ever | bring you | box and | box of | + + + date

and ev | ery day | ... [make | the ta | ble full]
You lift | you eye | to he | ... you | go up | to he
'Garden | boy you | be strong | and beau | tiful
Hold out | you hand | and ~~touch~~ | ~~I sex!~~'
The gar | den boy | say to | you ...
'What do | you want | from I?
Mother | if you | do not | cook + + + | I do | not eat
Shall I | [eat the | bread of] | ill will | ... the | food of | evil?
Shall grass | + + + pro | tect me | against | the cold?'
You hear | he an | swer ...
You strike | he and | turn he | in to | a fish
You set | he to | live ... | in the | middle | of the | garden
Where he | can move | + + + nei | ther up | or down

So you | will love | [DICTA | TOR in | turn] ... | and he | will
pay | for it"

When the | woman | sex god | hear this
she an | ger + + + | ~~she fly~~ | up to | the sky
and go | before | she fat | her the | sky god
Before | she moth | er the | wife of | the sky | god she | cry ...
"Father | DICTA | TOR in | sult I"

Cut iii

"DICTA | TOR speak | to I | of ill | will ...
he speak | the bad | word a | bout I"

The sky | god make | of he | mouth a | shape and |move he |
tongue ...
he say | to the | ~~woman~~ | sex god
"Hold on | + + + you | come on | to DIC | TATOR
and DIC | TATOR | point out | you no | good
speak ill | of you | and send | you ~~word~~ | ~~bullet~~"

The wo | man sex | god make | of she | mouth a | shape and |
move she | tongue ...
Speak to | the sky | god the | father

"Father | make the | MAN COW | of the | sky he | will kill |
DICTA | TOR in | ~~he home~~
make the | MAN COW | feed on | the bone* (?) | of DIC |
TATOR

*or "body"

If you | do not | give me | the MAN | COW ...
I will | break op | en the | gate of | the un | der world
I will | fire up | the judge | of the | under | world + + +
I will | make the | dead rise | + + + and | they will | eat up | the
~~peo~~ | ~~ple of~~ | ~~the earth~~"

The sky | god move | he tongue | and speak | to the | woman | sex
god
"If you | ask me | for the | ~~MAN COW~~
for sev | en year | in the | land of | big ci | ty of | the an | imal |
noise no | thing will |
    grow but | ~~brush wood~~
Have you | enough | + + + corn | for the | people | in store?
Have you | enough | ~~grass~~ for | the an | imal?"

The wo | man sex | god move | she tongue | to speak
Say to | the sky | god the | father
"I have | enough | + + + corn | for the | people | in store
I have | ~~set grass~~ | ~~in store~~ | ... for | the an | imal
If there | must be | seven | year + + + | of no | thing but | brush
wood
I have | enough | corn + + + | for the | people | in store
I have | set in | store grass | for all | the an | imal
... to | he ... | .... + + + + + +
.... + + + + + + + + + + +
...... | ~~of the~~ | MAN COW"

The sky | god lis | ten to | the word | of the | woman | sex god
[He cre | ate for | she + + + | the MAN | COW of | the sky]
The wo | man sex | god + + + | drive [he | down to | the earth]
... [to | big ci | ty of | the an | imal | noise] ...
... +
He go | down the | river | + + + + + + + + + + + +
When the | MAN COW | of the | sky sneeze | a hole | open | up

in | the earth
two hun | dred peo | ple of | big ci | ty of | the an | imal | noise
~~fall~~ | ~~in to~~ | ~~it~~ ...

Cut iv

...... | people
At the | second | sneeze a | hole op | en up | and two | hundred |
people | fall in | to it
Two hun | dred peo | ple ... | three hun | dred peo | ple ...
Even | three hun | dred peo | ple of | big ci | ty of | the an | imal
| noise fall | in to | it ...
Even | four hun | dred peo | ple of | big ci | ty of | the an | imal |
noise fall | in to | it ...
Even | five hun | dred peo | ple [of | big ci | ty of | the an | imal |
noise] fall | in to | it ...
At the | third sneeze | a ...| hole op | en up | before | ~~WILDMAN~~
WILDMAN | fall on | the MAN | COW of | the sky
WILDMAN | jump up | and seize | the MAN | COW of | the sky
| + + + take | hold of |
    he head
The MAN | COW of | the sky | throw sand | in the | face of |
WILDMAN
he show | he ~~bot~~ | ~~tom~~ to | WILDMAN

WILDMAN | make | of he | mouth a | shape and | move he |
tongue ...
he say | to DIC | TATOR
"Friend we | have be | come ~~great~~ | ......
How will | we + + + | over | throw he?
Friend I | know ... | ....
and strong | ... + + + + + + + + + + + +
We will | destroy | ... + + + + + +
I ... | + + + + + + + + + + + +
~~We must~~ | be strong | ... + + + + + +
We must | fill* (?) ... | + + + + + + + + + + + + +
       *or "kill"
... + + + + + + + + + + + + + +

... and | stick* (?) he | behind* (?) | he* (?) neck"
*or "kick"   *or "in"   *or "the"
....
WILDMAN | circle | about | ... he | run ~~round~~ | ~~the MAN~~ |
~~COW of~~ | ~~the sky~~
WILDMAN | hold he | ... and | [push he | face in | the dirt]
....

Cut v

And DIC | TATOR | like a | bad ~~moth~~ | ~~er~~ + + +
strong and | ...... + + + + + + + + + + +
strike [with | he knife] | in the | + + + ~~neck~~ | [behind | the ear]

After | they kill | the MAN | COW of | the sky | ... they | ~~tear
out~~ | he heart
They lay | it be | fore the | sun god
They sit | down like | two blood | brother

The wo | man sex | god go | up on | to the | wall of | big ci | ty of
| the an |
    imal | noise ...
In the | dress of | ~~one who~~ | ~~cry~~ she | speak the | bad word
"May ev | il come | to DIC | TATOR | ... who | make light | of I
who kill | the MAN | COW of | the sky!"

When WILD | MAN hear | the word | of the | woman | sex god
he tear | off the | leg* (?) of | the MAN | COW ... | and throw | it
in | she face
            *or "cut of meat"
"When I | can reach | you + + + | I will
tear off | + + + you | ~~leg too~~
I will | ~~push the~~ | ~~in side~~ | of the | MAN COW | in to | you face!"

The wo | man sex | god call | togeth | er the | holy | woman
the ~~top~~ | ~~shelf girl~~ | and the | hotel | girl + + +
and ov | er the | leg of | the MAN | COW of | the sky | they start
| ~~to cry~~

DICTA | TOR call | togeth | er the | expert | of [the | city] | the
art | man the |
    science | man all
The young | expert | look at | the head | of the | MAN COW | of
the | sky ...
It be | cover | with beau | tiful | ~~blue stone~~
as thick | as two | finger | + + + side | by side
He bring | [the head] | and hang | it in | the house | of he | father

They wash | they hand | + + + in | the great | river
They ~~seize~~ | each oth | er as | they walk

Each on | a horse | ... they | ride through | the street | of big | city
| of the | ani |
    mal noise
and the | people | of big | city | of the | ani | mal noise | gather |
to look | up at | they ...
DICTA | TOR speak | to the | people | who ga | ther there
to the | woman | he say

Cut vi

"Who be | the jew | el of | all ~~bat~~ | ~~tle man~~?
Who have | great pow | er a | mong man?
DICTA | TOR be | the jew | el of | all bat | tle man
[WILDMAN] | have ~~great~~ | ~~power~~ | ~~among~~ | ~~man~~ ...
... they | be strong | + + + + + +
...... | [the last | gift they | have not]
...... | [sick] ... | ....
In he | house + + + | DICTA | TOR hold | a big | party
[At last] | ~~they lie~~ | ~~down and~~ | go to | sleep in | they bed
WILDMAN | when he | lie down | see a | dream ...
WILDMAN | jump up | + + + to | set the | dream free
he say | to he | friend ...

"Friend ... | why do | the great | god sit | ~~in court~~?"

Note:

Gilgamesh was originally written in Mesopotamia, current day Iraq, on clay tablets in cuneiform script, a script which developed at first as a method of recording business transactions. *Dictator* translates this text into modern-day Globish – a limited vocabulary language designed for use in international business communities – and in so doing hopes to paradoxically return the epic, whose theme itself is profoundly occupied with trade, to its strange and distant roots.

Letters Inscribed
In Snow

❧

Laynie Browne

Snowflakes grew bigger and bigger. At last they looked like big white hens.

Games glass in your eye. I almost saw, held up in the rim of. Not
quite pressed to lips. As if you were ducking. Dunking in frustration
night after noon after riding all day. I don't know what to call you
from such a distance.

How could you still populate letters with lucid thoughts? How could
you place them in that sheet of snow in the gallery? Not doing so,
but then publishing as if you had. Without asking permission? Even
just those you wrote to me. One half of our conversation has ended.
Become fluent. Even after I write these words, and then delete them,
they reappear. Do you recognize your name, from among your
many names? Undertake- to apprentice your name?

You came up behind me and touched my shoulders as I was reading and I put the pages down. I put down the damp eyes of the non-sleeper, and the birded darkness, and the river of unsent messages. Yet as you questioned me, as to whether I would be able to undertake the performance of the tale I thought that though your pages rested on the table between us, and though I was taken now nowhere else but had been nimbly threaded inside your eyes, I would be unable.

Why, you ask?

I won't be performing. But inhabiting. It's already happened.

shoes— river
flowers— earth

dear—

Go alone threading   — echo

You sleep at the feet of distant planets. Newly discovered cold,
orbiting

Written sky or bird. A bird isn't written. Isn't immune to darkness,
isn't taken to bed.

Your eyes close damply.

Is there another name for you as in darkness when you cannot be
seen?

I don't believe you aren't actual just because I can't hear your
language-object song, just because rest is not to be found upon the
back of a reindeer, just because I tried to inhabit a river, to sleep on
an absent sleigh.

Dear Kai,

Are you still freezing?

Once you were close enough to touch, walked out amid flower
boxes. And in the winter, one eye seen through glass. A smile in
eye— I could not mistake for mine. Now I don't know what to call
you. Where you have gone? I consult the dictionary for advice. I
find: a crucial point reached in a course of action with no possibility
of turning back. A substance that can impair. A chemical action
inside the body. Two opposite poles, as in a magnet. A purposely
expressionless face. A sharp or tapering end. A mark of punctuation
surrounded by large bright-red petallike leaves. To furnish a point,
as in a pencil. Starting point — yourself: within water.

Love,
Gerda

You wrote the name *Gerda* for me. You watched my thought just
as easily as Gerda watched Kai when he no longer existed. I had
already become her. You knew that I would never submit to being
a character who did not know her own tale. You knew that in
trusting me to take up this role that each act of divination would be
created anew and complete. You knew that in this way you'd made
me responsible for locating yourself. For bringing you back from the
land of winter. Never mind that we had already, in the outer worlds,
drifted to Spring. You knew as you closed your eyes each night and
did not sleep. I knew you had departed, like the artist who never
arrived at the gallery. Like the blank sheet of snow. You left yourself
and therefore me. How could I possibly blame you for separating?
You had already separated from yourself.

River rejects shoe
Flowers deny earth

dear—

If there were a way to invoke messages I would without stopping, through my fingertips. I fathom your reversals amid silt and ice. I can speak in sepals, from the underside of narrative—I'm not allowed to do this, but I go on because another time ago speaks a different language. Of what consequence is the word "unknown" or even "forbidden" to a dimensionless character, a string of letters? Of what consequence to retrace a speech of thumbs, buttons, breath beneath breath, fallen to the floor? Would you follow me, pick up each invisible utterance? Place the weightless pile delicately upon a chair? Would you stand and leave me there to unmend every space between known obstacles? Would you pull back the curtains and ask me to wait?

Dear Kai,

Now, look in the glass.

What if I were to carry this bundle of letters, breath beneathe breath, weightless, those opposite to the ones published anonymously. Letters which have been erroneously attributed to others. What if I were to carry mine, and place them in that empty space, where once was a blank sheet of snow, in a gallery? As we are tested we fund power. Wood of a yew tree becomes bow. Wait on the will of broad, thick or course brushstrokes, a villainous character, a barrier or boundary. Heed— the state of a body perceived of generating sky — firmament.

Love,
Gerda

Paris Métro I

The Second Mourning of Cole Afcott, Chapter 1[1]

Chris Eaton

Some creatures don't deserve to live.[1] Those without use, which should go without saying; but also those that are too useful, because they rob us of the opportunity for our own use, for achievement, greater self-reliance, the opportunity for purpose; the mules, the oxen; the camels; the ones who carry us into complacency until neither ride nor rider lurch right; those that are good; those that are merely good enough; those who are merely good enough for something; those that are but pale copies of use; the bichon: a pale copy of the poodle and the barbet who are, in turn, pale copies of pale copies of pale copies, teetering back to the first tamed gray wolf; the Bali tiger: runt of the species; the Arabian ostrich: mother of negligence; the ape: a laughingstock, a personal embarrassment; the Arabian horse; anything domesticated but especially cats; those that are meek, those who flatter, those who beg, those who gather; the whining collie, bleating meerkat, the emasculated bottlenose (*kookaburra, kookaburra*), gentled bear; those who expect things, even if it's only bad weather; those who work and also those who will not, who never expect to do anything strenuous, or heroic, or even

---

[1]From a novel-in-progress about the life of Camille Saint-Saens, the death of art, and how he was quite possibly Jack the Ripper. Forthcoming from BookThug Publishing in 2016. .

moderately active during the off-season; those who adapt; those
that don't; those who fly because they have wings; those who crawl
because they do not; those who have neither wings nor bellies but
still make the attempt, perhaps especially those, who aspire, the
raccoons, washing their food like tiny little men, that can be dressed
in all sorts of humiliating waistcoats and bobs; the immensely
relatable; the uncomfortably honest; those who believe; those that
long, even for the peaks of pointlessness, forging aimless work out
of instinct: the sea turtle, swimming steadily against the current all
the way to Ascension Island to mate, so the next generation can do
it all over again, through all that golden-green water over the dark,
over the chill of the deeps and the jaws of the dark, the sun over the
water, the sun through the water, the eye holding the sun, being held
by it with no thought and only the rhythm of the going, the steady
wing-strokes of the flippers in the water, I can't believe it, do the
turtles know about sharks, do they not think about the sharks when
they're swimming that 1,400 miles, I can't believe they'd swim 1,400
miles thinking about sharks; those that feed off the weaknesses of
others; those who seek community for protection; those with puss,
those that preen; the peacock, the Lopshire leopard; those who
seek attention merely by standing out; the parvenu, those sudden
kings of France: the American mink, American bullfrog, sitting out
on the edge of a mud puddle, fast asleep, American cottontail, the
American loons, with their long-drawn unearthly howl, more a wolf's
than any bird; the mimics, whose ambition calmly trusts itself to the
road, instead of spasmodically trying to fly over it; those who are
fierce; those who are of affectionate disposition; those who abide the
laws; those who write them; those who aim for immortality; those
who beach themselves like great pods of whales on the shores of
fate, one eye pointed up at the sky, like Isaac to Abraham, the other
planted more gratifyingly in the sand, and accept death as the end.
Those who care too much about this particular moment and their
particular place in it.

On the other side are those who also deserve to die not
because they are similarly without use because they are but because
they are just too good for this world, have done nothing to warrant
this life besides being born, majestic and true, without even dreams
because theirs is naught with envy; Verreaux's eagle-owl: feasting
on the pregnant hare; the king cobra: eater of snakes; the fin whale:

solitary beast of the sea, the banished and unconquerable Cain of
its race, whale-hater as some men are man-haters; the Barbary lion:
King of the Beasts, Lord of the Gladiatorial Rings. They barely
exist in this world (could care less what the rest of us do), and are
yet so often brought low by it. Surely this is why God gave the
razorback its great fin, a constant reminder of its truth, projecting
like a sundial pointing to the time of its own death. I once saw one
swarmed off the coast of Argentina by fewer than a dozen orcas, in
the Samborombón Bay, as though this should have been a warning
to us upon our arrival in Buenos Aires. She was a magnificent
creature, near seventy feet in length by the captain's estimation,
her dorsal curse as tall as a man, and her straight and single lofty
jet rising like a tall misanthropic spear upon a barren plain. She
was gifted with such wondrous power and velocity in swimming,
as to defy all pursuit from man. Our captain, who rarely perceived
the necessity to speak with us, said the whalers had once avoided
them, too fast for the trouble, but then the tide of the sperm whale
receded, the tide of the right whale receded, and trouble took on an
entirely new monetary value. And there they were, her small black
cousins, ennerved to slaughter by newly perceived weakness, their
increasingly less furtive teeth upon her fluke. Would they have dared
in her day? Like the gangs of Brutus upon Caesar? This is how God
rights the world, his pity wasted on those who already receive enough
of it. Imagine what this world would be like if He backed the winners
for once, the strongest beasts He bore upon the Earth, rather than
this constant redistribution. At one point, the razorback violently
heaved her tail loftward, brought it crashing upon her attackers. She
had some fight remaining. But we could see the bloody gash, the log
jam of rolling black snakes. We saw the dorsal fin nod and keel, her
curséd fin, the fault of design, the sea jeeringly kept her finite body
up, and drowned the infinite of her soul. Once she knew the game
was up, she carried her shame down to wondrous depths, where
strange shapes of the unwarped primal world glided to and fro before
her passive eyes, imprisoned not by man but by possibility. Strands of
flesh began floating to the surface.

We found the lion later, perhaps too late, in the winter of our
life if the fin whale was the fall, to teach us humility, forgiveness, to
rebuild our living house, to tell the Truth, with His golden mane and
great, royal, solemn, overwhelming eyes. We could not even look at

Him directly, even trapped behind bars in the botanical gardens of the *Parc Zoologique Ben Aknoun*, went all trembly, my brother from the impression of a delightful strain of music, I myself from the sensation of mysterious horror. And yet, at the baring of its teeth there was no more winter. At the sound of its roar, no sorrows. We named Him Calando. If we humans had not come along, He would have likely ruled the world. Instead He was forced to witness His own slavery, the last of His kind. Even if the semblance of His life could have been reproduced in its entirety, in some form of clear dome drawn miles wide, with an entirely replicated food chain, a blazing sun over some North African mountains, a tree branch for reclination, a lioness, and one or two cubs, would He still have been a Barbary lion? Would He still have been Free, would He still possess dignity? Would He know from the smell of the lamb, the loose folds of the antelope's limb, or the bland smack of the wounded waterbuck, that it had been placed there by uniformed attendants with their own poor personal hygiene? Likely He gave it no thought, that is what life was and this is still what life is. *Ben Aknoun* existed as a deterrent to Hope, or a monument to human mastery, depending on which side of the fence you stood. The lion's entire space was no more than fifteen feet across, devoid of any natural clutter, with its shredded wooden flooring, two large rocks and a ragdoll, surrounded on three sides by walls of brick, a large rubber ball it never touched, a fallen tree. He had worn a path from the wall to the trough and seemed unable to deviate from it. And yet He also seemed oblivious to all of it, as though He existed on another plane, a separate dimension, looked at us like we look at rocks. We were nothing more to Him than rain, less than rain, less than a breeze, He may even have felt pity on us, as we pined for the recognition of accomplishments, of victories, for objectivity. The Barbary lion taught that the way was to become subjective, to become the subject. The Barbary lion was not a human being. It was not important for the Barbary lion to have visible evidence so that He could see if His cause had been victorious or not; He saw it in secret just as well. He looked at us as if to say: *As long as you are always looking down at others, you cannot see something that is above you.* And we listened. And we reconsidered. And my brother made a wretched compromise with the beast, in a language it could understand, called to the lion each day until it saw him, recognized him as an equal, coaxed it to the bars of its cell and slipped it bits of flesh through the fence when no one was paying attention, which was often, gradually increasing the amount of poison so that it would remain undetected by the great beast until it was gradually lulled to a final sleep.

Most everyone in this world is either a camel or a lion. (The reference to Nietzsche is not lost on me. Have you read him? You should. He was a venerable, humble and honest thinker, with impeccable music taste, whose writings surely no one can read without the deepest emotion. He did what he said and said what he did, a great rarity in any time.) The big question: Which one are you?

When Camille Saint-Saëns died, there was a parade in the streets of Algiers, beginning at the *Hôtel de l'Oasis*, where a man named Hautbois unceremoniously slit my brother's throat and drained his blood slowly into a porcelain bowl, sprayed a diluted mixture of phenol and arsenic into his eyes, then filleted him from the lower margin of his rib cage to the superior crest of his hip, tore out his liver, his pancreas, cast his entrails momentarily to the side and dug deeper to remove his lungs, his stomach, reeling in his intestines like a fisherman coiling a rope. (Recounting this does not come easy for me; but the task has occupied me totally, occupied me religiously, I have understood the completion of this authorship as my duty, as a responsibility resting upon me.) Hautbois went to the balcony for a cigarette, left the heart and kidney alone. When he returned, he trimmed my brother's beard, set his mouth in a slight, uncharacteristic smile, shoved wads of cotton and gauze into his anus, and dressed him with the help of our least Arabic servant in Camille's most expensive suit in preparation for the two-day steamer trip to Paris.

Hautbois was, not a camel or a lion but a vulture, a tool, the mortician, his only purpose to introduce my brother to the crowds that had gathered outside, the body escorted by squadrons of cavalry, a mounted corps of Chasseurs d'Afrique, a full regiment of Zouaves in formal *sirwal*, a dozen Senegalese, and five companies of imperial fusileers, carrying the body on the backs of the people from the hotel to the pier, down rue Tripoli, along the Boulevard de L'Armée de Liberation Nationale, past the beaches, the aforementioned zoo, the *bassin Anglais*, in full view of the lycée, the customs offices, and Aristide Briand Square, snug between the Opera and the Theatre.

When Camille Saint-Saëns died, there was a ceremony at the docks presided over by the archbishop, the governor general. All the players and singers from the Opera – in fact, every musician within a hundred miles – took to the streets to mark the occasion, to celebrate the passing of France's greatest composer – and at this point this statement was still true, especially in Algiers – by performing together one last time in his presence. When Camille Saint-Saëns died, they performed Beethoven's *Eroica*.

A state funeral back in France was held, as I recall, at La Madeleine. Franck, for obvious reasons, was not in attendance. Neither was Stravinsky, whom Camille once called *a political anarchist throwing bombs indiscriminately around Paris*. Monet sent his regrets by telegram from Giverney: Suffering from cataracts STOP Unable to travel STOP Painted a weeping willow in Camille's memory in a general reddish tone. Anyone else could not avoid it, politically, not even Debussy, who once met Camille on the Channel ferry for an introduction to Sir Hubert Parry of the Royal College of Music, yet whom Camille later called, after a confrontation over the use of bassoons, *obsessed with the bizarre, incomprehensible, unplayable, his timing always a step or two behind the beat*, nor de Givreuse, who had courteously reached out to Camille after being chosen over him for admission to the French Académie with *My dear colleague, l'Institut has just committed a great injustice*, only to receive Camille's matter-of-fact reply from The Canaries: *I quite agree.* In the end, Camille was their victor, it would be like not attending a treaty signing with Napoleon. Those who clearly posed no threat, whose stolid mediocrity remained the unwavering benefactor of Camille's support: Messager, Widor, Duparc, Fauré, even Liszt and Dubois; those who did pose one and he did everything to crush: in secret, Ravel, Chaminade, Massenet, and Dukas, whom he never forgave for also befriending Debussy, or more publicly, d'Indy and his acolytes (Canteloube, Auric, Poulenc, Milhaud, Satie, Honegger), who gathered toward the back to shake each others hands and yawn in unison; d'Indy, who'd never had an original idea in his head, though not as bad as Vinteuil, who ran off with the melody of Camille's *Violin Sonata in D min* then had the nerve, when confronted, to say my brother was *a musician I do not care for*; the Americans: Hemingway, Stein, Valentino without his beard, Fitzgerald and Zelda; and Enrico Caruso Jr., just seventeen years old, who had quite rightly distrusted the coroner's report on the cause of his father's demise as pleurisy with an intercostal neuralgia, instead blamed Camille, and refused to leave the coffin's side and then the grave all night in case the whole thing were a trick. Diémer had clearly rehearsed – and very nearly pulled off – the story of the time he had been prevented, by atmospheric inclemency, from performing with Saint-Saëns in a two-piano version of Liszt's *Preludes*; Camille had, on that occasion, simply placed both scores on his piano and played both simultaneously; the master Dutch cellist, Joseph Hollman, recounted to the delight of at least a third of the attendees his experience of performing the debut of the *Cello Concerto no. 2*, written specifically for him, forgetting the score in a taxi in his haste to make the performance at the Conservatoire, and Camille, without a word of blame or blitheness, rewriting it from memory, as it was being performed, handing the pages up to Hollman from the prompter's box; even Dubois, whom everyone had supposed was already dead, told the story of one of Camille's first appearances as a live performer, when he not only surprised the entire audience by playing his Mozart pieces from memory, but then also offered up as an encore whichever of Beethoven's sonatas would please Her Majesty, Queen Maria; though d'Indy was no doubt already considering his next move, it was still generally accepted, on that day, in the way that these things are when someone has just recently passed, which is to say with the fantastic hyperbole of fact steeped in grief, that Camille Saint-Saëns was one of the best men France had ever known, that he had some faults but that, in the end – and in all things one must take the end into account – he was indeed as good, if not better than, when also taken with all of their faults, Mozart or even Beethoven.

I was not asked to speak.

Of course, music isn't about a community of mutual support. Music isn't pleasant. Music isn't nice. Composing music isn't about entertainment or distraction. It isn't a compass, moral or otherwise, isn't therapy, isn't about revealing the true essence of life, the beautiful frailties and strengths of the human spirit. Music is about composers with no humanity not noticing other humans – as the rest of us don't notice ants – while engaging each other in war.

And one could question, after reading all this, whether it was all worth it, whether the lengths to which Camille went to destroy some of the most promising artists of his generation was in the best interest of art, or beauty, which is to say nothing of the others, the innocent bystanders, myself included. Otto Mahler could not take the success of his brother another day. Unable to deal with the emergence of Handel, Jeremiah Clarke supposedly flipped a coin to decide if he should hang or drown himself, and when the coin landed on its edge in the mud, used his pistol. Who knows what more Tchaikovsky might have achieved had he not met my brother and taken his life at fifty-three?

Then again, we won.

from A book with no name

Ken Edwards

Frequently asked questions

Would you like to come this way? Would you like to sit down? Do
you know where you are? Do you know why you are here? Would
you like something to drink? Why not? Do you know your rights?
Can you please focus your attention? Can you answer the question?
What was that? What was that you said? Why did you say that?
What was that about? You don't know? Can't you remember? When
was it? Can you give more detail? Where were you? What happened?
Was that what was supposed to happen? What was supposed to
happen? Did it? What are you doing? Where are you going now?
What are you up to? What's that? When? What do you mean? You
don't know? What was that again? Where? With what? So what
exactly happened? Can you cast your mind back? What were you
doing? With whom? How did it happen? What happened next? How
did that come about? What did you think about it? Did you even
think about it? Do you even think when things like that happen? Are
there any thoughts going through your mind and if so what? What
does that mean? What do you mean by that? So what do you expect?
Why do you say that? What was that? Can you answer in more

detail? Can you add any more? Do you expect us to believe that? Do you expect us to believe anything you say? Can you speak up please? Are you having us on? What do you mean you don't know? How can you not know? If that's what you meant why didn't you say so? Why did you make that statement? Would you like to retract that statement? Do you regret saying that? Why not? Was what you said true? Can you please answer? Why did you lie? Did you even think of the consequences? What are you thinking now? Is there anything at all going through your head? If the question was put to you in a different way would your answer be different? Why do you say that? Can you say more? What do you expect anyone to believe? Is that so? How can you justify that? Can you please speak in English? How do you expect people to understand you? Would you like to think about it? Would you like more time? Would you like more time to think about it? Why not? Can you please compose yourself? Do you think the world owes you a living? Is that right? Why do you say it's unfair? Did you ever think about fairness when all this was happening? What do you mean by that? Is there any point in saying that? So why did you say it? Are you saying that's not what you said? So what did you say? Can you explain? Do you know what the consequences will be? Do you know what is likely to happen next? Have you given this any thought? Have you given any thought to the gravity of your situation? Would you like to reflect on this? Have you anything more to say? Do you realise this is your last chance? Is there anything more you would like to add?

Dialectics

This. This is. This is not. This is this is this is not. This is this is this is not the way. This is not the way. This is the way. This way this is not the way. This is not the way not the way. Not the way this is not the way. Not the way it was. This is not the way it was. This is not the way it was not the way it was. It was not the way it was. It was not the way it was not. The way it was was not the way. The way it was was not the way supposed. The way it was was not the way this is not the way. It was not supposed. It was not supposed to be the way. It was not the way supposed. It was not supposed to be this way. The way it was is not the way it was supposed. This is the way it was not supposed. This way was not supposed this is not the way it was supposed. This is not the way it was supposed. Not the way it was supposed to happen. This is the way it was not supposed to happen. This is not the way it was supposed to happen not the way it was supposed to happen. It was not supposed to happen this way. It was not supposed to happen this way it was not supposed to happen. It was not supposed to happen. This is not the way it was supposed to happen.

It

It is this. It is. Or is it? It may be. But then again it may not. It can't be determined. Could it? No it couldn't. We can't determine whether it is. Or what it is. It isn't possible to do so. We can speculate about it. We can make assertions about it. We can construct narratives about it. But it's not possible to do much more. That's what it comes down to. It comes down to not much more than that. And that's about it. So it's time to look outside. What is it doing? It's raining. This is it.

Nobody there

Is anybody there? Is anybody there? Is there anybody there? There's nobody there. Is anybody there? No there's nobody. Nobody there. There must be somebody. There must be somebody there. Is there anybody? No there's nobody there. There's nobody. That can't be right. There must be somebody. Somebody must be there. Is there? There must be. There must be somebody there. It can't be right that there's nobody there. Is anybody there? What's the matter? Is there nobody there? There used to be somebody there. Now there's nobody. There's nobody there that's what the matter is. There was always somebody there. Was there? Was there always somebody? There may have been somebody but now there's nobody. Something must be the matter there's nobody there now. Somebody used to be there. There was somebody. There always used to be somebody. Somebody was always there. Somebody was there and nothing was the matter. Nothing used to be the matter. Nothing was the matter when there was somebody there but now nobody is there

so something must be the matter. Something must be the matter
because there's nobody there. What is the matter now? Is somebody
there now no there's nobody there. There used to be somebody. Now
there's nobody. Nobody's there but somebody used to be. Something
must be the matter. Is anything the matter? What is the matter?
What is the matter something must be the matter. It seems there's
nobody there that is what seems to be the matter. That can't be right.
Somebody must be there.

Fall

We find ourselves falling. And we try to pick ourselves up but pretty
soon we're falling again. Everybody around is falling. As far as
we can see there are people falling. Each falls in his or her very
personal fashion. Some fall elegantly but for others there is a lot to
learn. There remains a great deal to be desired in the manner of
falling of certain of us. We hear a great deal of criticism of this even
as we are falling. Some lose all their dignity as they fall shouting
and screaming and flailing their limbs while others preserve theirs
and do not cause such embarrassment. We hear the conversations
as we pass. We are passing each other as we fall at different rates
in our different manners some faster some more slowly some with
grace and style others merely plummeting. Some have a need to
maintain decorum others argue that such vain attempts are simply
foolish since we are all on the way down and there is nothing to be
done about it. Yet others attempt remedial procedures for example
constructing parachutes improvised from scarves and pocket
handkerchiefs stitched together and attached to belts and some have
limited success in that their fall is temporarily slowed or halted or
even reversed in some instances at least for a short time so that there
is some amelioration but it rarely lasts because sooner or later the
improvised parachutes fail and the rate of fall once again begins to
pick up. And some attempt to join hands and at least fall together
in a co-ordinated fashion while others have closed their eyes and
appear to have retreated into their private internal world as they fall.
Some have become reconciled with their falling and seem to be at
peace. Some make jokes about falling which are greatly appreciated
by those around them if we are to judge from the level of hilarity and

so pass the time in this way. And some deny that we are falling at all saying it is a psychological illusion saying that we are all still in the same place and that it is the world that appears from our point of view to be forever receding upwards but that this is of no significance and we should stop worrying about it. Others claim falling is a punishment for past transgressions specifically citing the sin of pride that inevitably precedes a fall and these people appeal constantly for collective repentance and atonement as the only solution to the problem if problem indeed it is and they solicit donations in order to better spread the word but none of this appears to have the desired effect. And so we continue to fall. We continue to fall to the bottom. There is a great deal of speculation and fear about the bottom. There is even panic about what reaching the bottom may mean and about the extreme pain and carnage that may ensue. But this is premature some argue. The bottom could still be some way off. There is no point in speculating and worrying about reaching the bottom until we actually arrive there or until we have some hard evidence that it is approaching and this is not the case. We haven't reached the bottom yet and probably will not for some time. But if or when we do it will at least be a new experience. There is always something to be said for new experiences. Some of those falling say it will be a milestone. That's the buzz around here. Reaching the bottom will be a milestone and so those of us who take that view say that we shall look forward to that. But some say there may be no bottom. They say that if there is no bottom then we shall always fall we shall always be falling without end and that this is our only destiny to be forever falling and it is possible or indeed very likely we shall never reach bottom because the bottom is merely an illusion produced by our minds. Others argue that there must be a bottom because the fall would otherwise be meaningless because the whole idea of a bottom gives purpose and dignity to our falling and we should look forward to and welcome our arrival at the bottom whenever it should happen. And the arguments become quite heated at times on occasion resulting in disgraceful scenes of violence and it seems there is going to be no resolution to this conflict any time soon.

Persons

I am saying this this is what I am saying. I am saying this I said it
before but you disagreed. You said this was not what you said you
said you disagreed with what I said. You disagreed with what I said
you said. You said that what you were saying was something quite
different but I said that's not what I said. What I said was this and
I have said it before on many occasions in fact you heard me say it
but you disagreed with me when I said this you said something quite
different. I can see what you're saying but what I am saying is this.
What you are saying is something quite different and I can see that
this is something you are saying and that you have said it before but
this is not what I am saying. This is not what I said. What I said was
something quite different from what you said and I disagree with you
about what you said I said. You said that what you said was different
from what you said before and I said that I agreed with you. I agreed
that what you said was different. But you are saying that I disagreed
with you about what I said before and I did not disagree with you I
did not disagree with you at all but I said that what I said was what
I said and that's what I am saying. And you said that you agreed
with me but what you are saying is different from what I said before
on previous occasions and I agree with you on this. I agree with you
about this and I am not saying that. I am not saying that at all. If I
said this once I said it many times and you agree with me about this
that I have said it many times and on many previous occasions. And
you said that he said it too and I agreed with you that he did say this
too. He said it before and you heard him say it. I heard him say it.
He said it to me and he said it to you and he said the same thing on
each occasion and I agreed with him when he said it but you said
you disagreed. He says that he has spoken to you and you said you
disagreed with what he said about what I said and what I said you
had said. I have spoken to him and I said to him that I had spoken
to you and that you and I had agreed what to say and that there was
no more to be said. But he says he is not in agreement with this he
agrees with some of what I said and with some of what you said but
he does not agree with what both you and I agreed on. What he is
saying is something quite different and he has said it before and will
say it again but it is something quite different from what you and
I previously agreed and what we now agree about. He says he will

speak to you and to me and he will also speak to her because she has something to say about it too but we don't know what that is. I have heard her say something about this and I am not sure whether she agrees with him or whether what she is saying is in agreement with either you or me or with what you and I have agreed. What I am saying is that she may disagree with him or she may agree with him and she may disagree with what I said or with what you said or she may agree with both you and me. If she agrees with him or with you or with me or with all three then I agree that it should be as agreed and what I said before should stand but if she disagrees with him or with you or with me or with all three we shall all have to speak together and come to some agreement. And if we cannot come to an agreement then we shall have to agree to differ.

Three Pieces

🌿

Craig Foltz

Place Your Faith in the Impossibility of Flight

One version of the truth involves the detuning of encyclopedias
and the creation of hazardous waste management reports. Another
version involves cracked headstones and slippery crevices. Still
another is linked to the future through disparate mandates. Mandate
1: History should not be whittled away without toothpicks. How
else to calculate fungal circles? Mandate 2: Win me over with sump
vessels, duplicate me with fossil records and old growth forests. One
distils foreplay by escalating questionable issues. Another licks and
licks and licks and licks until there is no frost line on the vessel.
Mandate 3: Replicate this month of salty verbs. Mandate 4: Oh, to
incur the wrath of honeyeaters, sunbirds and sugar gliders! So, this
is how we ended up in the lowest point of the basement. Mandate 5:
A bed will separate foreign objects from complex oracles. Pale, green
men shall parade through your dreams selling protonated molecules
disguised as sacks of potatoes. In this one, they deftly remove your
legs from their sockets, season them, and slowly begin to cook them
over fire. Soon, you find yourself gnawing on the bones right along
with them. Marrow tastes best at ambient temperature. Mandate 6:

A factory floor is no place to don galoshes. Memories churn through language the way a paleo diet dissolves in bouillon cubes. Genitals appear to us as pieces of recently chewed fruit. Gourds, for sad guitarists Mandate 7: Creation myths allow you to transform yourself into the female form. Oh, to induce the wrath of her septagram! Before warding off evil, let us refresh your most remote follicles.

You Will Not Be Taken Alive

Before extinguishing fire, we capture silhouettes to remit the dimensions of a cave. In front of you something carved, something engraved. Incidental research suggests this vessel will only divulge her secrets under certain conditions. Condition 1: Mysterious beeps and clicks are detected from the depths of the ocean, but they are not foreboding enough to keep our silky protagonists on dry land. Their dismissal of the pleistocene age makes no sense until one considers the sexy tug of molluscan fauna. Condition 2: Know this. There will always be patriots for our bulky arrangement of florets. There will always be those who endeavor to extract meaning from the loosest compendium. But despite their best efforts, there can be no narrative without an endless parade of loops in which the needle can run around. Meteorologists reach the same conclusion. What's the use of summer rain without the scent of soggy cardboard? Condition 3: Is it inappropriate to imagine touching strangers through their clothes? Man with beard, woman with stone beads. Is it trespassing to eavesdrop on the sounds from previous generations? For contemporary peoples, segmentation is the featured content. Condition 4: In this one, the past is so distant as to preclude the invention of mountains and any associated plateaus. A lovely aspect composed of flat, monochromatic fields of light. Spectral analysis shall reveal the paths of arrows, while trippy diagrams of valve locations shall reveal the dissonance in our names. Condition 5: Those who commute to work are the same as those who would remark on dreary conditions. One says, "How can we confide in flesh without the removal of bones and cartilage?" Another says, "Can you hear me? Are you there? Over and out." Condition 6: The people who build the road intuit our future travel by placing their fingertips on the ground and checking for small vibrations. They mulch their hands through the soil, homing in on nematodes and other reminders of the last glacial period. Condition 7: Arch. Arched. Arching. Condition 8: During the descent we instinctively brace for impact, but impact is a quaint concept from an era we have yet to document. If anyone asks. We're talking about the time before USB sticks and classic rock. We're talking about the time before fishes could bleed. Actually, we're not talking at all, but if you close your eyes you might hear us anyway.

The Contents of the Box Will Not Reveal Themselves

When we fall to earth, rivers will bifurcate, in the order received. Authorised version to follow. The girl whose fingers resemble discharge valves arrives despite displaced curls. Her arms and shoulders are a jumble of scars and tattoos that are impossible to distinguish. Some say you share many of the same characteristics as your salamander kin. Others comment on your penchant for blue cars and soft, almost mushy, taxonomies. Still others say nothing, but file you away with the rest of the tricksters and frauds. Carved in stone, saturated in color. One removes themselves from the narrative. Another suggests that narrative exists simply to validate the local terrain to outsiders. But then, sensitive poets cannot empathize without the aid of pastoral images or the fractional distillation of water. She says, "You are better off alone." In some cultures, throwing shade is nothing more than the hippy version of war. The periphery giggles, then discards. You want to tell her that you once attempted to reach the rarefied air of slo-mo. She, who would lead you to believe that hearing protection is optional, offers two hopeful versions of truth, "Punish yourself or be punished." How else can these things play out? Placed over hot coals and suspended by your inners. Raw materials rather than living tissue. Truffles of war rather than system takeover. Turns out that this is the happy place you remember when you can't remember the happy place you remember.

The Book of Suzanna

ᘉ

Bernard Hœpffner

There dwelt a man in Godforsaken, called Burden:

And he had a companion, whose name was Suzanna, the daughter of Pergrad, a very fair woman, and one that feared no adventure.

Her parents were righteous, and taught their daughter according to the laws of their country.

Now Burden was not a great rich man, and had a fair garden joining unto his house: and to him grew a goodly number of vegetables; because he was known to speak to his plants, and knew them almost as living beings.

One year he had been appointed to speak about colours, such as the American spake of, and he spoke of that wickedness, the double-blue-bind, which came from Bateson and seemed to govern many people.

And in the same place also spake Suzanna: and her subject was the blue, the bluest, she spake like a blue streak, and thus they went off into the blue.

Now when the people departed away at dinner, Suzanna went with Burden to walk.

And the others saw them going in every day, and walking; saw that their lust was inflamed toward each other.

And they perverted their own mind, and turned away their

eyes, that they might not look unto them too much, nor remember past judgments.

And albeit they both were wounded with their love, yet durst not one shew another his love.

For they were ashamed to declare their lust, that they desired to have to do with each other.

Yet they watched diligently from day to day to see each other.

And the one said to the other, Let us now go home: for it is dinner time.

So when they were gone out, they parted the one from the other, and turning back again they came to the same place; and after that they had asked one another the cause, they acknowledged their lust: then appointed they a time both together, when they might be alone together.

And it fell out, as they searched for a fit time, that she was to go to a far country with two children and a sort of husband, and she was desirous to do what was correct and proper: for it was a time to be watchful.

And there had in a previous time been no body with them save each other, and they had hid themselves, and had kissed.

Then he said to her, Tomorrow, bring me your self and we will shut the garden doors, that we may speak to each other.

And they did as he bade, and shut the garden doors, and went out themselves at privy doors to fetch the love that commanded them: but they saw not one, because they were hid.

Now when they had gone forth, the two rose up, and he said unto her,

Behold, the garden doors are shut, that no man can see us, and we are in love with each other; therefore consent unto me, and lie with me.

If thou wilt not, you will bear witness against our love, that we are desired to be with each other: and therefore thou stayed.

Then Suzanna sighed, and said, I am straitened on every side: for if I do this thing, it is a sure sign unto me that I love thee: and if I do it I cannot escape your hands.

It is better for me to fall into your hands, and do it, and to sin in the sight of my husband.

With that Suzanna cried with a loud voice: and the two cried together.

Then ran Burden, and opened his garden door, and into his garden they went.

So that no one heard them cry in the garden, and they rushed in at the privy door, and no one saw what they did there.

But later, when somehow someone had decided to declare the matter, as he wanted the husband to be greatly peeved off: for there was never such a report made of Suzanna.

And it came to pass the same day, when the man was assembled to her husband, he came also full of mischievous imagination against Suzanna to put her to shame;

And said the husband before the man, Send for Suzanna, the daughter of Pergrad, Burden's lover. And so they sent.

But she did not come with her father and mother, her children, and all her kindred.

Now Suzanna was a very delicate woman, and beauteous to behold.

And these wicked men commanded to uncover her face, (for she was covered) that they might be filled with her beauty.

Therefore her friends and all that saw her wept.

Then the husband stood up in the midst of the people, and laid his hands upon her head.

And she weeping looked up toward the West: for her heart trusted in her lover.

And the husband said, As you walked in the garden, you were not alone, and you shut the garden doors, and went there where no one would see you.

Then your lover, an old man, a Jew from the North, who there was hid with you, came unto you, and lay with you.

Then we needed not to be in the garden to see this wickedness.

And when we imagined you together, the man we could not hold: for he was a foreigner for us, and he opened the door, and he leaped out.

But you being my spouse, we ask who the old man was, but you would not tell us: these things do we testify.

Then the assembly believed them as having been shameless and they felt they were judges of the people: so they condemned her to shame.

Then Suzanna cried out with a loud voice, and said, O everlasting Blue, that knowest all the secrets, and knowest all things before they be:

Thou knowest that they have borne false witness against me, for, if I did what I did, there is no shame attached to it, and, behold, they fill me with shame; whereas I did such things, and the shame these men have maliciously invented against me they must now turn upon their own head.

And the Sky heard her voice. And the Sky had been given the name More Hedgehog hog hog.

Therefore she went away, and so many tribulations she had to suffer, the blue sky itself was wont to weep seeing what suffering she had to undergo:

And thus it cried with a loud voice, I want to clear the blood of this woman.

Then all the people turned their eyes toward the sky, and said, What mean these words that were just now spoken?

So the sky standing high above them said, Are ye such fools, ye sons of the Sava Dolinka and of the Sava Bohinjka, that without examination or knowledge of the truth ye have condemned a daughter of your land?

Return again to the place of judgment: for they have borne false witness against her.

So when they were put asunder one from another, and the sky said unto them, O thou that art waxen old in wickedness, now thy sins which thou hast committed aforetime are come to light.

For thou hast pronounced false judgment and hast condemned someone who, if not innocent, had many reasons to do what she did.

Now then, if thou hast seen her, tell me, Under what tree sawest thou them companying together? And he answered, Under a mastick tree.

And he received the sentence to be cut in two.

Therefore it was asked of every one to retract shame of Suzanna, with Burden her companion, and all the kindred, because there was no dishonesty found in her.

From that day forth was Suzanna in great reputation in the sight of the people.

And so she should.

Two Pieces

David Miller

Spiritual Letters, Series 7, #2

The neighbours threw raw eggs at us from their balcony, while we sat
talking in the courtyard. – Don't you realise you could have scarred
someone? you shouted angrily. *Schwarzkopf*, the purple leaves so
dark that we thought them to be black. Dead of a heroin overdose,
he'd turned bright blue by the time he was found. *Of night, lonely,
blind-eyed.* We were being held captive, my mother, my friend and I,
by a tall, thin, sinister-looking literary academic, in an abandoned
flat; he told us that he hated his mother and that his colleagues
were arseholes: I drew my own conclusions, and effected an escape.
Without even waiting to involve the police, I gathered some friends
together and we broke into the flat, fearful of what we'd find: we
found it empty. *Your shadow is a squirrel, mine a bobcat.*

> It wasn't you after all
> or anything like you
> but when the figure first
> appeared in the room
> it didn't seem

an apparition let alone
sinister
but then the animals came
and proliferated
a cat attached itself
to my back with its claws
and I couldn't detach it
yet I did kill its companions

The old man stood in my doorway, with rain pouring down outside, asking if I'd look after his flat, next door to mine, while he was away. It didn't make me uneasy that he had black silk hangings and covers in his bedroom; but on a later occasion he telephoned me while I was staying at a friend's, although I could have sworn I'd never given him the number or mentioned my friend's name. *At the time he entered the asylum, he was very handsome, like a movie star – in fact, he'd acted in films. When he was released, nine years later, he looked like an old witch.* – That kike mentality, he said, that kike spirit exemplified in the Kabbalah... I want to hear no more of it, ever. An old image comes back to me, of black fire on white fire – a writing of fiery black letters on a ground of fiery white. *Half bricks on whole bricks.* The doctor inscribed a cross in red on the patient's record, signifying extermination by lethal gas. *The intricate lead crystal window above the door crashed into the street and pieces of furniture came flying through doors and windows.* A Brownshirt climbed onto the roof, waving the Torah scroll and shouting: 'Wipe your arses on it, Jews!' *The Snake has been liberated. We must crush the Snake's head.* All he could engender in his disciples was despair. But a rival's disciples were brought false elation. *...we were not only shut out of our houses, the baths, and the public square, but they forbade us to be seen in any place whatsoever. For we praise the fish of the living.* An owl flew off into the trees, its eyes orange and black. In the park, two small girls, one white, one black, were on swings and both laughing. *The skies open for you: may you live in peace.* Words inscribed on stone, tile or marble slab, with images of acrobat and gymnast, fisherman and shepherd, martyr and saint. *Nor is the fire ever lulled to sleep,* he wrote, *but it will consume the sea, the mountains, and the woods; God will destroy everything with it, judging every soul.* I took up a conch shell, and blew into it; you took up a ram's horn.... Neither of us ceased from weeping.

Jay and the Flamingo

Jay, who was in her early thirties, was an artist. She had been working on a painting that afternoon, but it had not been going well, or at least, as well as she'd hoped. She'd already been working on it for some time now, and it had come to be the only painting she was involved with. Her husband Wally was painting in his own studio in the house, so Jay went by herself to a nearby park – a large park with a zoo in it.

Jay walked around the park until she came to the zoo, then she walked around the enclosures until she stood in front of where the larger birds lived. There were no other people about, and it felt peaceful to be there. Jay leaned against a tree and took out her cigarettes.

'That's very bad for your health, dear', someone said.

Jay looked around her, but this part of the zoo still seemed deserted. 'I must be imagining things', thought Jay.

'However, I know it's really none of my business', the same someone said.

'Who said that? Where are you?' called out Jay.

'I'm right here.'

The only creature at all close to Jay was a pink flamingo. It had been edging its way closer for some time now, but Jay had thought nothing of it.

'Are you... are you able to speak?' Jay asked, as surprised with herself as she was with the idea of a talking flamingo.

'Yes, dear, I am', replied the flamingo, coming even closer. 'My name is Beatrice. And what is yours, if I may ask?'

'It's Jay.'

'Ah, what a nice name, my dear! And what do you do, if you don't mind my asking?'

'I'm an artist, but my painting isn't going very well, I'm afraid.'

'Why don't you paint a rose, my dear?'

'Beatrice, that's uncanny – I *am* painting a rose! Well, in a way... it's a rose and it's also not a rose.' And Jay struggled to explain this to Beatrice, while the flamingo listened attentively. When Jay had finished, Beatrice asked:

'What else do you do, Jay?'

'I love to dance, for one thing.'

'Well, I don't dance, dear, but I like to *move about*', replied Beatrice.

Jay promised to visit her again, and then left.

⊖

On the way home, Jay took a route that led past a hair salon which she was curious about. She knew the owner slightly, and she knew that he'd been intending to staff the salon with apes and monkeys borrowed from the zoo – gorillas, baboons and orang-utans, all known for their love of grooming. He felt they could be trained to be hair stylists. It would be a fashionable novelty, he thought, and it might make his fortune.

When Jay reached the salon, she peered in and indeed saw an orang-utan using its fingers to style a woman's hair. The woman seemed to be highly pleased with the way her hair was being stroked into place (presumably after being searched for insects). The owner, Bill, noticed Jay and waved. Jay waved back, but she didn't go in.

⊖

When Jay arrived back at her apartment, she told Wally about her encounter with Beatrice.

Wally didn't believe what she said about the flamingo. 'Jay, you've been working too hard!' he exclaimed. Jay didn't know how to persuade him.

Later, in the evening, their friend Wallace came by the apartment. Wallace was also an artist, and he published an unusual magazine with loose cards and pages in an envelope or small folder, with his own art and poetry and that of his friends and others. Jay told Wallace about Beatrice, and he was intrigued. He suggested that Jay, Wally and he go to the zoo together the next day.

⊖

'Beatrice, this is my husband Wally', Jay said.

'Hi, Beatrice', said Wally.

Beatrice didn't reply. She just looked at them in a steady kind of way.

'And I'm their friend Wallace. But some people call me Wally as well – so feel free.'

Beatrice remained silent.

'You know, I have a sister named Beatrice', said Wallace. Jay and Wally both looked at him, surprised; he'd never mentioned this before. Indeed, Wallace rarely said anything about his background.

Beatrice the flamingo didn't reply.

Jay, Wally and Wallace looked at each other. Wallace shrugged. Wally shook his head. Jay looked at Beatrice. Then Jay, Wally and Wallace turned and walked away.

The next time that Jay visited the zoo, Beatrice said to her: 'Are all the men you know called Wally, dear?'

'No, Beatrice, they're not', said Jay. 'And why didn't you speak to Wally and Wallace? I felt like a fool.'

'Oh, I'm sorry, my dear. You see, I'm a little... capricious like that. It wasn't anything personal: I'm sure Wally and Wallace are very nice.'

While they'd been talking, Jay had noticed two Canada geese moving closer and closer towards the flamingo.

Jay quickly climbed over the railings and jumped down into the enclosure.

'Oh dear, you *did* startle me!' exclaimed Beatrice.

'I just saved your life!' said Jay. 'Don't you realise that? I mean, if I hadn't been here...'

'Now, Jay, don't be so dramatic. I do appreciate your friendship, my dear, but *saving my life!* Let's not get carried away.'

Beatrice really could be utterly unaware of things, thought Jay. 'But there were two Canada geese – coming towards you! I'm sure they were going to attack you.'

'That must have been Guy and Anne. You didn't frighten them away, did you? Jay, they're my good friends – they're the nicest, most *civilised* birds you could ever meet! Dear, dear me, now I'll have to go and apologise to them.'

'I can't seem to do anything right,' thought Jay. 'Why on earth did I think Guy and Anne wanted to *attack* Beatrice?' She sighed.

'Goodbye, Beatrice', she said. 'I'll see you again soon.'

'See you soon, dear', said Beatrice.

⊖

On her way home, Jay looked in the window of the salon again.

An orang-utan, a gorilla and a baboon were grooming the hair of three stylish-looking women seated in front of mirrors. Other women sat waiting their turn. Bill was standing there, in a corner, and he noticed Jay and beckoned her in.

Bill introduced her briefly to Rosalind, the gorilla, Muriel, the baboon, and Annabelle, the orang-utan. Rosalind and Muriel stopped work just long enough to nod hello, but Jay could have sworn that Annabelle winked at her.

As she resumed walking towards her home, she wondered: Did they have long enough lunch breaks? And what happened to them in the evenings? Did they have a TV? And where did they sleep? Did they go back to the zoo?

⊖

Jay tried one more time to get Beatrice to talk to other people. She asked her poet friend Jack to accompany her when she next visited the flamingo.

Beatrice wasn't really familiar with people being drunk, but she could tell there was something wrong with Jack.

'Beatrice, this is Jack', said Jay.

Beatrice didn't say anything.

'So, you can't talk!' said Jack in a slurred voice, and he began laughing. 'Can't talk, can't talk!'

'Jack!' exclaimed Jay. 'That's not nice.'

'Of course I can talk!' said Beatrice.

Jack fainted. When he came to, he swore he'd never drink alcohol again. And he didn't – for a day or two.

⊖

Jay struggled with her painting for a long time. Some days her work on it went well, while other days felt discouraging. She persisted. The painting changed variously, and she could have made a series of related paintings instead, but she didn't. Why? The painting was extremely large and heavy, for one thing. There wasn't space in her studio for more than one work like it. However, there was also a sense of wanting one final image, not several.

She didn't visit the salon again, but she heard that Annabelle, Muriel and Rosalind had become celebrated hair stylists.

She did continue to visit Beatrice.

Finally, Jay took a photograph of the painting to show Beatrice. 'Beatrice, the painting is finished – or at least, as far as it can be', she said.

'Oh my dear, how wonderful!' Beatrice exclaimed.

Jay held the photograph for Beatrice to see.

It was and was not a rose. It wasn't red. For the most part it was grey and white. It was centred, like a rose, but it didn't really look like a rose in any conventional way. Yet it did somehow seem flower-like.

It was a painting, but the paint was so thick that it was almost a sculpture, as well. Parts of the encrusted surface seemed carved rather than painted.

There was something raw about it, yet sophisticated at the same time. It had the look of something long considered and meditated upon, but there were hints of the impulsive and the energetic as well. Despite the grey and black, it wasn't dull in the slightest.

In fact, more than anything else it was like an extraordinary burst of light, along severe radiating lines, out of and back into what might be clouds and might also be plant forms. At the bottom of the painting these forms became more like mounds of earth or stones. It had an intensity to it which was like dazzling sunlight breaking through the boughs and leaves of trees or the gaps in a wall.

Guy and Anne had been edging nearer and nearer, until they looked at the photograph over Beatrice's folded wings. 'Splendour!' said Guy. 'Brilliance!' said Anne. Jay was taken back: she had never realised that they too could talk; but she didn't say anything.

'Dear, dear Jay', said Beatrice, 'it's beautiful! Not pretty, mind you, not at all. Indeed, I think this is even more than just beautiful – it's magnificent.'

Guy and Anne nodded approvingly.

'Do you really think so, Beatrice?' Jay asked.

'My dear, a flamingo always tells the truth. Didn't you know?'

(For Dodo.)

Reginald Edward Morse
The Lost Episodes, 1-6[*]

❦

Edited by Rick Moody

N-Hotel, Bergen, Norway, June 13-20, 2011

We have stayed in some really bad ones. Where to begin? 1) N-Hotel had us berthed in a room with a full-sized bed, despite having confirmed a double king. 2) Upon walking into the room there was unmistakable musk of waste water and mildew. 3) The walls were AbEx'd with dirt and ominous smears (just the hooks remained where the art formerly hanged). 4) Others on this very web site have commented on the *noise* at the N-Hotel which could, in fact, force hardened insurrectionists to *confess*, and we were on the back of the hotel, but we could still hear the hooligans in the *fotball puben* at the front. 5) Stampeding on the floor above us, overnight and early in the morning, as if there were a bona fide madwoman in the attic, or perhaps a family of hogs in rut. 6) We came in June, amid the glory of the midnight sun, and yet the curtains were of a *thin white gauze*. 7) We requested vegetarian sandwiches for breakfast (one had no choice but a sandwich for breakfast), and still we received ham; we were told we would have to walk the unsafe and tobacco-reeking stairwells to reception to get a replacement sandwich if we

[*]Excerpted from *The Complete Writings of Reginald Edward Morse*, a compendium of online hotel reviews by one of the preferred reviewers at the RateYourLodging.com website.

wanted one, because the staff was *too busy* to bring the sandwich
to our room. (Meanwhile, to be thorough, the infantile juice boxes
in our breakfast sacks had no straws, and repelled all attempts to
be opened.) 7.5) The staff was sullen on all occasions. 8) The tiny
lobby was always crammed with dozens upon dozens of roller-board
suitcases, so getting in and out required Olympic-caliber vaulting.
9) A retinue of disconsolate persons constantly smoked outside door
of hotel, likewise in the dingy *fotball puben* day and night, and as we
passed we could feel our bronchia sprouting aggressive malignancies.
10) Tea service in the lobby had no hot water. 11) Dryer did not
dry clothes (two hours, clothes still damp). 12) The bathroom had
human hairs generously beribboning the tile when we arrived. 13)
It seems too easy to mention that the beds were uncomfortable, but
they were thin palettes of insomnia and misery. 14) No closets, no
coffee/tea making in room, no hair dryer, no *soap*, except for one
of those wall dispensers with liquid "body wash," which was about
as effective as waving a clove of garlic near to your private bits. 15)
Meager selection on the television, all Norwegian, for which we
should have been grateful, as I have read that many people didn't
have a television that worked at all. 16) Effect on my relationship to
K: negative! ★

*Liverpool Grace Inn, 1258 Transistor Parkway, Liverpool, NY, October
4-5, 2011*

To get to Transistor Parkway, you have to turn off of Electronics
Avenue, and if you think I make this sort of thing up you are wrong.
Appropriately, in this tumbledown sprawl outside of Syracuse, there
is everywhere a susurring of interstate, all of its traffic intended
upon *away from here.* The Liverpool Grace has faux-Greek statuary
out front--a naiad in a clamshell, enfountained, toes cushioned in
a bloom of algae, this the only indication of the elevated spirit of
human possibility, the *grace*, the forgiveness, the redemption, that
has been all but stamped out elsewhere on the premises. Well, there
is a complimentary coffee bar in the lobby that operates all the
day long (but was down to dregs of house blend when we arrived
at 9:45 PM). The girl at the front desk asked us if it was okay that
we were on the second floor, as though the second floor were
a profound inconvenience. There were only the two floors. The

first floor apparently leaves one close to one's vehicle, and what is planet earth, amid the susurring of Liverpool, but the terrain which must be traversed in the progress from climate-controlled interior to vehicle? The second floor, the girl said—Gothic black outfit and eye makeup—was preferable because on the second floor you did not have children on the floor above you. Who could quarrel with this logic? To solve the problem, as the motivational speakers say, *be* the problem. We could be the clog-dancers on the floor above, because we were getting ready for tomorrow's clog-dancing convention in Syracuse. It's all true. A cursory room check of room #232 indicated the usual oppressive floral patterned interior and machined imitation watercolors of *barns in autumn* bolted to the walls. There was a sofa that sagged in the middle beside the king bed which was the indication of a *suite*, the only indication. Our view out the second-story window was of tarmac and big boxes. I do not want to have to, in all of my reviews, mention the problem of mildew in the bathrooms. I do not want to appear preoccupied with mildew, of which *aspergillis* is one particularly lethal variety, which has been known in certain cases to cause dementia. I would like to spend a night where I didn't have to mention *aspergillis*. Is that so much to ask for? In this instance: it was like someone was manufacturing Roquefort in the bathroom. Like they had an assembly line devoted to round-the-clock Roquefort manufacture. It was like our neighborhood homeless gentleman decided to stay with us in the Liverpool Grace, camping out in the bathroom where he strung up some of his shreds on a line to give them a complete airing. Did you know that the word "mildew" originally came from "honeydew?" We were barely in the door of #232 when K. became trapped in that loop, in front of the mirror by the entertainment console, in which she needed to assess her imagined level of obesity. There is no obesity there at all, but that does not stop K., who, without a moment's hesitation, will start removing garments in order to check the size of belly and posterior, grabbing bits of flesh, *tisking* at herself and the handfuls of flesh, grabbing up skirt, pulling down underwear, doing several 180-degree pivots, from which activity she will not be dissuaded. There needs to be a substantial amount of mirroring in a hotel room to make possible her *body mass surveillance*, in which she began spitting out numbers of pounds she needed to shed, and apparently the Liverpool Grace did not have the *grace* to allow one to be entrapped in a dialogue of mirrors. Oh how quickly one wants to get to one's car, and out of the Liverpool Grace, which was not, in the end, a place of elevated spirit, a place of redemption, but rather a place of *aspergillis* and mediocre foam pillows and a twenty-four hour coffee station without coffee.★★

Bingham Dormitory, #18, Lewiston College, Lewiston, ME, June 22-23, 2010

We were feeling rather excited when we borrowed the $5000 for the "Expressions of Travel" class at Lewiston College. I personally have always wanted to leave behind a memoir of my journeys, including my theories about international currencies, a sketch of my grandmother, Charlene, whose birth was the result of a profane assignation between a ruthless Southern landowner and a domestic aid. K. intends to compose a full-length prose poem about her youthful eating disorder and a sweet but sexually voracious gymnastics coach she knew once. Neither of us had written more than a few lines reviewing, e.g., our internist, or films we don't like, which is to say: we knew we had a lot to learn. Who knew that what we really were going to learn was about the horrors of dormitory life! These Lewiston dorms are like tumbledown New England barns. Speckled with green-gray bacterial life on the exterior, mossy, overrun with squirrels and hornets, grim fluorescences in the hallways, and a general vibe of the *sexually transmitted disease*. How many children of rich persons have ended their lives in dormitory hallways like this? We entered these neglected, dimly lit hallways with an intense dread, as though each darkened corridor could contain a German philosopher, and, in fact, in the communal kitchen, which had almost nothing that one might associate with food, excepting an espresso maker that had a sign on it, "Property of Aaron Marsh!!!!," a shirtless gentlemen was riffling the lower shelves mumbling, "Shouldn't have drunk so much." Still, the hallways were nothing when compared to the room to which we were assigned. It was ninety-three degrees Fahrenheit that day, with high humidity, and of course the college resisted summer air-conditioning. I get that. It's a liberal arts institution. Only a couple of weeks a year require a.c. As a result, the room was hot enough to cook limbic tissue. The two beds, if that's what you call them, chastity insurers, whose box spring was just a lattice of extremely rusty springs strung across a crude wooden frame designed to alert the entire dormitory whenever coitus took place, and the mattresses themselves were more like slabs of inert building material. As each was a foot across, we placed these on the floor, among the earwigs. K. went to the communal bathroom, which had no mats of any kind, nor were there any hair care products, etc. One small bar of Ivory Soap had been provided in the room. We went immediately to the Home Depot in town and bought a box fan for $15.95. It was loud enough to drown out the alcoholic couplings of the writers around us. This description herewith is the only writing I accomplished while at the workshop. ★

The Alpha Institute, 15 Pond Roundabout, Rhinebeck, New York, August 14-17, 2010

The Tantric Sex workshop had been suggested to K., who was going by the name Astra briefly. Someone she'd met in Marin County back in the nineties, had suggested the workshop. We told her that we liked to travel, and she suggested the Tantric Sex workshop at the Alpha Institute. There were a lot of great teachers at the Alpha Institute, or at least there were a lot of names I remembered dimly from the late seventies. There were several echelons of lodging possible at Alpha. First, you could live in a dormitory with several other people, in a hostel type environment; second, you could get a semi-private room with one roommate; third, you could pay for a private room. The rooms were priced accordingly. According to Astra's friend, no one really used the private rooms. They weren't considered in the spirit of Alpha. After all, it was a community workshop. We were not too concerned about the price point, though we should have been., but we nonetheless booked the middle alternative, the single roommate. Perhaps our roommate, a drummer named Jorge, who was there for the Drumming and Masculinity workshop, was not prepared to share the room with a couple, especially a couple who needed to be able to practice Tantric sex, as we were given homework between classes. This certainly cannot have been easy for Jorge. But I'm digressing. The room was small, and the pillows were very Indian, as was the case with almost all the furnishings, small, brightly colored, completely uncomfortable, as if comfort were somehow bourgeois. There was a tray for burning incense on the little desk, and that implies, yes, that there was a small desk, but Jorge had piled here many of this things—his loincloths, his clavé, his castanets, his bongos—and there was a tiny shower stall that we were often fighting over. Astra and I could not fit into the bed, and she even pushed me out one time, and told me go ahead and sleep on the floor if I couldn't stop biting her nipples. Jorge woke up from his fitful snoring and complained, and this is when Astra told us we could both *fuck off*, as far as she was concerned, and if you knew her, you knew that this was not the kind of language she ordinarily used, but was more a reflection of the fact that we had not yet achieved tantric release. Jorge's snoring sounded like a sump pump discharging the backwash from a flooded basement. I was worried that Astra was somehow attracted to him. We hoarded food from the dining hall, were constantly stuffing muffins into Astra's kinte cloth shift and carrying them back to the room and broadcasting the crumbs everywhere. After two nights, Jorge found a young woman with a Mohawk who was living out in the trailers at the edge of the institute, where all the staff resided, and he moved in with her and taught her to feel the skins of his bongos. They had us to dinner there one night, and we roasted gluten-free cutlets over a propane fire and talked about the predictions of the Mayans. After that dinner, our lodgings seemed more capacious, and we still had Tantric release to look forward to. ★★

Howard Johnson Inn, 1052 Boston Post Rd, Milford, CT, circa April 1, 1985

It was near here that I went to a funeral on a certain day long ago, namely the funeral of a last surviving grandparent, and I can remember nothing about this funeral, though it is known, among those to whom I am related, that the funeral included a brief stay at the Howard Johnson motor lodge. Why can I remember nothing about this hotel? Are there certain hotels of which you can remember nothing? It is true that my grandmother had a fondness for Howard Johnson's restaurants, those bright orange roofs, and that as an inhabitant of New England in my childhood, I can well remember when all the rest areas, along the interstates, were outfitted with Howard Johnson's restaurants. It was a time in the life of your reviewer, if not in the life of the nation, when Howard Johnson meant quality. The interstate road system was created in order that there would be efficient routes out of the cities during attack by any foreign agent, and having created these routes out, we also needed a way to pull over and get some gas, without clotting the towns nearby, and thus the rest area. The divine rested from its labor, and even Joseph and Mary needed a place to put down for the night. (And how would you rate the manger where Jesus of Nazareth was born, the manger in which western civilization was suddenly transformed, for good or ill, would you rate it highly based on the outcome of night spent there, a definite five-star outcome, or would you rate it poorly based on some of the criteria we use here for discussing the places we stay now? 1) it probably did *smell* in the manger, and you would need to evaluate kinds of livestock stink and how you feel about them—for example, K. is personally affronted by the smell of goat, and will not eat any goat products, no matter the alleged health benefits of goat products, and it is fair to say that I personally like the smell of horse manure, and this is because of a couple of family vacations from my childhood when I once or twice spent time in the company of horses; I love the whimsy of horses, the way they are capable of expressing so much emotional warmth and so much variety of mood so simply, and so if the manger of Bethlehem had stabled the occasional nag I would have been tempted to rate it highly; 2) the straw may have been rather comfortable, and, in fact, just the sort of thing the Virgin and her consort were well used to, because of what were beds composed in those days if not straw, 3) I personally am always worried about making too much noise in a hotel (see the entry for the Plaza Hotel that I have posted elsewhere on this site), and am therefore occasionally happy to learn that a hotel in which I am staying is *empty*, and on this occasion it stands to reason that the guests were staying in the available lodging without human company, and thus the Virgin was free to make as much noise as she needed to during the labor process, and my ex-wife, who once gave birth at home, described to me how there is definitely a need, under these circumstances, to make a certain amount of noise, though the belief that women scream during labor is prejudicial, and masculine in origin; that is to say, I was present when my wife gave birth at home, though admittedly I came in toward the end, because I had been travelling for work, and I did see my wife, in the beginning of growing *away*, transformed by the pain of labor into some raving, sweating, goddess of transcendence, some willing sufferer who knew that this pain preceded the ordinary miracle of childbirth, who knew that this was both the moment we had stayed together to experience and also the moment in which we would stop needing one another for any purpose at all; however, it is possible that the Virgin, who may have been only dimly aware of the significance of the child she was carrying even though she had lived through the Annunciation, was disinclined to make a lot of noise, to cry out, because, after all, she was the Virgin, and was therefore *mild*, and so the fact that she was in labor in the manger was somehow comforting—it was a place to stay and she could elocute as much as necessary, and if you are one of those people who believe that just because she was the Virgin she didn't make any noise during her labor then you are, as far as I'm concerned, *living in a fog bank*, because the thing about her child was that he was at least half-human, and so he was going to come out like a human baby, which means there was going to be a fair amount of discomfort, because, this is the lot of all women since Eve, as I myself once saw, a pain that you have to admire, that you have to wonder at, and 4) that brings us to the issue of the mess and fuss of labor itself; now maybe in these dark days before the light of Christianity it was not uncommon for people to put up in an inn in order to give birth to a child, but these things are not without significant blood loss (there was a sort of *Cape Fear* effluvium to the whole thing in my experience), and a great variety of human fluids, and perhaps the virgin and Joseph were only too happy to stay in a setting that would make this blood and muck completely *routine*. They, Joseph and Mary, understood the great dignity, and grace of the animal world. The animal kingdom knew about the blood and pitch of childbirth, understood, accepted the blood and pitch, and the animal kingdom knew how it was the lot of the animal kingdom there to dwell, unable, in most cases, to do much about the blood and pitch, but to endure it, to find in endurance something enviable; Mary threw in with the animals in that particular lodging, and she knew, in that way, the tremendous dignity of the animal kingdom, and this we would have to consider admirable, and likewise 5) the lodging was extremely inexpensive. I think Luke, the gospel writer in this particular case, does not indicate whether the owner of the manger required payment for the overnight in this case, but I think we have to presume that the lodging was free, and there are free hotels in my catalogue of hotels but I have to say most of the time when things are free you have to trade away quality, and this day was no exception; but Joseph and Mary were free to save the money that they might otherwise have needed for lodging and to spend it on food, which means that they could have a really top notch breakfast the morning after Jesus of Nazareth was born, and 6) if they needed milk, it's possible that they could just go across the stall to where the cow resided and give her teat a good squeeze, because animal husbandry was such, in those days, that probably everyone knew how to do it; on the other hand, 7), rats, and I'm afraid this just a big *downer* and has to be counted as a demerit in any rating of the lodging in question, because as everyone knows rats are the one thing that you don't want in any temporary lodging situation, it's just a drop dead requirement for me, *no rats*, it's so important that as a reviewer of hotels I would say I have no other absolute requirement, in the end, but that the room have no rats in it, and I wouldn't even admit into this list a hotel that had rats in it, I just wouldn't even bother, because I would not allow you, the consumer, reader of my reviews, to have to stay in any hotel that had rats in it, and, unfortunately, Mary and Joseph had to contend with rats, there were definitely rats in the manger, and the rats were fighting with the other animals in there for the grain strewn around and clumped in piles; though we have not considered the possibility therefore of 8) cats, and even though pregnant women are meant not to handle the feces of cats, because of *toxoplasmosis*, everybody likes a cat, or most people do, and therefore perhaps Mary had the option to pet a cat during the labor itself, and maybe this calmed her, and the cats in turn were a scourge to the rats and mice of the manger, and, furthermore, Joseph and Mary had visitors, namely guys with fancy perfumes, and these guys masked some of the earthier odors of the stalls, and the grim dark, which would have been hard, the candlelight, in which Joseph stumbled around and ran into sheep, tripped over them, while trying to get a compress for Mary, kicking dogs out of the way, and this darkness, after a time, was mitigated by the bright light of one alleged star, though maybe the illumination was simply the light of a marriage, which for at least one moment, dealt with the reversals like a team, and so for every problem in the manger, from the point of view of RateYourLodging.Com, there was some equal and opposite success, and so I'm going to go out on a limb here and say that the manger in Bethlehem probably rated about ★★★). The Howard Johnson *rest area* fulfills a need, which is the first order of business. Howard Johnson, by reason of its bright orange roof line, its faintly oriental roof line, meant progress and quality, and for myself and my siblings, it meant *sausage*. Which is to say that the primary food group of the Howard Johnson, in those days, at least for us, was *sausage*, and that was enough. In the end, Howard Johnson's gave away its license to the rest areas, and many of the inns closed, and that's partly why I can remember nothing about them. One time I made a journey up the Boston Post Road, from New York to Boston, an American journey, and I came through Milford, and in due course I was adjacent to the cemetery where my grandmother and grandfather were buried, and I had not been there in fifteen or twenty years, and I walked into the graveyard and without any sense if it was the correct graveyard, or where the grave was, exactly, I walked right up to it. Death and lodging are intimately related. Death is something that happens immediately after lodging. ★★

The Belamar, Manhattan Beach, CA, August 6, 2010

The valet parking situation in the greater Los Angeles area is not to be borne by the faint of heart. The parking lot at the Belamar is about the size of a sigmoid colon, and the cars are fitted into it like tiny cancerous polyps, which can only be extracted from surrounding healthy tissue by an expert surgeon, or by an excessively friendly fellow from the movie-making world who says *bro* a lot, though just out of earshot. We did not realize the valet parking arrangement and thus traveled from end to end of the parking lot like octegenarians, K. yelling at me that the sugar-free taffy that we had purchased at PDX were *profoundly laxative* and that we needed to gain entrance to the hotel immediately. I apologize greatly for the use of this language in this review, but you know when you have become a *regular reviewer*, a trusted voice, a voice of reason on a site like RateYourLodging. Com, you must be able to use whatever criteria are at hand. So, first of all the parking situation, and then the matter of the lobby, which smelled like a swimming pool. A pair of excessively casual front desk people assured us that there was absolutely nowhere to eat, nowhere to walk, nowhere to drive, not nearby, and then they gave us a couple of those credit-card sizes keys, and we set disconsolately off toward the elevator. Upon our insertion the hotel seemed entirely empty. We ambled through the piscine or ichthyic interior as though looking for smaller fish to swallow, and eventually crammed ourselves into the elevator heading for floor three. Upon disembarkment, we smelled a smell almost impossible to describe, but because I am a distinguished hotel reviewer I will now attempt to do so. Description of reputable lodging *must* include the olfactory sense. The Belamar, third floor, smelled like some amalgam of hashish, sunscreen, and cheap cologne. Upon entering our chamber, the smell was of such gravity that K. did what she only does every third or fourth trip, she called the front desk immediately. The unconcerned, bespectacled young lady from reception arrived and began smelling immediately, and then the two women were each smelling, wrinkling their noses in this way that was both attractive and somewhat ominous, after which the young desk lady did indeed give us another room on the second floor, and this was kind of her, because had she not, my review would have been of *utmost seriousness,* how could she know that I was an esteemed reviewer on this site, RateYourLodging.Com. The second floor was different entirely, and must have been the floor where they sequestered society women who were trying to overcome cosmetic procedures. Upon imagining that we could, at last, relax, that we might enjoy the room that we had procured at a massive discount by using *a discounting website*, a non-English-speaking handyperson knocked at the door and with some grunts and hand gestures indicated that he would, at this juncture, install our shower curtain, which we so far had not missed, and it was just as he was leaving, having thanked us in two languages, that K., still as yet afflicted with the taffy referred to above, at the outset of this review, could no longer contain herself, and, for the first time in the course of our epic romance, broke wind in a most delicate way, like a balloon releasing air so as to rise. At last we were berthed for the night. ★★

Moccasin Box

for Pauline Johnson Tekahionwake

٭

Meredith Quartermain

Drive north on any of Vancouver's main streets, and the blue-grey forested hulks of Grouse and Seymour mountains lunge up a wall into the sky as your road disappears over a cliff-edge into the inlet. In East Van the hulks dwarf false-fronted wooden stores reminiscent of frontier trading posts laced together by electricity wires on leaning cedar poles. In the West End they loom over tower blocks and head-office skyscrapers, reminding the busy city, in its antlike toings and froings, of all it is not and can never be. All the more so because even the immense, implacable blue-green hulks are superseded by their crown, a pair of snow-covered peaks which Vancouver fondly calls The Lions.

With they grey cables of its Lions Gate bridge, Vancouver ties itself to the Lions' immensity.

Logs of wood and stumps of trees innumerable, Captain George Vancouver wrote in 1792, staring at driftwood on the delta of the Stó:lō, the river at the foot of these mountains, which did not lead him to the Northwest Passage. Trees, trees and more trees on the wall of peaks blocking his way. Up the coast in the traditional lands of the Skwxwú7mesh, he found a stupendous snowy barrier lurching from sea to clouds and spewing torrents through its rugged chasms. He logged the weather: dark, gloomy, blowing a southerly gale which greatly added to the dreary prospect of the country. Desolation Sound he called some of the coast: forlorn gloomy forests pervaded by an awful silence, empty of birds and animals.

Trees haunt the city: the old giants whose feet spanned a cart and horses – their stumps slimy with moss – still lurk in the salal and ferns of Stanley Park or up the slopes of Grouse Mountain in the Capilano Canyon where they feed the roots of new giants several arm-spans in girth. Their distant tops creak and moan in the wind. Myriad spiny points of needles, long drooping fronds of

cedar, catch shafts of sun and rake tatters of fog from the ocean. The air drips. Trunks, limbs, moss soak up the grind of city planes and cranes, holding in their cavernous understory the rush and trickle of the Capilano river, the peep of a nuthatch, the snap of a falling branch, and, high above, the combing of wind, the chortle of a raven.

Up above, high – sagalie, in the Chinook jargon Pauline Johnson used with Chief Joe Capilano, recording his stories of the Skwxwú7mesh people and the Sagalie Tyee. I imagine

Johnson searching like I was for stories, not from invaders, but from here, stories from the first people of the blue-grey hulks, the moaning giants, the chortling ravens.

The snow-covered Lions are not lions to the S<u>k</u>w<u>x</u>wú7mesh people; they are the Twin Sisters who were lifted to the mountaintops by the Sagalie Tyee. It was they, so Johnson records in her *Legends* from Chief Joe Capilano, who brought the Great Peace between the S<u>k</u>w<u>x</u>wú7mesh and the Haida by the simple act of inviting them to a feast. Another legend tells how the Sagalie Tyee sent his four giants to challenge a swimmer, claiming they would turn him to a fish, a tree, a stone if he did not give way to their canoe.

Back and forth and right toward the giants' canoe he swam so his child would have a clean life. The Sagalie Tyee made him Sl'kheylish (standing-up-man rock) to remind everyone, Defy everything for the future of your child.

Thanks to the Sagalie Tyee, Shak Shak the hoarder suddenly found himself a two-headed serpent, one of his mouths biting the poor and one mouth biting his heart. He who pierces the serpent's heart will kill the disease of greed – so said the Sagalie Tyee. A young man of 16 remembered those words and brought down the monster.

A young woman could get help too from the Sagalie Tyee, if she wanted to know which suitor really cared for her. What if she was looking for other things? Like stories that had grown with the forests. Stories of women who dared, women who blazed trail? Women who spoke? Would the Sagalie Tyee come to her aid?

The front-desk casually mentions a pair of Pauline Johnson's moccasins held somewhere in the library, she's not sure where. A Special Collections librarian says she'll look into it and disappears to inner regions, some time later bringing out a large archival box with reinforced metal corners. We have no provenance for these, she tells me, unfolding tissue paper around a pair of pale, soft moccasins covered with beaded flowers and woven bands of grass, the soles smooth as the bottom of a foot. Their ankle-high cuffs flop over next to curled balls of delicate lacing. Lack of provenance meaning, I suppose, that someone could have found a pair of moccasins in Johnson's possession when she died which actually belonged to someone else – her sister, say, or a friend – and mistakenly passed them off as Johnson's, or even that someone claiming to be a friend of Johnson's had given them to the library when in fact they had belonged to the friend's grandmother and never been touched by Johnson. I try to think this but I've opened a box I can't close: I'm certain they are Johnson's. She's supposed to be wearing them in this picture. The librarian retrieves from an envelope a photocopy of E. Pauline Johnson Tekahionwake in her Mohawk stage costume, that she made of buckskin, and we see her as through a window smoked up by a house fire, moccasins illegible.

In 1909 she retired from the stage at 48 to a two-bedroom Vancouver apartment three miles from Siwash Rock, one of her favorite destinations in Stanley Park. For 20 years she'd been Canada's most famous author (known throughout the English-speaking world), constantly touring and living in hotels. Now her days turned around a small apartment on a treed street in a town

clinging to the far edge of North America, a town barely keeping its
own against wind and sea and the forested mountains looming in its
face. Yet here she found something grander than ever: her Cathedral
Trees. Every day, heedless of the rain or sea soaking her clothes,
she would walk to Siwash Rock, and then to the nearby Cathedral
Grove, one cedar and six Douglas firs from the old-growth forest,
also called the Seven Sisters.

To support herself with no stage performances, Johnson
wrote stories for *Mother's Magazine* and *Boys' World*, stories like "The
Wolf Brothers," "The Silver Craft of the Mohawks," "The Potlach."
Chief Capilano came and sat in silence at the round oak table that
had come from her father's house. She had met him in Buckingham
Palace. After several visits he began to tell her his stories and she
began retelling his Legends of the Capilanos. She visited the offices
of the *Vancouver Daily Province*. Lionel Makovski began paying her
$7 a piece to publish the stories in his weekly magazine, adding
photographs to make them and Princess Tekahionwake his star
attraction; elsewhere the paper had the called the Chief an agitator
and blamed him for disputes and uprisings. Johnson then could
not meet his deadlines; she canceled appointments without notice;
Chief Capilano died; and breast cancer spread into her right arm.
Makovski himself became her writing hand as she dictated the stories
from her couch.

An unsigned page in the moccasin box says that Makovski
made a lot of royalties from Johnson's Legends. He was a member of
the trust that gathered them into a book to raise funds for her living
and medical care. More than 10,000 copies were printed at that
time and the book is still in print. Makovski received the copyright
of *Legends* in Johnson's will, which also left him on her death in 1913
the moccasins she wore on her first trip to England, he perhaps then
leaving them to the library.

She left her pens and the copyrights of *Shagganappi* and
The Moccasin Maker to her manager and stage companion Walter
McRaye, who had started his career doing Drummond's Habitant
verses and who later did hilarious impersonations of celebrities.
Dink, she nicknamed him. During their long journeys on boats
and trains and stagecoaches, they invented together a family of
traveling companions: "the boys" – four of them – who took their
mattresses along and slept on the hat racks, using this vantage point

to play tricks and comment on their friends. At the Steinway Hall in London, the boys bought four tickets for Pauline and Dink. They amused themselves with a cat called Dave Dougherty who slept in Johnson's dressing bag; a bug called Felix Joggins with his very trying wife Jerusha; and a mongoose called Baraboo Montelius.

In 1915 the balance of the proceeds from *Legends*, after paying Johnson's debts, was divided between McRaye and Johnson's sister Eva who then divided her share between the cities of Brantford (near Johnson's ancestral home) and Vancouver, sending $225 to the *World* newspaper to spend on something of assistance to the arts or literary life of the city. Mr. Nelson, the Manager of the *World*, was puzzled as to what to do but at length hit on the idea of purchasing a Pauline Johnson room at the hospital which could be devoted to care of artists, actors, poets, newspaper people and "others of allied interests who might be in hard circumstances (a not unusual condition in these occupations)." He was then "very much moved" by reading about the city's 29th Battalion at the front who were "lamentably short of machine guns where the enemy was well equipped with them." The Vancouver boys seemed to be fighting with their bare fists. Why not buy a gun?

The *World* launched a subscription. How very easy it is to rouse individuals around a sentimental cause. Only to suffer slow and miserable deaths or violent and brutal ones in the Great Ongoing Wars of humanity against humanity and humanity against the earth. Buoyed up by inner spirit or driven by drugged imaginations, people launch into their ventures with little idea of where they'll lead. Or they launch in knowing all too well where it will end: their fate. Yet boundless and unpredictable beginnings save the world from its normal and natural ruin. Thus writes Hannah Arendt: in the fact

of natality lies the root and faculty of action. We act, we speak, and
each time make a beginning toward the possible, just as we entered
the world from our mother's wombs.

The money poured in. Children walked the ten and a half
miles from New Westminster to Vancouver and gave their car fare
for the Pauline Johnson machine gun. By August 1915 the *World* had
$1000 (more than the annual wages of most working men), which it
sent to The Hon. Sam Hughes, Dept of Militia. The manager of the
World was delighted that Lt-Colonel Tobin of the 29th Battalion
would receive a gun for his "gallant corps." Would Tobin see that
the gun bore the name 'Tekahionwake'? Tobin wrote that American
munitions manufacturers could not deliver the gun before January
1916; the Russian and Canadian governments took the firm's total
output, but he hoped to obtain two guns before the battalion left for
the front or certainly shortly afterwards. He promised to engrave
'Tekahionwake' on one and send a photo, but in December 1916
the battalion was still without its Tekahionwake. In December 1918,
the manager of the *World* wrote to Tobin wondering whether "the
Tekahionwake which we gave to the 29th" could be returned to
the *World*? "We are all so proud of our British Columbian men,"
he wrote, "that I am hoping the story of the war, from the British
Columbia standpoint – and with special reference to the exploits
of the BC units – will be collected and become a textbook in our
schools." In July 1920 the *World* regained possession of the gun,
and showed it with a poster saying it was first fired at Kemmel Hill,
Belgium. During a raid, it jammed and Corp. Snowden tore the
red-hot gun apart, fixed the feed-wheel pin, reassembled the gun and
fired again in less than ninety seconds. At St. Eloi, the Tekahionwake
was manned by Ptes. McGir, Owen, Bourke, Annandale, Cooke,
Davidson and Williams (all killed later). At Ypres, three tripods were
shot from under her. One of thousands of machine guns deployed in
the Great War.

I lay out my scraps of research – the haunting trees,
Johnson's walks to Siwash Rock, the things she left in her will, her
stories (from Sḵwx̱wú7mesh chief Capilano) of the Sagalie Tyee, the
strange spellings of words in the Sḵwx̱wú7mesh dictionary, the 7 to
be sounded as a glottal stop like *oh-oh*, the *x̱w* sounded like whispered
wh in *what*. Puzzling over how the Sḵwx̱wú7mesh language might
talk about the Sagalie Tyee, I find *walh7áýnexw* is a Sḵwx̱wú7mesh

word for *spirit*. The dictionary gives no pronunciation. I'm left to imagine what sounds I can. *Kwelh7áýnexw* translates as *spirit of the water. Spirit touches one and one goes numb* – this comes from the word *tení7i7. To go on a spiritual quest for power* is held in the word *ts'iyíwen. Nexwslhich'álhxa* is a *spirit who cuts people's throats* whereas *ch'awtn* is a *spirit helper. Sna7m* conveys a *spiritual power exercised through dancing and singing*, while *siẃtń* evokes a *spiritual power exercised through words*. I let the words figure my tongue. As though words were boxes, and, lifting their wriggling lids, I could find moccasins to slip on, become other than what I am: a taster of letters, a chaser of whiffs humming with threads to other alphabets, echoing glimpses beyond words, always a beyond – an end to a rainbow that flits away to a creak or a moan, a chortle, a rattle streaking the heartbeat, gutwrench, the thousand bitmaps wired in my eyes from born-into wars owners ancestors conquerors cities. As though I could wear them like masks. Tree – Spirit – I tie with tongue taps, certain they exist somewhere with Forest S̲k̲wx̲wú7mesh Self Moccasin. Laces evaporate leaving foot tied to ear, mouth to armpit, eyes all knees and elbows adrift in my house of mirrors. Tap tap tap along the rhythms. Anyone there?

Approaching, in June 1792, the long tongue of land that separates Vancouver's harbour to the north from its boating and beach playground to the south, Captain Vancouver met Chief Capilano's ancestors, who, he wrote in his Journal of Discovery, "conducted themselves with the greatest decorum and civility," and presented him with "several fish cooked and undressed." They "shewed much understanding," Vancouver thought, "in preferring iron to copper." The welcoming party paddled alongside Vancouver's ship as it headed between their communities of Homulchesun on the north shore and Whoi Whoi on the south, and twice assembled their canoes in order to perform ceremonial acts whose meaning

remained "a profound secret" to Vancouver and his men. Afterwards they showed even greater cordiality and respect to the pale-faced newcomers.

The secret was revealed by Qoitchetahl, secretary of the Skwxwú7mesh Indian Council from 1911, who told the city's archivist, his people believed "a calamity of some sort would befall them every seven years. . . . Capt. Vancouver came in a seventh year. . . . When strange men of strange appearance, white with their odd boats, arrived, the wise men said 'this may be the fateful visitation' and took steps to propitiate the all-powerful visitors" with the white eiderdown scattered at festival or potlatch houses. As Vancouver arrived, his people "threw in greeting before him clouds of snow-white feathers which rose, wafted in the air aimlessly about, then fell like flurries of snow to the water's surface, and rested there like white rose petals scattered before a bride." That painted icon Johnson chose not to be, preferring instead to hail the world from the stage with a "cry from an Indian wife" bidding her husband, go to war: "by birth we Indians own these lands,/ Though starved, crushed, plundered."

It's not the immensity of Lions but the immensity of Twin Sisters that rules Vancouver's antlike toings and froings. The immensity of trees and the immensity of sisters. Pauline was passionate, spontaneous and generous; her sister Eva was dutiful, frugal and practical. They argued and wrangled all their lives about Pauline's unseemly stage career, about her raffish friends, about her loans to finance recital tours, and about who was the better teller of Iroquois history. Right up to her death, they quarreled about why she must be buried in a gloomy forest of incessant rain far away from her homeland. They even fought over whether you had to wear a raincoat in Vancouver: Eva said you did; Pauline said you didn't.

The Seven Sisters in Stanley Park were Pauline's daily haunt. "In all the world there is no cathedral whose marble or onyx columns can vie with those straight, clean, brown tree-boles that teem with the sap and blood of life," Johnson wrote of her trees, "no fresco that can rival the delicacy of lace-work they have festooned between you and the skies." When she was too weak to walk she drove to the park in an open carriage. There must surely be some trace of them in the Stanley Park forest – women who dare, women

who stand for all to see, and one woman especially, who wrote, "I love you, love you, . . . love you as my life./ And buried in his back his scalping knife."

With my sister I set out along the seawall from Third Beach, the west wind forcing us to double over like question marks. Fortunately the tide is out leaving a good stretch of bared rocks between us and the crashing waves that have hurled piles of sand and seaweed along the pavement. We hug the edge of the forest seeking lee from the wind till we get to the steps up Ferguson Point bluff. Wind blowing away our conversation and chilling us right through our rain gear, we head across the grass to Johnson's shrine and burial place not far from Sl'kheylish: "standing-up-man rock." The shrine's rough-hewn stones, enfolded in the shadowy roots of 70-year-old forest, form a cairn holding a carved relief of Johnson's face above a pool catching rainwater. And it now comes to me that we've made this pilgrimage in a kind of amazing cosmic rhythm during the same week in March that Johnson died 100 years before.

Inside the forest, our coats no longer balloon with wind, our eyes adjust to the shadowed cavern that spreads in all directions 100 feet below the canopy. Half a kilometre away, other walkers drift along other trails; at one point several young men stand in a ring smoking pot. They disappear and we are alone again with sword ferns and trickling streams looking at stumps bigger than four-door sedans. Thick ridges of their growth, laced with moss, still surge up over our heads from the forest floor – the remains of virgin forest. Some have holes in their moss-encrusted bark, reminding me of a story from S̲k̲w̲x̲wú7mesh chief Khahtsahlano about men cutting down a tree to carve into a canoe. They found a mask inside the tree. He told how they harvested trees by chipping into a leaning trunk from both sides and driving in wedges along its length till the weight of the tree pulled it down splitting it well up the trunk. If in the forest you find trees with holes some way up, these are likely test holes to find out whether the tree was hollow or rotting inside. Or, my sister said, they could be holes for the springboard notches where loggers rammed in planks to stand on while they worked their two-manned saws.

That day we do not find Johnson's Cathedral Trees. They are not where one website says, where Tatlow Walk crosses Bridal Path, or where another suggests at Bridle Path and Lovers' Walk. We are lost. The trees are lost.

I wake at night wondering why I'm searching for them. Am I prey to the Lure in Stanley Park, a rock hidden not far from the Seven Sisters, where Johnson tells us the Sagalie Tyee imprisoned an evil-eyed woman who brought disease and sorrow, a rock so powerful it will drive to insanity or death anyone who goes near it. So evil was the power from this rock that the Sagalie Tyee protected people from it by transforming the kindliest, most benevolent of them into a grove of trees to stand as a shield. If the shield is gone, we could go too close.

A few days later we return with more accurate directions. Although the wind is not as fierce, it is far colder, coming straight from the heavy snow on the Twin Sisters. Even under the canopy we must keep moving to stay warm, pausing just long enough to marvel, in our strange, scientific innocentness of the rock's lure, at a harlequin pattern of moss tufts coating the trunk of an enormous fir, or the cedar stalks thick as cathedral pillars split from a single root, or bulges of wolf-sized burls thirty feet over our heads. Delicate pink-budded shrubs grow out of the virgin forest stumps. Or giants grow on these stumps who began their seedling life on a high platform left by the loggers, and now half swallow the old stump in writhing octopus roots.

At last we find seven stumps of the Seven Sisters with a battered plaque whose scarred and smudged Plexiglas shows a faded photograph of grey columns. Park officials felled the trees in 1956, believing they were a hazard to humans.

from Growing Dumb: The Village

🌱

Peter Quartermain

Life in Wheaton Aston wasn't like the farm at all, and it wasn't like
Birmingham either, a tiny village miles away from anywhere, twelve
miles or more from Wolverhampton, a good hour on the bus, it ran
just twice a day except on Saturdays and Sundays when there'd be
extra. At the start of the War Mum went with me and Our Kid
along with Alice the maid to live there with Mr and Mrs Davis,
me five-and-a-half and Phil almost eight, Dad took us in the car,
him going back to lodgings in Birmingham, he'd come and see us
weekends. The Davises ran the village shop, her a distant relative of
Mum's, but I expect Dad made most of the arrangements, he looked
after that sort of thing. On the way there Mum said "There won't
be any indoor plumbing, you'd better be warned, except for a couple
of taps over the kitchen sink and perhaps in the scullery, not even
a flush toilet, and there's no electricity." We'd have to get used to it,
Dad said, "but it'll be just like the farm that way. Use the pump in
the yard, but they've got an Elsan" and we hadn't been there more
than ten minutes before I had to try it out. Mr Davis led me across
the yard and pushed open a door, cold white-washed room, clean
cement floor and a small window at the side, in the corner a metal
barrel with a lavatory seat on top and a pipe running up the wall

behind it to let the smell out, a draft of outside air coming in where it went through the wall up above my head, toilet paper in a holder, "You can wash in the scullery when you're done," he said, the smell pungent at the back of my nose, the cold air and the chemical smell not at all like the privy at the farm with its holes cut in the wooden seat. My skin tightened on my face a bit damp and sticky, Mum told me after that "it's just disinfectant, to get rid of the germs," but it all felt strange, on a shelf a tall square tin with a screw top with dried blue stuff all round it where it'd spilled, *That's what smells so strong!*, I touched it with my finger but it wasn't even sticky, and I lifted the scrap of curtain over the window, it was just the yard outside and a low brick wall. *Well what did I expect?* and I shrugged because I'd been so daft to want the window to do something new.

Our kid and I'd never even heard of the Davises until a few days before, and goodness knows what they thought of it all what with their two kids but they never complained, five almost complete strangers two of them small children dumped on them for the duration, but a lot better than having a bunch of scruffy townies who'd been evacuated from the big city or would be. Nobody knew how long the War would last but it made us move so us kids knew it was serious, and looking back now I realise the Davises must've been glad of the extra ration books as well as whatever money it meant. They ran the village shop slap bang in the middle of the village kittycorner from the church, Leabank Store, houses all around, and outbuildings across the cobbled yard at the back and side. Three rooms wide and two deep but most of the front and part of the back given over to the shop or to storage, a pump in the yard, a bit crowded sharing it with the Davises. Phil and I had a room up a dark staircase, blackout curtains on the widow, two beds side by side with a chair between them, a candlestick on a chest of drawers, crinkly red cellophane in the grate just like at home or at Grannie's in Spalding, but no fire screen, a few bits of soot that'd fallen down the chimney.

Peggy and Timmy were older than me, Peggy the biggest and Our Kid just a bit older than Timmy, "You two show them around," Mrs Davis said the morning after we got there, "not that you're likely to get lost," and she laughed. The village school was just down the road from the shop, and Phil and me started there the very next morning, Peggy and Timmy walking along with us till they

pointed where to go and ran off to play with some other kids. Lots
of kids kicking stuff about, throwing balls, girls skipping, playing
conkers, a lot of shouting and running about. I went up the stone
steps to the big double door above my head, shiny brass handles,
small windowpanes, and a teacher's loud scornful shout *"You!* Don't
you know you're a *boy?"* "GIRLS" it said on the sandstone lintel
miles above my head *How could I possibly 've seen that?* "Boys over
there!" She gestured and spoke to somebody else, another teacher,
they both laughed. Back down the steps, *"You!"* another shouted,
"You'd better run!" Cross the front of the building, up the other
flight. It looked just the same. Another laugh. "Run, boy! or you'll be
late!" I could feel the hot flush sweating my face in the middle of all
these strangers, other kids looking, Peggy and Timmy out of sight,
Our Kid nowhere to be seen. Nobody ever told you anything.

Through the tall door, clatter of kids' boots on the lino, high
ceilings, a grown-up pointed and I scuttled, scrape of seats and bang
of desk lids, "Sit *there.* We'll sort you out later." A big map of the
world on the wall behind the teacher's desk, like the one we'd had
in kindergarten only bigger, the desk taller, all the seas in blue, a
Union Jack at the top, coats of arms round the edge, the British lion,
and a lot of the land in bright pink, especially Canada so big on one
side and India and Australia on the other and dotted lines leading
to tiny Great Britain in just about the middle, we all knew without
being told that we lived in the centre of the universe. We'd seen maps
of the world with all that pink or sometimes brilliant red all over
the place, in post offices and shop windows, but not long after Phil
and I 'd begun to settle down in Wheaton Aston, only a few weeks,
they started to take them all down and put them away along with
the signposts which told you the way to the next village and how far
away it was so that the Germans wouldn't know where they were if
any got shot down and got loose in the countryside or even invading,
"Somerford ½ " or "Codsall 6." Pretty well every classroom had a
map on the wall, a lot of them with "The Empire on which the Sun
Never Sets" or "Highways of Empire" written across the top, and
you'd see the same map but smaller and without the label at the very
front of your school atlas, and in a home atlas too. And of course
you couldn't help seeing the King's head on your pocket money and
everywhere, we all had our stamp collections, we all wanted Sammy
Roe's 2¢ Canadian stamp dated XMAS 1898, a map of the world

with the British possessions in red and "We hold a vaster empire than has been" across the bottom. We breathed all that in through our pores, we never had to think about it. The idea of Great Britain was just *there*, and we knew it'd been there for ever.

A couple of years ago thinking about me writing this Our Kid sent me a battered copy of *The Little Oxford Dictionary of Current English* the child's big red-crayon handwriting cramped into the small inside front cover, "14/6/42" we'd long left Wheaton Aston by then, he'd put his name above the date as well as his two addresses one at School and one in Rugby, they filled the page, they reminded me how almost all the kids'd add as much as they could to make their address longer, adding "England, Britain, Great Britain, the British Isles, Europe, Western Hemisphere" before adding whatever else they could think of, "Earth, The Solar System, The Milky Way, the Universe," we all competed. One kid crossed out "Europe" with a thick black line when his dad told him to, "England is *not* a part of Europe" he said indignantly, "we got *nothing* to do with them!" and we all admired what he'd written instead, "The British Empire." A lot of us copied that.

At the end of every day Mr and Mrs Davis'd count the money in the till, sometimes fussing over it, and sometimes Mrs Davis'd call us over, "Here's George the Second" she'd say, or whoever it was, "come and see" and we'd peer at a thin copper disk worn almost smooth, a date like 1748 dimly traceable, faint strange-looking head, "It's a ha'penny, looks like a roman emperor, doesn't he. Won't spend *that*," and she'd put it to one side. People always had a few old coins tucked away somewhere, odd little curiosities to hang on to, to mull over the way us kids did with that Canadian stamp, you couldn't escape how old everything was, and I've still got an 1806 farthing with George III's head looking off to the right. Marlow Grandfather collected almost everything, birds' eggs, coins, stamps, and told us, every time we saw him, to look for old coins and carefully inspect the stamps on letters that came to the house. "They tell you who you are, " he said. "Look for differences among them," he'd tell us, "compare colours, see if there are any mistakes. That's the proper way to build a collection, that way you'll build a good one." But of course we didn't, not in Wheaton Aston at any rate, and of course we all saw lots of pence with Queen Victoria's head on them, it was just money, part of the shop really, though the last

three pages of that little dictionary of Our Kid's, all about "Moneys,"
told us how important it was. With their lists of "Some Foreign And
Colonial Moneys With Equivalents" to the value of the pound "at
par of exchange before suspension of Gold Standard in U.K. 21 Sept.
1931," they really did tell us what Mum and Dad and the Davises
thought, and what we learned every day at school, that we lived at
the centre of the universe. Nobody questioned the rightness of all
those pink bits, and people changed the subject if General Smuts or
Mahatma Ghandi got mentioned, or they turned away.

    Not that we paid much attention to what went on at school,
and when I think about that place I really get quite confused,
partly because I can't remember very much at all what being in the
classroom or the playground was like except for the smell that stayed
with you even after you got home, ink and chalk and wet clothes,
and the noise, clodhopping boots on tiles or lino, but I can remember
the building all right, it loomed so over me with its two sets of doors,
one of which you were absolutely forbidden to use no matter what,
tall identical doors at the top of two identical flights of stone steps
at either end of the brick building, the tall narrow windows and the
frowning roofline. And once you got inside, you ended up anyway
in the same classroom as the girls, who'd been made to use *their*
entrance just down the corridor. I think I hated that building because
of that encounter with "GIRLS" at the top of the steps at their end
of the building, but it was just so daft that it made me laugh when
Phil took me back to see the village a few years ago, and on *that* visit
I looked at those steps and turned round and saw the small red-brick
bungalow across the street, and said "Why, that's the headmaster's
house, Mr Button's. We never went *there*!" and he grinned, "We
all dreaded him, didn't we. I think even Mum did." We both
marvelled a little, Mr Button such a fierce little man, his plump tight
flesh filling his pin-striped three-piece blue suit, always stern and
impatient with us if we were playing in the street. "You children
clear off!" he'd shout, sometimes he'd wave his fist, "take your noise
elsewhere! You've no business near here!" and that was just as daft
really, where in the village would we play if not by the school. I was
a bit shocked when as we ran away one of the kids said "It's our
village too!" but he didn't say it very loudly, we all felt indignant. If
Mr Button's daughter was there he'd grab her and her tricycle and
wheel them back into the house, "Stay away!" Not that we saw her

very often, nor her mum, hiding away from village life. Mrs Davis and Mum said that with his schoolmasterly ways he thought we were all beneath him, "We're just shopkeepers to him," Mrs Davis said, and "Really!" Mum said, "he's such a vulgar little man." We all had nothing but scorn for the sore thumb of that little red bungalow so new-looking and out of keeping with the other buildings on the street. "Too big for his boots," Mr Davis said once when he came in from the shop. "Look at 'im, in 'is *suit* when 'e's got 'is *boots* on."

We kids didn't see much of Mr Button, in school or out. He looked after the senior kids in their room, other teachers but I can't remember who looked after the rest, and us smaller ones were in the hands of a young woman who I only knew as "Miss." She had us do a lot of reading aloud out of the schoolbook, and I was good at that, I liked the sound of it and I liked reading, all of us liked long words, and the sentence I got described a church and the high-up windows in the clerestory, cler*é*story I said without a pause I liked the rhythm of it, it sounded right and I loved how posh it sounded, but she smiled and shook her head and said "clear story." Years later Mum said her name was Miss Chapman, she can't have been more than about nineteen years old and she taught us reading, writing, and simple arithmetic. It was like being in a one-room school with the older kids helping the younger ones, and I didn't find out she'd got it wrong until I was ten, I'd just got into the Third Form at Brewood, Nosey Parker was talking about churches in Scripture class and he asked what those windows were called and after nobody answered he said "cler*é*story." I wasn't half glad I'd kept my mouth shut and not said "clear story," his scorn was so crushing, and I was really quite astonished years later, when I was browsing in Banister Fletcher's *History of Architecture* and found that it was called both, sometimes with a hyphen and sometimes without. I wasn't at all pleased to find out that for all those years all of us had been wrong, at School you just weren't allowed to be, there couldn't be two proper ways to say things, both of them correct, and we all loved it when a know-it-all got it wrong. We all knew how to be withering. But Miss Chapman wasn't like that at all, she never made you feel daft or resentful, she was so friendly we all behaved ourselves, and she taught us everything. When we started Arithmetic the bigger ones in the class would help the younger ones do simple sums. We did a bit of French, geography and history of course, not much Scripture except for a few

bible stories, and a lot of reading. Hengist and Horsa were supposed
to be heroes, but I couldn't sort them out from Ethelred the Unready
and the Alfred who burnt the cakes, they none of them had anything
to do with anything, and the silly empty pictures didn't help. But
it didn't seem to matter, Miss Chapman didn't insist the way other
grown-ups did, and with the news of evacuees and people moving
from one place to another perhaps we all knew we wouldn't be there
very long and as it turned out we only went to the village school for
two terms, up till Easter. And Miss Chapman didn't last long either,
what with a critical shortage of labour she might've got called up,
anyway she moved to somewhere else perhaps the way Alice did
before we left Wheaton Aston, when she got married. Dad stayed on
in digs he'd found, some place in Moseley Phil says, and we didn't
see much of him except at weekends, and a couple of times not even
then.

      He had some petrol coupons because farming was an
Essential Activity so now and again he'd drive, but to save petrol
he usually took the bus, an uncertain and tedious journey what
with lots of changes getting about inside Birmingham and then to
Wolverhampton and if he missed the one to Wheaton Aston he'd
have a long empty journey back to his digs, him not getting off work
on Saturday until six, closing up for the weekend, and he must've got
a bit anxious, especially if they were held up by an Air Raid the bus
picking its way through rubble-strewn streets, and most times even if
he had the car he'd get in when we were in the middle of bathtime,
and he'd leave again next day. The car looked ever so funny with a
cowl hooding its headlights so that only a little shaft of light could get
out, it was easy to drive off the road at night and one weekend he was
late because in the car he got caught in an Air Raid and couldn't get
through for hours, and another he didn't get in at all because he was
in an accident. There wasn't any phone there were only two in the
village that we knew of, telephones were like telegrams, scarce and
only used to tell bad news, but he'd got a message through somehow,
and when we came downstairs to breakfast and we asked "Where's
Dad?" Mum must still have been worried sick, but I don't think we
paid attention except to notice he wasn't there. Grown-ups worried

all the time.

On bath night Mum and Mrs Davis or Alice would drag the great big galvanized tub in front of the fire, put a screen round it while us four kids – me and Our Kid, and Timmy and Peggy Davis they were a year or two older than us – sat around the oil-cloth table with its pooled light from the oil lamp, carefully not looking at the screen and its glow, blackness because we had drawn curtains, quick little glimpse of bare skin through the screen when someone shifted a towel, sudden rush of cold air as Dad came through the door careful of the blackout, one of us in the bath the others hunched over a comic or a book or a game, dark shadows round the room, pools of yellow light from the fire and at the kitchen table, a glimpse through the screen *Don't you dare look!* So eyes half-closed, face pointing the other way, we looked. Sidelong. *You should be ashamed of yourself! Want a good hiding?* Peggy often went first she was the eldest so if the weather was nice the rest of us would be sent out to play so we *wouldn't* see, and it didn't matter if you got a bit dirtier, towels hanging on a clothes horse near the fire not in front of it so you might feel its heat when you were in the tub or getting dry after. Lots of splashing and laughter, voices from behind the screen nattering away at whoever was in the bath. You'd get out of the bath and shiver away before the fire while a grown-up fiercely rubbed you down, and someone else poured another kettle of water in for the next child, but the water got colder and colder and the towels got damper and damper soggier and colder no matter how hard the grown-ups tried, they'd hold the towels real close to the fire while you shivered away in the lukewarm water, skin prickly from the cold, goosebumps on one side and fireglow on the other, every little move you made making a new bit of cold, eying the others all wrapped up in their dressing gowns looking warm and pink and sparkly-eyed. Because I was the littlest I should've gone first, but my knees were always muddy, the dirt engrained no matter how I struggled to clean myself off at the kitchen sink, I went last, especially when Timmy and Phil'd let me tag along to play Pooh Sticks where the stream ran under the road at Lloyd's Farm. *You'll have to wear those clothes until they dry, you know* Peggy'd smirk at my discomfort and maybe a bit envious as I came back muddy and wet, *Serves you right, you'll be the last again!* The bath by the time I got in a thick scummy mess round the rim, grey mucky suds floating on lukewarm water, *had anyone peed in it?* everything soapy and slick, and you got your hair washed, scrub of carbolic Lifebuoy soap, a big enamel jug of water to rinse it off. That was usually warmer than the bath, but it wasn't much relief because by the time it had trickled through your hair it was stone cold running down your back and chest and under your arms and you'd climb out pink and shivery and still feeling a bit mucky, only now the muck was all over instead of just here and there, some of it wiped off on the towel, and you'd get into your pyjamas and dressing gown, almost fall over from the hard scrub Alice or Mum'd give your head with a yet another towel damp from drying someone else's hair, and be given a bit of something to eat and drink before being sent up to bed, the others sitting at the table talking and reading or playing a game.

The first Saturday we were at Wheaton Aston, "I've got a treat for you lot before you go to bed," Mrs Davis said, and I perked up, still feeling a bit sticky from the bath. "Bread-and-milk!" cried Timmy and Peggy, "Can we have a dab of butter in it? please! please!" and Mrs Davis plonked a bowl down in front of me full of chunks of bread soaked through in a bath of hot milk. But it smelled horrible, cloying the back of my mouth, my tongue felt thick, and I shook my head. "Go on, try it," she said, and I dipped my spoon through the oily scum of butter greying as it spread and took a bit, the bread all hot and slimy in my mouth. I put the spoon down again. "Don't you like it? Here," and she took a precious spoonful of sugar and dumped it in, "Fancy that! Never heard of anyone not liking bread-and-milk!" and Timmy looked a bit scornful as Peggy laughed. I stirred it up, and it just smelled worse, the sweetness hanging on even more stubbornly in the back of my mouth and I knew, simply *knew*, that I'd never be able to get it down, my stomach rebelling in a lurch. I couldn't swallow, and I sat there shaking my head and looked down. The others lapped theirs up just about record time, *Can we have his, then?* "You'd better have a glass of milk, then," Mrs Davis said, "but it won't warm you up the way hot milk will!" "Can I have a piece of bread with it?" I asked, I loved bread, I still do, and they all laughed. "You won't get any jam!" Mum said, and chuckled as Mrs Davis gave it me. Most weeks it got to be a ritual, them with their hot bread-and-milk and me with my milk and a piece of bread. Unless we went short.

What with four adults and four kids, the Davises living

behind the shop and us sleeping in a couple of rooms up a steep staircase above it, we kept getting in each other's way, the grown-ups trying to find things for us to do, an old set of Ludo and a much worn pack of Happy Families lying on their shelf, all of us irritably aching about the place in wet weather, unravelling old socks and pullovers, carefully undoing seams on shirts so Mum and Mrs Davis and Alice could turn the collars and the cuffs, we got to be real handy with scissors cutting up old trousers to repair not-so-old trousers, Mum really hated putting a new seat in a pair, "Honestly," she'd say, holding a piece of cloth against the light, "you can see right through this, it won't be any good," and Mrs Davis'd nod in sympathy as she huddled over her task, "It's enough to try the patience of a saint!" Peggy tried to teach Phil and me to knit, "Sewing socks for soldiers!" she said, but when I picked up the knitting needles after she'd done a couple of rows and she took my hands in hers, sitting behind me, I couldn't see what she was doing her fingers got in the way she threaded the needle through a loop and then hooked the wool over it, we did it over and over "Hold it like this" she'd say, and "This goes over this, here" and what we got was a bedraggled mess of wool, loose loops sticking out and hanging down. "Pull on that" she said, "Gently" and the whole mess simply unravelled until there was only one row of stitches left on the needle. "This is hopeless," she said, "I don't think you'll ever learn" and Mrs Davis said that even if we learned to knit a nice clean row and move from one needle to the next we'd never learn how to turn a heel or finish up a toe. "You can't teach boys how to knit, not properly. And anyway," she said, "me and your Mum have too much to do, you'd better take up corking, Peggy can teach you that easily enough," the old wool too crinkly and the bits too short to be good for anything else. After a while one of the kids would sigh, "Can we go now?" and Our Kid and Timmy'd hare for the door to get into the village maybe grabbing a rubber ball and Peggy'd be off to play with her pals, dolls or something like that, but chattering away and I'd sit there with the corking or perhaps with a drawing-book.

Two or three times after dark with the distant sound of planes, the sky full of stars and the moon, "A bomber's moon" said Mr Davis, and if one came close "'Ear that? that's one of ours, German engines sound different," we'd cluster outside listening and looking out towards Wolverhampton ten miles off, searchlights crisscrossing sometimes smoke rising from distant lights on the ground "that's bombs" somebody would say quietly but they were very faint, the War was very far off, it was easy to forget it most of the time. "Look at the moon!" said Peggy, and Timmy said "I can see the man-in-the-moon, look, he's ever so clear." But no matter how hard I tried I couldn't see it. Peggy crouched down a bit right behind me and pointed her arm over my shoulder, "Look along my finger! There's his eye" but that didn't work, from where I was her finger hardly pointed at the moon at all when I looked along it, and Mum said "cover one of your eyes" but that didn't help, and after a few minutes of trying they all began to sound a little bit annoyed, *why can't you see it?* but they didn't ask straight out. I felt quite bewildered, and it may be I was looking for the sort of thing I'd seen in a fairy-tale book or on a calendar with the phases of the moon, as clear as a line-drawing, and all I could see was fuzzy grey shapeless bits on the moon's yellow. When we got to bed that night Our Kid said it was funny I couldn't see it, everyone can see it, it's just *there*, but it was a long time after Wheaton Aston before I actually did.

"You can't always be going off with Timmy or those girls," Mrs Davis said one morning before the others all went out. "Here's a book for you. Timmy and Peggy both loved it, I did when I was young. It's got lots of pictures, it's a good story," and she put it on the table, *The Water Babies*, a greeny-brown picture on the cover two big fish, red speckles on their back, peering at a small child looking out at them from a cleft under the water, "You'll like it a lot, it's about being the youngest," she said, and Peggy said "Tom the chimney sweep, what a wonderful time he had living under water, wouldn't you like to do that?" but it was such a lot of words and there really weren't many pictures, I had a hard time getting into it, I couldn't understand the white room that Tom fell into from the chimney, it just didn't make much sense, and I didn't believe anybody could be as namby-pamby as Ellie was. Mum said she'd read it when she was little, "It gets much better after Tom falls into the river and becomes a water baby" so I kept at it when there was nothing else for me to do, but what with words like Naboth and Cinque-cento, when I asked nobody really knew what they were, it was too hard to enjoy. Who'd ever have a name like Mrs Doasyouwouldbedoneby and Mrs Bedonebyasyoudid? What could I do with a word like *anastomosing*, none of the grown-ups had ever heard of it and Miss

Chapman didn't know when I asked, she couldn't even find it in the dictionary. Dad thought the book was too old for me and called it "a bit preachy," and I thought it was a bit bossy. Things like "Sir John was a very sound-headed, sound-hearted squire," saying he was "just the man to keep the country side in order" was like listening to Mr Button, or strict Grandmother at Marlow, everyone so very proper and polite. Why would anyone telling a story call its hero "Naughty Tom?" *You never did like to be* <u>told</u>, Mum wagged her finger at me long after.

But that depended on the telling. One day when we got back from school a wizened man'd turned up outside the shop wearing a worn and grubby grey suit, he'd leant his bike against the wall with a bag in the handlebar-basket, he wasn't quite clean, he just talked to us as though we mattered, winked at us, listened when we said something. Peggy knew who he was, he worked on one of the farms nearby, he'd been there for years, and he'd got a ferret in a bag, he took it out and stroked its neck. Mum saw him through the window and came out, "Don't you all have chores to do? Timmy, you sweep the outhouse, Peggy you're supposed to be in the kitchen, Philip and Peter, you come with me" and the four of us scattered, but he stayed where he was and we soon clustered round him again, the ferret still there. "Don't touch!" he said as he leaned over it, "'E ain't 'alf got teeth, sharp 'uns too! Gobble y'up!" and he laughed. As we examined this lean fierce creature with its small red eyes and off-white fur he told us he used it to go rabbiting, "Got two last night" he said, "You'll be 'avin' one of 'em for your dinner I expect," and he showed us a string contraption he'd put round its head and snout before shoving it into the warren, he called it a cope, and he told us the ferret chased the rabbits out of their burrow and he could catch them with his dog, or he'd sometimes set a snare or two. "You got to put the cope on," he said, "or it'll kill the rabbit down the 'ole and eat it and then it'll go to sleep it'll be so full, and you've lost your ferret" and he laughed, we wondered at that tiny ferret eating a whole rabbit all by itself, and Peggy asked him if he'd ever lost his, he said he had a couple of times but he'd got one of them back, sometimes they got rid of the cope down the hole. "But they're quite tame," he said, "and you don't really 'ave to train them, no, just get to know them a bit and get them to know you, keep 'em 'appy" and he laughed again. "They know you but they don't like you, no, they don't 'ave any love in 'em, not like a dog. No loyalty" and he laughed again. "But they don't 'alf breed, worse'n rabbits, they've two litters a year" he said, he loved talking to us and we liked it too, remembered what he said, he just explained things to us because we wanted to know, he wasn't like a lot of the grown-ups we met. "He's a poacher, isn't he?" said Timmy, and Peggy said "Of course not!" and "I bet he is," said Timmy, "he's bound to be. He swopped that rabbit for something from the shop." "*Rabbits* aren't poaching," Peggy said. "Other animals are!" said Timmy, and I wondered.

One of the things the ferret-man had said became a catch-phrase of ours for a while, and we'd chant and chortle it whenever we could, we must have been pretty tiresome with it, he'd got it from a book of some sort, an encyclopaedia I expect, he told us when he warned us about the ferret's bite, "When irritated, it is apt to give painful evidence of its ferocity," said in a posh voice, and he laughed. "Just like Mr Button" Mum said, and a day or two later she told Mrs Davis she thought he was a very irascible person, "Always whacking the kids at school," Mrs Davis said, "That's what I've heard." "At home, too, I shouldn't wonder," Alice chimed in, "honestly, you'd think someone with a name like that could think up a better name for his daughter than Pearl," and they all three began to laugh. "But Pearl's a pretty name for a girl," Mrs Davis chuckled, shaking her head. *Why was it all so funny?* Shy little three-year-old Pearl who looked a bit like her dad and always wore pretty little dresses and never said anything very much. She didn't play with the village children and she always looked clean.

But the world of adults was not the world of the child. "You're coming with me to deliver the bread," Mr Davis said as he came in from the yard one breakfast, and Mum smiled. He put a big basket of bread on the handlebars of his bike and another over his arm and gave me a smaller one and door to door we went round the village. Two big loaves for the Joneses, a Hovis and a malted for old Mrs Crooks, four white and a brown for the Purdy family. We got back to the shop after about an hour, everything carefully counted and remembered, and he wrote it all down in a little book. "Are you tired?" he asked, "we're going out again, we've got a long way to go."

And he slung a great sack of bread over his shoulder, and gave me
a bag with a shoulder strap, four two-pound loaves in it, crisp fresh
baked crust warm against my coat. And in answer to my question,
"We can't take the bike. Come on, then." And we set out across the
fields, the long wet grass swishing against my socks, the odd thistle
or burr scraping my legs. Watch out for the cowpats. Climb the stile.
Open the gate. Close the gate. My bag of bread kept sliding down
my shoulder and I kept hitching it up, holding it with my hand.
"'Ere, let me move it to the other side," he said. "It's a lot further
by the road," he said, "and it's 'arder on me feet." "It's Mrs Philps,"
he said. "A big family. 'Er 'usband's in the Army. 'E's a Sergeant.
In the South Staffs regiment. Somewhere in the War. Overseas
I think" – the short sentences punctuated by the grassy sound of
walking. It was hot. I wanted something to drink. "There's a stream
coming up, under that 'edge." My pace quickened a bit. I cupped
my hand, licked up some water, splashed it in my face. It didn't taste
very much. "In the winter," he said, "when it snows, they sometimes
get cut off, and they 'ave to pinch to make do. It's a bit remote." We
stopped for a bit of a rest. "Don't want to rest too much," he told me;
"it gets 'arder to start each time. Come on." My bag of bread was
a bit damp from the grass, and my crisp loaves of sandwich bread
were beginning to lose their sharp four-square edges. "Don't worry
about that," he said; "not much farther." My bag kept getting closer
to the ground, dragging on the odd tussock. They usually fetch
the bread themselves, he told me, every Wednesday. But this week
they're poorly. I stopped. "Doesn't the bread get stale?" I asked. And
he told me they wrap it in damp cloth. "You're just wrapping it a bit
early," he said, looking at the sodden bottom of my bag. I thought
of horrible soggy bread and bread-and-milk and made a face, and
he laughed. "It gets a bit mouldy by the end of the week," he said,
"especially in the summer. Scrape the mould off." I was glad we lived
in the village. "And you can toast stale bread," he added; "makes
good toast." He looked at me and winked. "Or fresh it up a bit in the
oven." And then we were there. A red brick cottage, patch of garden,
a gate, some chickens out the back, empty pigsty. Mrs Philps gave me
a drink from the pump, and chuckled as she looked at my battered
loaves of bread. "You're a bit of a small one for that long hike," she
said. Friendly. Glad. "Couldn't 'ave managed without 'im" Mr Davis
said, and he ruffled my hair. My socks were covered with burrs. I

could smell my own sweat and I said "I liked that" and felt proud.
We turned round and walked the mile-and-a-half to a big cup of tea
at home, with sugar.

So we got away from the Air Raids and we escaped the
shelters with their noisy crowds but it wasn't long before lots of
evacuees escaped as well, billetted to what village houses had room,
they'd come to *us*, townies who reminded us constantly and forcefully
that the War was not very far away. We could feel *its* effects, no
doubt about *that*, as rationing began to bite, shivering outside and
getting chilblains in the cold raw weather, not much of a fire indoors,
if any, a spoonful of cod-liver oil every morning after breakfast to
keep the colds off and all day burping oily fishy taste up into the back
of your nose, now and again you'd smell it on someone's breath, it'd
even penetrate the boiled potatoes at dinner no matter how much
gravy you managed to drown it in. The only thing that helped really
was a great doorstep of bread to gnaw on, with a bit of dripping if
there was a bit to spare, Mr Davis called it mucky-fat, the melted
beef or pork fat strong enough to overcome the fish oil. But that too
was in short supply what with the butcher having none to spare, and
there wasn't much fruit except for a few wizened winter apples, cox's
orange pippins if you were lucky, good storers they were and we
loved *them*, we only knew about bananas because people sometimes
said they'd like one and we hadn't had an orange since before the
War. It was a real treat when Mrs Davis managed to get hold of a
jar of Radio Malt, just as good for you as cod-liver oil and you could
even spread it on bread if you wanted, but a jar didn't last very long
with four of us getting some, and the older kids began talking about
the summer when we could have fresh fruit, cherries and strawberries
and plums. But we still got colds all the time. Timmy and Peggy
told us that some of the village kids would be slathered all over their
chests with goose grease in October and sewn into their underwear
for the winter, we didn't really believe them until Our Kid ended
up sitting next to one of them in school, "I changed desks as quickly
as I could," he told Mum when we talked about it years later, I'd
forgotten all about it till he said that, "by the time December rolled
round they were pretty ripe I can tell you." But Phil got away from

that in December, that would be 1940, when he started as a weekly boarder at the Grammar School in Brewood, the next village over.

We all sneered at the rough London and Walsall townies billeted with village kids, "They all think milk comes from bottles!" Mum laughed. "Bunch of ignorant little B's," Mrs Davis called them, they all got slathered with Vick's Vaporub every night or had great wodges of some patent cotton wool like Thermogene, bright orange and smelly, sewn inside their vests, itchy stuff, we bet – we weren't quite sure whether to laugh or to be jealous. We all had terrible colds all the time, and it wasn't long before we wore Thermogene too, only ours was held with safety pins front and back. Phil remembers asking one of the townies where he came from and he said "Wa'sa'," we'd heard about Warsaw on the BBC and Phil was amazed that he spoke English at all and asked Mum "Did he come from Poland?" She made a face and laughed and said "No, no, Walsall's an industrial town in the Black Country, it's all factories, working-class Staffordshire." And then she told us "I can't really understand a word they say either, their accents are so thick, they're just urchins really, they don't have much to do with us." We four kids began to feel a bit ashamed of the Thermogene, its mix of capsicum and wintergreen oil *it doesn't half stink!* we said, the Vaporub made your chest all sticky, the Thermogene all itchy, as bad as wool. It said we were just like *them*, and if the thick cotton wadding kept our chests warm it didn't stop our noses running or keep the colds off like Mum and Mrs Davis said it would.

Phil really had a hard time of it, he got a terrible pain in his ear, most of us got an ear-ache now and again of course, kids do, but his simply wouldn't go away, it kept him awake half the night and more in that pitch-dark room with ice on the inside of the windowpane and its unused fireplace, the hot-water bottle slowly getting colder and colder, and in the morning his pillow would be all stained with what had come out of it, yellow pus sometimes with a bit of blood, his earhole all crusty and red-looking deep inside. He had an awful temperature, the doctor had come more than once, and sometimes on that side he couldn't hear what you said. After a bit of a search Mrs Davis found a roll of prewar cotton wool in the shop snug in its blue paper and every morning Mum would warm up a bit of it in front of the fire and put it in his ear to keep it warm, but it didn't help much, just sopped up the mess coming out of it.

But while she was looking for the cotton wool Mrs Davis found some fireworks from before the War, and Dad found a few more in the stockroom at Woolworth's in Birmingham. I think she even laid hands on a Christmas pudding all wrapped up, though it might've been in a tin, everybody was pleased about that, you couldn't get all the ingredients to make one not even at that stage of the War.

Guy Fawkes was on a Sunday in 1939, so Dad stayed late and set them off in the garden outside the window so Our Kid could watch them. He nailed a Catherine Wheel to the fence just outside the window but it didn't go round the way it was supposed to. "Never mind," said Mum, "they never do," but the Roman Candle and the Burning Schoolhouse were amazing, and I wanted him to let off some rockets not that we had any, but you couldn't do that not in the War, and you weren't supposed to have fireworks during the blackout anyway. Some other kids from the village came to watch, Dad made them stand back, and Our Kid sat up in the window in his pyjamas and dressing gown with a hot-water bottle and all the lights off in the room, a bandage round his head to keep his ear warm.

Everybody was terrified that he had mastoiditis, and a few days later Mum and Mrs Davis shooed Timmy and Peggy and me out of the house and told us to *stay out!* They spent the whole day washing and scrubbing floors and brushing all the cobwebs down and cleaning the curtains and the carpets and the furniture and the stairs and our bedroom and lighting a fire to get that bedroom warm, and at the end of the day when it was getting dark we at last came in, everywhere filled with a strong carbolic smell *Take your boots off before you come in!* and *Keep quiet!* One of the grown-ups kept a close watch on us as we got a thorough wash at the pump outside and then let us near the fire to warm up a bit before bed. Next day after school we were all sent out of the house again, but it was so cold and wet we came back into the kitchen and stayed there *No noise, mind! Read a book or play a game!* but before we settled into that two men wearing dark raincoats each with a small suitcase and scarves and trilby hats drove up to the shop, so shiny and tidy in the rain they looked as though they'd just been cleaned in a laundry, and spoke for a bit very quietly at the bottom of the stairs to Mum and then went up to where Our Kid was. We were all bursting with curiosity, so to keep us quiet Mrs Davis told us they were two doctors come from Birmingham to operate on Our Kid's ear. A few years later a new kid about my age who came to Brewood had a monstrous hole behind his right ear, big enough to put a baby's fist in, where they'd chipped and ground away the mastoid bone because of the infection, you couldn't do anything else about it. That night, when they'd gone back to Birmingham, Our Kid had the bedroom to himself.

Next morning Mum and Dad told us Our Kid didn't have mastoiditis after all, *What good news that is!* they smiled a bit, but they still looked tired and worried, *He's going to need a bit of attention, and we'll need your help too, you know.* He'd had an abscess in his middle ear and the doctors'd cured it up there in the bedroom by puncturing his eardrum to let the infection out, and he'd need a warm poultice over his ear to draw all the poison out *That's why we need your help, all of you, Mum can't do everything.* It took Phil two or three weeks to get really better, but he'd still now and again get terrible pain, and he never complained, but just sat quiet. His eardrum never really grew back properly and if there was any chance of getting water in his ear he'd have to put his earplugs in, hard rubber things, they must've been really uncomfortable, and they didn't work very well, he once tried them out swimming and one fell out and water got it, the terrible pain took more than two days to go away. He was mad about joining the Navy, loved sea stories and pictures of ships, and the abscess may have put paid to his hopes of being in the Navy, but it didn't make any difference to his dreams. His favourite book became E.C. Talbot-Booth's *Ships And The Sea*, a wonderfully thick little book with fold-out pages of drawings of ships and parts of ships and flags and funnel insignia, as well as specific information about length, tonnage, displacement, and all sorts of technical stuff. I think Dad found it in a used-book store in Birmingham and gave it Our Kid for Christmas, he'd spend hours and hours going through it, and after the War he spent nearly all his pocket money on books like *Jane's Merchant Ships* and *All the World's Fighting Ships*, hundreds of pages of silhouettes, aids to recognition really, along with technical details about each ship.

In the War of course we were all mad about joining up. I wanted to be in the RAF just to be different from Our Kid, and I'd draw camouflaged planes shooting at other planes or dropping bombs on them, curly loop-the-loop lines to show how the planes flew, the RAF roundel carefully coloured in, the swastikas in black, crooked rows of dashes making sure that the British guns didn't miss their German targets. When the Battle of Britain was going on we'd sometimes see dogfights high up, a distant intermittent buzzing they were so far away, we'd look for Spitfires and Hurricanes, now and again you'd see a Defiant, you could tell them by their gun turret, not many got made but we were proud of them they were made by Boulton and Paul in Wolverhampton. All of us'd be looking and pointing, cheers if a plume of smoke a plane span out and down, a long slow plunge to the ground faster and faster a long way off out towards Wolverhampton way or even Birmingham, and you could hardly see the planes at all just small dots and the blurs of the trails and we'd begin to argue and fall quiet trying to see if it was one of ours or a Jerry wait for a parachute and we'd argue quietly about it, always somebody absolutely positive it was a Messerschmitt, or a Hurricane or a Spitfire, but too far off to tell.

   Not long after Our Kid found he couldn't be in the Navy I decided I wanted to be in the Navy too, and we both cut pictures of ships out of *Picture Post* and *Illustrated* and the newspaper and glued them in scrapbooks. The drawings in my drawing books began to be of ships, page after page of them, harder to draw but more exciting because they had more on them, pompoms, torpedo tubes, huge guns, HMS *Nelson* had sixteen-inch guns sticking out of three big turrets, you could draw smoke coming out of funnels, men walking on the deck, shells flying through the air explosions and flags flying. And you could draw German ships sinking, men crying "Achtung!" and "Kamerad!", words we'd picked up from comics and cartoons in the paper, and parachutists being shot at. At Christmas and birthdays all through the War not just in Wheaton Aston we'd get picture books of *Our Fighting Forces* and *Our Glorious Navy* full of photographs of tanks and ships and planes and soldiers in full battledress and you could copy pictures out of them. Impossible heroics. I began to fill my drawing books with pictures of tanks knocking down buildings and crossing ditches and crushing German soldiers and shooting down planes while getting blown up. Someone in the village said that the only news we heard was what the Ministry of Information let us hear, and somebody else said "Ministry of Propaganda, more like" I was really puzzled, *How could anybody be so disrespectful and unpatriotic?*

When Phil at last began to get his strength back and him completely better, Mr Davis arranged for us to get a ride on a barge, "fixed it up at the pub," Mum said, "a day trip really, a day off from school." We weren't allowed to play down by the canal but we knew it well enough. On Sundays if it wasn't raining Dad and Mum would take us for a walk along the towpath, often towards Brewood, only three miles off, sometimes the other way, towards Church Eaton. Under the bridges the canal narrowed and the path curved out under the arch so horses could get through. Fastened to the corners of the sandstone or brick arch and reaching from the ground to somewhere level with my head, big tapered pieces of smooth black iron full of deep grooves at different angles. None of them were the same, but at the top and the bottom the grooves were quite shallow, some bridges you'd see faint grooves in the sandstone or brick corner above the iron, some of the grooves in the middle were so deep I could only just reach the bottom when I poked my fingers in, in the summer the iron at the bottom of the groove cool in its own shade, sometimes there'd be a bit of grit, sometimes it'd be a bit wet. The first time we went along the canal I asked Dad "What are they for?" and Dad just said "Wait and see." In a little while we met a horse pulling a barge along the canal, a nosebag over its face, brasses on its harness winking in the sun, the long rope dipping now and again into the water, the bargee at the back of the boat leaning on the rudder to steer the boat so the horse didn't pull it into the bank and we all stood still out of the way until the horse got past us. "Watch," said Dad, and we all turned round and moved

slowly along behind the barge. When it got to the bridge the horse
moved out towards the middle of the canal as the path curved out so
that it was almost right in front of the barge and then it was through
the bridge and it disappeared as the path curved back, and as the
rope lifted out of the water the groove caught it, you could hear a
faint singing as it rubbed water off the rope. "It took a long time to
carve those grooves," Dad said, "a lot of barges." Like feet on stone
steps, I thought. "It's a bridge guard," Dad said. "Sometimes the rope
slips off, and wears a groove in the brickwork. Not here, though."

It was Alice who walked us up the towpath towards Church
Eaton, to the bridge at Dirty Lane, everyone else had too much to do,
"That way," Mr Davis told her, "they'll get to ride right through the
village, they'll get a longer ride and won't have so far to walk back."
The barge really slowed as it went under the bridge it almost stopped
and we hopped on, Alice said who we were, it wasn't horse-drawn
but had a motor and the bargee wasn't a man but a big comfortable-
looking woman with a bandanna round her head. She had a couple
of kids but they were off playing somewhere in the fields. I asked
her if they ever got lost and she smiled and said they could always
find the canal and told us "once we get through the village you can
help us get through the locks. Then you can steer us a bit." We
chugged through the village at a walking pace, a sudden chill from
the abrupt shadow under the bridge next to the Hartley Arms, the
engine boomed as the sound bounced back under the arch, the sign
for "Banks's Ale" so much higher over the canal than over the road
it almost looked as if it was falling on you, and the pub garden came
down nearly to the water. The village seemed smaller, a bit distant,
but some of it closer and higher, a bit over your head, one or two
houses and half-timbered cottages looked nicer, you could see into
the back gardens, quiet and peaceful, grass and trees and flowers
and old brick. The water was just below the level of my waist where
I was sitting in the cockpit, the wall between me and the water cold,
the wood at the top of the side painted and warm from the sun, *the
gunwale!* I thought, proud of the word, but *no it couldn't be that, not
on a barge.* The bargee's big round arm on the rudder handle, lots of
wrinkles, pink and freckly skin, she looked a lot stronger than Mum
or Mrs Davis, lots of lines on her face but comfortable and relaxed,
enjoying herself, smiling a bit, looking along the side of the barge
so she could see around the cabin, a great flat expanse of wood and

canvas beyond it covering the cargo. If we stood up on the benches
we were sitting on we'd be able to see over it, but I wasn't sure we
should.

Our Kid stood on the seat to see better and she didn't say
anything, I remembered we'd trodden on the seat when we climbed
down getting on, but I just sat still and just looked, everything was
so different, like nothing I'd ever done before, and then we were
through the bridge and we could see the locks coming up. "There's
a rise of seven feet here," she told us, and moved the barge towards
the towpath, here made of brick laid in ribs so the horses could get a
good grip. "You can work the gates." We ran down to find the gates
at our end pointing away from us, already open, the gates at the
far end sprayed streams of water where they met. Our Kid walked
on the far gate to the other side of the canal hanging on to the rail
with one hand, came back to the open gate across from me, and
when the barge was safely in the lock we heaved away, each of us
pushing the heavy balance beam to close the wooden gate through
the water behind the barge and she threw a rope up as the lock-
keeper came out, he tied the barge up and opened the upstream
valve, cranking the big windlass handle she'd given him to let the
water come spouting in the side wall of the lock. I stepped over to the
rusty iron ladder going straight down the lock wall so you could get
onto the barge while it was all the way down there at the bottom, its
narrow round rungs, but the bargee shook her head and we stayed
up top. As the water rose in the lock and the loop in the mooring
line got bigger and bigger strands of weed stretched out away from
the ladder and then disappeared in surging brown water, the waving
green tips the last bit you could see, the weight of the water kept the
gates closed and fat streams gushed between them on the downstream
side, muddy brown-green, weed hanging down. Once the lock was
full my gate was so heavy the lock-keeper had to help me start it off,
Our Kid could just move his, but once it got started it wasn't too
hard, straining against the great thick square baulks of weathered
rough timber rubbed shiny by years of hands pushing, smooth
enough not to give you splinters, bits of grass and weeds in the cracks
and crevices in the top. As soon as the gates were open we stepped
across the narrow strip of swirling brown water between the edge of
the lock and the barge, flecks of greyish foam and bits of twigs and
leaves, eddies and little whirlpools, it was already moving as we got

on.

"What stops the canal from getting empty?" I asked. "I
mean, it always goes down from the high bits when you use the
locks," and the bargee said "Well it would, ducks, but they keep it
topped up. I'll show where if we go that far," and Our Kid asked
when we'd get to steer. "Once we get past the next bridge," she said,
"the Wheaton Aston bridge" and she gestured, it was only about fifty
yards away, and then we were through it, that boomy echo again,
there was a long straight stretch through the Lapley Wood bridge
a couple of hundred yards away and she gave Our Kid the rudder,
he had to stand on the seat to see. "Keep it in the middle," she said,
"we don't want to run aground. There's no tide to lift us off!" and
she laughed at her own joke. She explained that most canals just
had a narrow channel down the middle sometimes not as wide as
two barges "What would happen if we met one?" and Our Kid said
"Come on, Pete, you've seen. One of them ties up to the bank,"
and he gave me a look. "You can do that without any trouble most
places," she said. "You can always push it off, but you don't want to
travel that close." She took me down below to make a cup of tea,
"Call out if you get any trouble," she told Our Kid.

The cabin had an oil stove for cooking, and a wash basin;
it was lovely and warm with bright colours and curtains over the
windows, a bit of a rug on the floor, a door at the end. "There's
bunks for the boys," she said, they let down over the table opposite
the stove. It was all very tiny, with a special place for everything,
buckets and mops and brooms. A small pole stuck out of the top of
the cabin, and another one at the front of the barge, they hung the
washing on a line strung between the two, "'aven't you seen that?"
she asked, but I hadn't, and I thought of the three grown-ups in the
back scullery on a rainy washday, hands and arms shiny and red
from hot water, big wet patches on aprons and pinnies, steam from
the copper in the corner smothering everything with damp, smell of
carbolic soap, Alice turning the mangle while Mum fed the sheets
through, Mrs Davis rubbing away at something in the sink, pools of
water on the tile floor, basket of wet laundry waiting to go on the
big airing rack to dry clothes on that let down from the ceiling in
the kitchen behind the shop at Wheaton Aston and at Grannie's in
Spalding and what a nuisance it was, the rack always too small for all
the wash, two bedsheets took up a whole rack and you had to keep

lowering the rack and refolding the sheets and hanging them again with the damp side on top and keeping the fire going so everything could get dry and getting the sheets off before they were too dry so they could be ironed properly, we had to dry a lot of sheets at Wheaton Aston with four kids and three grown-ups, four with Alice, and then once all the sheets were done, the rack would go up and down twice as often, the rope forever getting in everybody's way, hanging up everybody's underwear and pyjamas and towels and shirts, socks and hankies, the rack going up and down all day long, and what with rationing there was never enough coal to keep the fire going and you wanted the clothes *hurry up! hurry up!* to get dry.

"Don't pull it up too fast!" Mrs Davis would scold, "You'll hit the ceiling" or "You'll break it!" but when it was full of wet stuff it was too heavy for me to pull up to the top. I loved lowering it though, I liked running the rope through my hands, "Don't let it come down too fast! You'll break the pulley" and "Mind you don't get rope burn!" the table always cluttered with clothes being folded or sorted and chairs cluttered up with baskets of clothes, everything smelling of damp, the whole room clammy and hot and steamy, nowhere to sit, everybody in each other's way, we all hated washday when it was raining, the whole day got cluttered and all the grownups got short-tempered, somehow you had to eat dinner or tea among all the clothes, somehow somebody had to cook the food, the kids aching about the place, or running about playing some game or other, or squabbling. And there'd be the ironing too, going on with the wet clothes still all over the place, hanging over people's heads and draped over chair backs, piles of ironed clothes on the table, hot dry ironing-smell mingling with the damp, rumpled and wrinkled clothes in the basket, two irons on the hob, a swing trivet on the cast iron range each side of the grate, the irons big and heavy, you didn't want to drop one it'd smash up the big red tiles of the floor, so hot Mrs Davis or Mum or Alice had to wrap a bit of cloth round the handle before they picked it up. She'd reach over from the ironing board and pick the iron off the hob right next the coals, lick her finger and dab it on the iron real fast, or with a bit of spit, always a bowl of water on the table where she could get at it, test the iron. Mum'd dip her finger in the bowl and flick the water hitting the iron, a little hiss of steam, to make sure it wasn't too hot, and then she'd run the iron fast over the cloth, "If you stop it'll scorch!" she'd say, "you can't go slow!" the room a thick fug with all that steam from the damp clothes and the water to sprinkle on the clothes if they'd got too dry, all the women with shiny red faces from standing so close to the fire when they were ironing, one of them perhaps doing the cooking, hair in damp strands down the sides of their faces, all us kids hanging about and fretting because it was raining too hard to go out, grumpily folding clothes or putting them away because there was nothing else to do, too crowded and cluttered for any play, not even word games there was so much noise and bustle, everybody busy.

Our Kid shouted "There's a bridge coming up!" and we both scurried back to the cockpit, "Would you like to steer it through?" she said, and she slowed us down a bit so he could steer this long narrow boat through a hole not much wider than the barge, you could easily touch the bridge on one side and it was only a few inches to the towpath on the other, the edge of the towpath lined with stone and with black iron at the rounded corners to fend you off if you hit it. We sat in the cockpit drinking our tea, milky with lots of sugar, and I looked at the wonderful bright paintwork, flowers and vines and leaves on a red background just like a gypsy caravan, yellow and blue and green and white, the name of the barge in a panel with a fancy border, "Meadowsweet." After the War, when the barges were nationalised, they all got painted dull grey and given numbers instead of names, and we hated the Labour government for doing that.

All around us were fields and woods, copses on hillsides, farms, cows in pastures, bits of villages across the grass, a church spire in the distance, after we got through the bridge the cut we'd been going through ended and then the ground gradually dropped away and we were up above the fields going along an embankment, all the time we chugged sedately on through serene and quiet, the only sound you could hear the motor, water would splash now and then against the bank or against the barge, moorhens and rabbits, or some villager's dog rooting about the bank, and birdsong and the odd cow lowing and an erratic bit of breeze that made you half-close your eyes. We could have stayed there for ever. We asked her where she was going, and she said she was carrying a load of chocolate from up near Liverpool down to Birmingham, "I bet you're going to Cadbury's" I said, but she didn't answer, she pointed off to the right to a big lake behind a dam on the other side of the aqueduct that carried the canal over the Watling Street, we could hear the traffic now, probably an Army convoy, "That's the Belvide Reservoir," she pronounced it *Belvidee*, "there's a stream that comes from there, just on the other side of the aqueduct, that's where the water comes from to top up the canal." *But how can the water get from down there all the way up here?* But she said she'd better let us off at the start of the aqueduct, her children would likely be waiting there. I wondered where they went to school, but she slowed the barge down told me to steer and disappeared inside the cabin for a moment, the canal just a bit wider than the barge as it went over the bridge, a rusty iron railing along the towpath all narrow fancy arches. She nearly stopped the barge altogether as she pulled it over to the towpath. "You've got a bit of a walk back to Wheaton Aston," she said as we got off, and she handed each of us a brown paper bag, the traffic rumbling and roaring by underneath us on the Watling Street. "It's a bit of chocolate," she said. I looked inside at crumbly grey-brown lumps full of little holes, just like lumps of coke we burned in the stove, "It's ever so good," she said, "it just 'asn't been made into bars yet. This is 'ow it arrives at the factory." We tried it, and it was just like chocolate but not as sweet, and we thanked her and she laughed and said goodbye. By the time we got to Wheaton Aston hot and tired we didn't have any left.

Before Golden Handcuffs:
The Mystery of the
All-American City

❦

Lou Rowan

Chapter 1. My Pledge to You

Books let me down.

I go to a party. I know no one. I measure myself against
the perfect outfit, the resplendent gestures of the financial star near
the crudités--his smooth ways with women, with everyone. He's the
ultimate New Yorker, a phoenix risen from Gotham's combustible
grime to dazzle and triumph.

I must not lose this occasion to convince him my firm can
help his firm. What an opportunity! If we connect tonight I can
assure the handlers at his office he "knows" me, he's awaiting my
call. But how to detach him from the bejeweled glamour of his
bedazzled audience? How to shine, sing, impress?

No passage, no slogan in any book has dissipated my tension,
or unlocked my tongue at moments like this.

But I am a Californian: I'll never abandon my quest for
messages of healing, for a faith that works.

In these pages I distill my personal and business lives to
intense moments shining like beacons, to adventures impelling me
to quantum leaps. I ponder these stories for meaning. I am there for

you.

I got the account from the financial star, and I'll tell you how.

I've labored over this book for 6 years, interrupted only by life's demands. The business career is done, and I write full-time.

I hesitate to tell you how old I am; I have experienced five-to-ten-year periods that went by in a blur: each of them I had plotted to lead to something--a career improvement, a better school system for my children, a safer retirement—only to realize when goals materialized they were but steps, plateaus, not the resting-places that would afford the meaning and permanence I've sought for decades. We are all trying to go home.

I wish I'd never known most of the people in this book.

A New Yorker for 33 years, I thought I would be as likely to live in Washington State as Mississippi or Mongolia. But when the tawdry magic of leverage and derivatives made representing Bankers Trust Company intolerable, I began to take calls from headhunters. Soon I was doing sales and customer service work for the George NuzzleTrust Company from a midtown office building affording fine views of the club where Christie Brinkley worked out and the building sharing a Playboy Club with Imelda Marcos's thousands of shoes.

After two busy years finding my way around the new territory and the new client base I moved West to become the Managing Director of Institutional Sales at Nuzzle's historic Tacoma headquarters.

The Pacific Northwest is known for its good nature--some would say its naïve good nature. I will always maintain that civility, while no antidote to humanity's dark depths, is to be prized, and I considered my decades suffering the aggressions of Boston and New York a barbaric exile from my youth, however troubled, in a golden California whose postwar conflicts between sprawl and splendor the Northwest mimics now.

I was to experience all too quickly the sinister elements dominating greater Tacoma's development. But let me assure you, dear reader, my adventures in this tarnished paradise yield crucial lessons for us all.

2. The Mystery of the All-American City

for Yas

Gina was the most effective administrative assistant in Legal, and the buffest woman at Nuzzle Company headquarters. I scanned the layered muscle of her upper body with professional reserve as she "walked" me through the new-account documents spread in neat sequences across her desk. The final signature-lines brought my pen to the feet of a framed pro wrestler flying boots-first at a prostrate body, black spandex buttocks suspended like twin bombs.

Did she follow Wrestlemania?

"Everywhere."

Their grunts and roars belied their polite, cheerful natures when Gina and her husband Sylvio lifted in the company gym. We'd pause to watch them move with the sinister strength of gorillas. Sylvio's head was shaven and a dark bush grew between his lips and chin. He worked in Trust Accounting. The high-pitched voice emanating from his squat massive neck was eerie, until you experienced the soothing warmth of his large heart. These talented parents showered their beautiful, raven-haired daughter Juliana with Wrestlemania tchotchkes.

Juliana enjoyed additional nurture from the the network of grandparents and great aunts typical of Tacoma's close-knit Italian community. When she reached grade-school, her silky hair was hacked to a mullet matching her Mom's, and she became a regular at chili bake-off days and holiday celebrations at Nuzzle. From second grade she was consumed with the desire to yell and gyrate before crowds; her grandmothers and aunts sewed her cheerleading costumes in lieu of her Mom, to whose muscular fingers needles were elusive. Her third-grade teacher pronounced her hyper-kinetic, and the guidance counselor suggested an amphetamine derivative. Mom and Dad, who fed themselves jugs of powders and pills, had no problem with the medication, despite their elders clucking warnings of addiction and madness.

I was there to help Juliana with her language arts homework, with her fundraising for teams and charities when she reached high school. My assistant Laura, another member of the Italian-American community, helped Juliana with the delicate sides of a young woman's life her mother ignored, occasionally banishing me from my corner office so they could let their hair down.

Junior year angry red splotches mottled Juliana's smooth skin. Laura exhorted Gina to take poor Juliana to dermatologists, but Gina and Sylvio, intent on neck-down glamour, were baffled by the problem flaming across their daughter's face. Poor Juliana was too embarrassed to demand help, and she became listless, a shadow of the raven-haired angel-child Laura and I cherished. She hinted at something evil haunting her, something so overwhelming she feared to confide it even to her loving mentor Laura.

-2-

Sports are life in the Northwest; I trained lunchtimes for a half-marathon. Reaching the crest of the "Hilltop," whose reputation for spawning criminal Asian gangs failed to deter my New York brashness despite warnings from my colleagues, I was puffing, sweating, wondering why I subjected myself to such rigors in late middle age. Faintness and nausea brought my pace to a crawl, and as I considered whether to walk them off, a gunfight erupted between gangs in flippers and diving costumes.

I dove under a monster-truck, peering furtively around its massive treads. The combatants' dry suits were aquamarine, pink, and heliotrope. Scenes of coral reefs, sunken treasures and leaping orcas adorned their torsos. The aggressor gang caught its foe confabulating around double-parked delivery vans, advancing on them from abandoned buildings and burnt-out vehicles in flanking maneuvers from all sides. They bobbed and wove in flopping goose-steps, getting off fusillades from handguns and automatic-weapons.

Caught by breezes off the Sound, the shots were insignificant pops: screams of *motherfucking motherfucker* and *cocksucking cocksucker* sounded wistful. The attacking gang's ammo-supply outlasted the trapped gang's, and one by one the losers peeled away to flop past me downhill. No one fell, no one seemed hurt: the only casualties from the hail of bullets were shredded trees and splintered plywood. Was this a Homeland Security rehearsal? The warmup for a gun-dealers' community event?

But a lone gunfighter in civvies was too fat to flee. The victors shoved him to the concrete, kicked him till he rolled onto his back, and shot him in the knee. He lay screaming and twitching as they sauntered off like feral penguins. His pale polyester leisure suit reflected clouds scudding across a wide sky brightened by choppy waters.

I approached to help him, but he called me an asshole motherfucker and told me to fuck off or he'd kill me. Rage erupted like a lahar from the fatty distortions of his ruddy face and neck.

I try to assure the serenity of my runs by leaving my mobile phone at the office; pay phones were stripped of their receivers and coin-boxes, but four squad cars arrived soon after the victors vanished. The police ignored my excited descriptions of the shootout, and stood around the victim, chatting casually with him, "How're you feeling Tony?" They ignored bullet-holes in walls, vehicles, trees, plywood windows, the scores of shell-casings catching the sun. An unmarked ambulance arrived; silent attendants rolled Tony onto a gurney facedown despite his wound, and pulled down his trousers to reveal the hairiest rump I've ever seen. They plunged a long hypodermic into the layers of cellulite wobbling beneath the anal brambles, loaded Tony, and all vehicles departed quietly.

Nuzzle Security referred me back to the Tacoma Police Department, after chiding me for running on the Hilltop. Our COO refused to believe I was serious.

There was no news coverage.

-3-

When I moved West, colleagues in management proffered their wives to guide me through their exclusive neighborhoods in search of a home befitting a Managing Director.

They were kind, hypergroomed exemplars of Nuzzle's family-company ethos, but I found the immaculate tracts even more insipid than Eastern suburbs, and it seem pointless to have come all this way to buy a luxury condo or midcentury house whose graces were confined to interior and garage features and benefits typical of Akron and Canton.

My guides scorned nearby Vashon Island as an isolated haven for arty hippies, and so I decided to take a look.

Porpoises cut through the wake of The Rhododendron, the car ferry on the short run from Point Defiance. A winding road following a creek through a small rainforest led to Redding's Beach.

The rocky shore was bounded by dark evergreens and crazily-leaning madronas. Large birds nested on the stump of an old-growth cedar at the high-tide mark, the mother stuffing the fleshy heads of her brood with gray matter I imagined regurgitated fish. Eagles soared, raising squawks and commotion in the trees. Clams squirted from the low-tide mud.

I bought a cottage on a bluff facing Mount Ranier just before the winter solstice, when the sun rises red behind the icy mountain, an event sacred to our First Nations. I complemented the aerobic training of my jogging with the harsh upper-body-work of clearing dense brambles from the sunny side of my two acres, so that I could plant vegetables in the spring. I resolved to learn the local trees and birds.

I coexisted comfortably with the veteran hippies who'd colonized this farming community in the '60's: like them I found Vashon a "healing island," and soon I was visiting a massage therapist often as my travels permitted. Like most North-Westerners this fit woman considered her dog a source of insight; his yips and snorts interrupted the reverie her strong hands wrought, and his smell competed with therapeutic odors from her candles. I was careful to visit after dark, when the gun-club abutting her woodsy haven had ceased fire.

-4-

In a perfect world, a world where the child is indeed father of the man, we could instruct our parents on our evolving needs, if only with trantrums or sobs, and our parents would respond like the benign gods existence anoints them. Whenever they noticed it, Juliana's misery baffled Gina and Sylvio. They were kind, they gave her the extra attention that had worked before puberty: longer quality-time sessions at the pizza parlor and in the gladiatorial video game-room, jet-ski outings on American Lake. They roared encouragement when she cheer-led.

Recurrently Juliana *dreamed she was flying over Tacoma in the scalding talons of a dragon-pterodactyl. Her ripe flesh bled in the metallic grip. Snorting a stench worse than Tacoma's lumberyards, the monster told her with indifferent ruby eyes and hot ratcheting tongue all was lost, flying her in a tight circle from the office-buildings to the boatyards until dawn*

232 | GOLDEN HANDCUFFS REVIEW

broke and it corrected course to skim her along the incoming traffic on the Narrows Bridges, the I-5, 6th Avenue, Pearl Street, and the 705. Her skirt flew up, she was exposed, and the world knew everything. She implored her captor to tear her limb from limb, to end this unflagging despair, this hell on earth. The implacable monster hung her upended from the fine filigree of the Chihuly Glass Bridge. Her blood splashed glinting cars. Enraged elders of God's First Church poured from white Escalades to stalk her up the walls, roaring curses that shook her like the freight-cars passing along the waterway, "Now we've got you, you cunt whore bitch devil!"

-5-

Sports are life in the Northwest, our life-blood is business, and results are what counts. My sales team quadrupled the output of its predecessor without expensive hiring. I received an Excellence in Leadership award. Life was good and I wanted to keep it that way. I took the stairway not the elevator. I treated myself to a rowing-shell, whose website sported a muscular man my age braving the swells beneath the Golden Gate Bridge. The Vashon Island Rowing Cub recruited me for my long arms, and rowing buffs urged me to buy a racing-shell. But my slow-twitch muscles dictated endurance not speed: I wanted to row alone for the distance that would stimulate my endorphins. Before dawn I explored Quartermaster Harbor, followed by a harbor seal 10 yards astern. Rowing engages 92% of human muscles, especially the vital core, dormant when I jogged.

One clear spring Sunday I launched from Tramp Harbor at 6:00 AM to circle Maury Island, my maiden foray into the wakes and swells of the vast Sound. I hugged the shore. "Vashon is more than dirt" proclaimed placards protesting the expansion of the gravel mine to fill land for SeaTac Airport's controversial third runway. Nearing the controversial pit, I heard gunfire, shouts, screams, and metallic roars like jackhammers coming from deeper waters behind me. Turning to look over my shoulder risked capsizing. I continued towards the din, pulling even with two mid-sized trawlers.

Swarthy men in diving-gear backed by fat men in hoodies exchanged curses and gunfire, which echoed over me from the cliffs. One trawler slammed into reverse, engine whining, water boiling under the hull as it disengaged, positioning itself to ram the enemy. But as it roared near the very center of the enemy's hull, I heard noise like the humiliating sounds a loose bowel movement can unleash in a public stall amplified to a deafening din, and smelled the unbearable stench of a public latrine. The stationary trawler's cannonade of putrid mud laced with clamshells blew out the glass around the attacker's helm, shredding its superstructure. Aimed lower, the hideous spew blasted crew, equipment, and crates along the deck, hurling bodies and equipment flopping and flying aft and into the Sound. Hypothermia can kill in minutes. The devastated aggressor retreated to collect its bobbing, screaming crew. The triumphant trawler unleashed a final volley of gunfire in triumphant salute, as it dropped anchor to lower divers packing what looked like bazookas and leaf-blowers. The wounded trawler limped towards Tacoma. I strained to suppress spasmodic retching, lest I become prey to the victors. A defeated survivor staggered ashore near me, his jumpsuit in shreds, his fat body lacerated to marbled meat. He told me what to do to my mother when I offered help. A black van materialized from the gigantic gash Glacier Northwest Mines gouged into the cliffs of terminal moraine. Vashon Island's lone police car oversaw his pickup.

It took every ounce of the discipline that got me through the New York Marathon to finish my course. The soaring eagles, the rising breezes pushing me up the Harbor, my harbor seal's falling in behind--I saw but did not feel these Northwestern delights as I neared home.

I watched televised sports in a daze, eating a balanced diet to restore my electrolytes and kill free radicals. I turned in early, hoping to begin the work-week rested, fresh and serene.

I scanned *The Tacoma Tribune* and the Seattle papers in vain for coverage of this battle at sea.

-6-

The issue roiling Tacoma and Pierce County that winter and spring, releasing passions normally smothered at home or extinguished in sports bars, was Coach: she came out.

She was the first sportswoman in Tacoma history to deserve the honorific so important to society: when you said "Coach" you knew you meant this hard-driving woman who kept Tacoma girls' basketball so consistently at or near the top of state rankings that her teams merited the honorific— "a franchise." The advent of women's professional basketball to the Northwest coincided with Coach's dominance. Women's hoops were big-screened and debated at sports bars.

Throughout her iconic tenure, Tacomans referred to Coach's diminutive partner as her roommate, and treated their sleeping arrangement with the respect for privacy that Americans had accorded J. Edgar Hoover's with Melvin Tolson. But when Coach and her partner joined joyous Northwestern throngs flocking to Oregon to be married, we could no longer remain silent.

Editorials in the *T.T.* called for "a policy of vigilant tolerance." Organized troops of Christians roamed girls' locker-rooms; embarrassed athletes entering and leaving showers, toilets, locker-rooms negotiated a phalanx of Megachurch Moms. Supersized pickups and SUVs patrolled Coach's neighborhood. Multimedia blasts by Big Jim Jones, charismatic founder of God's First Church, prevented police from honoring the principal of Stadium High's requests to protect students from the militant mothers. Fox News performed saturation interviews upon former and current members of Coach's teams, but failed to ignite rumors of molestation. Coach was so tough and demanding she might as well have been a man. The standoff persisted throughout the regular season, dividing and discomfiting all levels of Tacoma society.

How to villainize a woman who would have joined the WNBA had she not volunteered for Iraq after her freshman year on full scholarship with the Huskies? How to turn a woman who had taken shrapnel "too close to my asshole for comfort" into a punching-bag? How to attack a lifelong member of the National Rifle Association spending a good portion of her leisure hours stalking large animals?

The newly-wed Coach began calling her spouse the "Little Woman," vowed that anyone who interfered with them would get a "good ass-kicking," and announced that she had nothing to say further, except that she was intent on getting her kids into the All-States again.

The Little Woman had been Coach's nurse at the VA Hospital. She demonstrated the normal behaviors of the sports wife in the stands: patriotic fervor, fanatic participation in cheers and waves--as well as the feminine humility that deferred discussions of strategy to Coach and the athletes. She baked cookies for the teams.

Gina and Sylvio, who worked out with Coach, stood by her: "Dammit, she's a winner and she's good people." They discontinued their inspirational power-lifting sessions at God's First auditoriums, and withdrew Juliana from the Christian Angels Sodality at the megachurch.

Despite my indifference to most team sports, Laura roped me into many an elk barbecue at Coach's neat bungalow; I learned to pop natural antacids before and after. Coach's lone enemies were broccoli and kale.

-7-

May 1 brought revelation. The front cover of the weekly tabloid Seattle Stranger carried a life-sized photo of a vertical geoduck beside the headline:

MOB SLOBS'
PHALLIC
FOOD-FIGHT!!!!!!

West Seattle mob kingpin Alphonso ("Airport Al") Brutale had been arrested for conspiring to kneecap his rival Burien chieftain, Anthony ("Tony Clams") Scungile. The mobsters competed to smuggle geoducks across the Pacific; Tony Clams had raided Airport Al's diving talent.

The phallic geoduck, king of Northwestern clams, proliferates in the deep muck of Puget Sound, where until recently huge beds have survived in peaceful majesty, some clams dating from the time of Abraham Lincoln. The giant bivalve is prized as an aphrodisiac by the vibrant economies of China and the Asian Tigers. Divers poaching for the mobs blast the clams loose with water-cannons, and the proximity of the shoreline to SeaTac Airport renders smuggling convenient.

The Stranger surmised that business as usual would have continued, had not the mobsters exchanged gunfire near the terminal for private jets as Barbra Streisand arrived to confer with the Gates Foundation about the fate of the world. Brutale's nickname derived from his hero John Gotti: just as the Dapper Don had risen to prominence by controlling the delivery of goods to and from Kennedy Airport, so Airport Al attached his criminal tentacles to

SeaTac.

Sensing a breakthrough connection to the battles I'd witnessed, I called the FBI, who referred me to Homeland Security, which directed me to the Coast Guard headquarters at the Port of Tacoma.

-8-

I marvel at the insularity of business: glancing at the Port of Tacoma from my corner office, I'd been oblivious to its magnitude. Lines on lines of containers to the horizon, tankers half the size of downtown, super-sized trucks competing with endless trains, a maze of overhead cranes grasping containers with magnets, armed helmeted drivers of security Humvees the only humans visible—the toxic abstractions of finance fusing with the engineered realities of commerce in a vast complexity trackable only in cyberspace.

Parking my Prius, I felt like a fleshly speck.

Captain Olaf (Ollie) Olson pointed at chair without rising to shake my hand. The intensely ruddy face, styled yellow hair, gleaming teeth, muscular mottled brown arms, the deep chest straining his tan short-sleeved uniform—even seated he was an inexorable presence, like the humming power transformers lining Tacoma's roads.

He recited my family history, my career, position at Nuzzle, my largest accounts.

"So what's a respectable captain of finance like you got to do with socalled shootouts, Lou?"

"We have a sports culture at Nuzzle: I'm outdoors a lot. I don't know why I happened on the battles. I wish I hadn't. But I it's my duty to report something so dangerous."

"I lift, I run, I do all the area tri's. But I don't go running on the Hilltop. And what's this rowing a shell in the Sound?"

"Well, Captain, I've never been one to confine myself to the places my business colleagues stick to."

"You should listen to your colleagues, Lou."

"Captain, I'm wondering why the police haven't gone after the gunfighters, why the incidents never appeared in the media till yesterday."

"What do you think you know, Mr. Rowan?"

"There were clues everywhere; the police stood around chatting with a mobster named Tony."

"Clues? A mobster? Are you trying to do our job for us?"

"No, Sir. I have a bag of the spent shells. I returned to photograph the bullet-holes. I'm trying to cooperate if someone will listen."

"Are you? The Coast Guard is not a law enforcement agency. We patrol the waters to protect our great marine industries."

"Homeland Security referred me to you. Seems like I saw gangs of smugglers and poachers shooting it out."

"You told them about bunch of guys in drysuits and flippers and a socalled gunfight on the Hilltop. Then there's some kind of battle off Maury. Were you seeing things? Were you dehydrated or sunstroked?"

"I take care to hydrate, Captain. And what about the Scungile-Brutale shootout at the airport?"

"That was a crap story in a lefty fag rag. All charges were dropped."

"Were dropped? Why?"

"Permitted weapons discharged accidentally during a lunch break. We believe in the Second Amendment out here, Mr. Rowan. I trust you're not one of those bleeding hearts wanting to take these babies away."

He led me by the elbow to a glass case where oiled assault rifles and machine pistols gleamed like jewels. He patted the giant revolver on his hip, staring me in the eye, and wheeled to gaze on his wide view of the docks.

"—Now, Mr. Rowan, can you see those great ships out there?"

"Yes indeed, Captain."

"That's what keeps us all on our toes ready for action 24-7. If our ports aren't running like clockwork, we'll slow the economy of this great city, this great state, this great nation, and the developed world. And you ought to know what that means." As he performed his oration, I mused on attack-dogs: how the eyes of even the maddest dogs coming at you lack intensity, focus—it's the body, the teeth.

"Sir, my company is a major taxpayer here."

He turned on me, blue veins bulging under gold head-chest-

and-arm-hair, face purple, "You giving me that crap about how you pay my wages so you can tell me what to do? Come back when you've got something real. I've got a port to manage."

I drove to a waterfront park and reclined my seat for a restorative power nap. That night we would deliver a portfolio review to the Hylebos Tribe, and I needed to be sharp. I wondered if Captain Olson was high on something beyond power. My brain and body were numb.

The black Prius absorbed the sun's rays as I slept.

Perspiration gushed from me as slimy tentacles forced the windows wide open, reached into my car, and dark beaks fed on my thighs. Sated, the octopi donned bright robes, spun on supple tentacles, and gyrated on my hood to the beat of "Louie, Louie." They preached The Rapture; breath like fish-farm waste steamed from beaky maws dribbling my blood. Bulbous preaching heads reddened like hot metal, grew blond hair; tentacles bulged like biceps and sported tattoos: Mother, God, Country. *The anchor-clutching spread eagle of the Merchant Marine festooned aquamarine, pink, heliotrope vestments.*

I woke in a drenched shirt and soggy briefs. I prayed the company shower would recruit my spirits for the late meeting.

-9-

When Nuzzle Investments' major full-service client, God's First Church, expanded its empire across the Port of Tacoma, buying out the Hylebos Tribe whose remnants huddled in abandoned hospital compounds along the toxic canal that had been their sacred river, we were certain that GFC would transform the tribe's Emerald Bay Casino into a synergistic church enterprise.

GFC controlled downtown Tacoma commerce: a portfolio diversified across marinas, upscale condos, office buildings, Christian mini-malls, hotel franchises, Bible Museums, Christian theaters, Old and New Testament amusement parks, abortion-free hospitals, conversion clinics for homosexuals. My company provided consulting, hedge funds-funds-of funds, pensions and deferred compensation to church executives, and an outsourced turnkey profit-sharing plan for select clerical associates. Our money market funds bought their short-term paper, which carried an A1P1 rating. Nuzzle executives combined their business and spiritual callings by serving on GFC operating committees, and on its board.

God's First Church rose from the Tacoma Dome parking lot, where Big Jim Jones preached from a simple bare platform to motorized believers. The platform has been bronzed, and attracts pilgrims from the Americas and beyond. His booming voice startled travelers passing the lot on the I-5. Autos, trucks, motorbikes honking and roaring for Jesus caused occasional pileups, but the Pierce County highway patrol, many of them congregants, hesitated to interfere with God's work. Complaints over the favorable terms under which Big Jim obtained the Tacoma Dome from the city quieted when the faded blues and tarnished whites of our signature monument were transformed to solid gleaming gold, and an A-list of celebrities headed by Vice President Cheney assisted at the christening of God's First's Holy Dome.

Big Jim blessed Nuzzle's annual meetings in the Dome. Many a work cube displayed his blockbuster *Jesus and Me*, a case study in marketing classes at the University of Puget Sound and Pacific Lutheran University, capturing step by step a career progressing from gangly nerd to muscular tailback to triumphant entrepreneur: his smashing success as a car-dealer, his victories over the worldly, fleshly temptations that accompany success, his nocturnal dialogues on the showroom floor with his Personal Savior, his elucidations of which car-models had been the most spiritually-stimulating, the visions calling him to the sacred parking-lot, the revelations dictating the bestselling *Jesus Champ* novels presenting Our Lord as a violent American nativist, his creative securitization and leverage of real and spiritual assets, his innovative tax-exempt structures, his dramatic excommunication of union organizers, his aggressive control of labor costs through volunteer work by women and children.

The life-expectancy of Hylebos indians dotted precariously along the Port of Tacoma's geometric waterways is 41 years, and so no one remembers the teeming wetlands—fertile estuaries nourished by the Puyallup River meandering from sacred Mount Tahoma. Pioneering Tacoma city fathers dredged and improved this former tribal livelihood, which explorers optimistically renamed Commencement Bay. A few years ago the City of Tacoma paid a broken-treaty settlement into an endowment whose income provides not only a small income to each tribe-member, but also social and administrative services in an abandoned hospital, from whose parking lot the tribe sells fireworks and cigarettes. Before it became a hospital, the blocky brick building housed schools that purged young indians of their language and culture. When God's First Church bought out the tribal commercial sites the legal settlement had extended along the engineered harbor and into Federal Way, the cash influx increased the tribal annuities to an average of $5200/annum — income denounced as socialism by Northwestern politicians.

Investment reviews are scarcely exempt from the fraught relations between Indians and anglos. Portfolio managers assume that tribal officers are unfamiliar with the basic principles of diversification and risk-return. But anxious that Indians would be insulted if presentations betrayed that assumption, they issue reports so detailed and jargon-ridden I lived in fear that, no matter how steady our performance, the Hylebos would fire us to end the affliction of our visits. I needn't have worried: the presentation was so soporific our clients would have needed powerful stimulants to summon the energy to dismiss us that night.

As with most clients, it was my practice to take the Hylebos to dinner alone, so that I could assess "the relationship."

Jimmy Smith was the treasurer: to train for his job he'd read up on finance and investments and stayed abreast with automation while doing the books for the Emerald Bay Casino. He was also the tribe's unofficial historian. A huge man, who walked only to get to the next seat, he devoured vast venison steaks—which he loved to urge on me.

"Come on, Lou, if you don't eat like us, we'll think you don't care about the account. Vegetables are fine in their place, but a man needs wild meat! Wild meat, Lou!"

Charlotte Rose managed human resources, moving up from a payroll accounting job. She was a plain, methodical woman whose knowing smile and raucous laugh could startle. It took two years of working together for them to confide in me what I'd suspected: they were an item. They'd made it work for 16 years by not living together.

"He's a big pain in the ass. I don't know what I'd do with him in my house," Charlotte chuckled. She liked to let Jimmy do the talking, so she could correct him when he went over the line.

Their new partnership with God's First was thriving: names of huge rock and country-western acts flashed from the Emerald Bay Casino's dazzling billboards on the I-5. Gaming revenues rose 32%, stimulating tribal employment, even though the benefits program was cut back to the minimal GFC system. Megachurch members crowded tribal museums and marinas. Young men and women found new work, about which Jimmy was vague.

"We love doing business with God, Lou! We're happy campers! We're making miracles!"

"But Jimmy, why is GFC OK with the casino, and the non-Christian performers?"

They winked at each other and laughed.

"Your God made money as a medium of exchange; He created Las Vegas, Tin Pan Alley, and the British Invasion: who are we pagans to question our owners, the instruments of His will? They know best what's good for your immortal souls.—And we have our assets safely diversified in your George Nuzzle Modern Portfolio Theory. I tell you, Lou, we're hogs in good stuff!"

Charlotte broke in. "But Lou, you don't look so good. You're one pale paleface. What's happening with you?"

I told them about the shootouts and my ordeal with Captain Ollie. They roared with laughter. Jimmy chided me, "Oh come on, Lou. Don't you know the Merchant Marine is the shippers' and cruise lines' private police? They never met a sludge dump or an oil spill they couldn't cover up. If we Hylebos depended on fishing and clamming we'd be dead. Homeland Security's a joke; they strung you along because you work for Nuzzle. We could tell you some funny stories, man! Funnier than your Hilltop blast or your water-fight! Why do you think God's First was so eager to own a seaport?"

Charlotte cut him off, "*Now Jimmy*, let's stick to business. --How're you doing with the ladies, Lou?"

I told them I was doing fine alone: it would take someone special like Charlotte to tempt me.

"Well, Lou, you're a pretty good-looking guy, and you make a good living. You know what your problem is?"

"Yeah, Lou, you listen to Charlotte, she's got the answer!"

"You go down to those fine car-dealers along the I-5 and get you a big Lexus or Beamer. Dump that Prius, it's no good with the women, Lou."

"OK, *OK*. I respect your opinions, so here's what I'm willing to do: how about a spoiler on the Prius, and giant tires. I'll drive the first Monster Prius."

"Yeah, that's good, Lou. Maybe we can get someone from the Culture Center to paint some totems on it."

"Well, that's settled."

"No it isn't. How about we find you a nice Indian lady."

"I'd like that, but you've already got the best one, Jimmy. –You can't leave me hanging like this: tell me what you know about the Hilltop gangs and the trawlers."

But they chided me for being a white man inventing legends—leave the myth-making to indians. I asked if they'd heard about geoduck smuggling; they cackled and asked if I needed to boost my manhood.

I knew they were playing—but at what game?

"Hey, it's past our bedtime. Sweet dreams, Lou. You're doing a good job; you stay on the account and Nuzzle keeps it.—Listen to a couple of stoical Indians: don't let all this stuff get you down. We don't; we eat meat. Get your blood up; you're too pale. You spend too much time worrying. Get yourself a good woman."

-10-

Choosing a therapist is arduous. You look when you're stressed, your judgment scattered. I couldn't go to Nuzzle Employee Assistance: I doubted their competence and their confidentiality, especially after my session with Captain Ollie.

One of those spring days so vivid you forget the gray and the rain, Coach held a sumptuous wild-meat barbecue for "her peeps:" Laura and her carpenter husband, their young son, Gina, Sylvio, Juliana--and me, the newest member of her inner circle. She had a rack of fresh meet too fine to freeze.

Juliana looked better, her rash fading into her early suntan, and she'd returned to cheering. But she remained quiet and remote. Laura, Gina, Sylvio had returned to the tiny Roman Catholic community. The Little Woman, the only Jew in our small circle, commuted to Vashon Island: the magachurches stifled Tacoma's synagogues, and on my eclectic island Jews gathered Saturdays in a converted schoolhouse.

I joined Coach as she flipped smoking flitches of elk.

"How did you and The Little Woman meet."

"When my ass was shot up, she was my nurse. Kind of like something out of Hemingway, except I doubt he'd be cool with a couple of dikes."

"He's too sentimental for me, Coach. —How're you holding up under all this noise and controversy?"

"Easy: I know those megachurch motherfuckers are full of shit. They want to run our lives, run everything. Who the fuck do they think they are? That Big Jim, he's a fucking war wimp. Look at the bastard: he's fat, he's greasy. Who asked him to run our town? They can kiss my ass."

She stabbed a flitch of elk with a mini-pitchfork, and dumped it on a platter ringed with ceramic salmon and squid on a background of filigreed sea vegetables.

"But I'll tell you, Lou, when it really gets to me, I see Tahini."

"Tahini?"

"Yeah, she's one kickass therapist. She's a healer. When shit gets me down, she gets me going. Sometimes the Little Woman and I go there together; sometimes I need the headspace just for me. You've been looking like shit, Lou. She's on your island. Give her a try."

I felt that I might prefer a style of therapy more traditional than hers. But as I watched Coach serenely preparing the sizzling feast, slamming Gina and Sylvio on the back, patting the Little Woman on the derrière, breaking down her guns with Laura's husband, letting Juliana beat her at bocci—as I watched all this good cheer I wondered if my hesitation was snobbish. My massage therapist had urged me to try Tahini: my hams were seizing up, and all my muscles knotted, "full of prime noogies, super-tight, Lou."

-11-

The advent of a new triple-wide prefab along Vashon's two-lane roads, happening weekly during the the real estate boom, caused traffic clots and fallen limbs. I proposed to Charlotte and Jimmy that we invest in affordable housing composed of vertical triple-wides. "Yeah, Lou, and I don't know why you won't enhance those prime acres of yours with a fine prefab. Nobody's going to confuse you with white trash."

But Tahini's neon jade triple-wide was a rich experience. Water-features undulated through patches of clumping bamboo and around boulders onto which images of the Buddha and kindly avatars of multi-limbed Hindu goddesses had been painted in styles combining underground comics with medieval illumination.

Tahini outweighed me, but in her tie-dyed muumuu she moved with the lithe dignity of a sumo wrestler. Silently she led me through the grounds in random loops, pausing to press her palm to the brow of a rock as if it were a forehead, or to merge her body with the bamboo. She directed me to breathe from the gut in time with her. Then she entrusted me with the story of the crisis, the "nervous breakthrough," that continues to inspire her work.

"It's how I arrived, Lou. I wasn't here, really *here*. I broke through to Now when I failed to summit Rainier.

"A tight band of us from the Island had trained for months with an experienced guide, wise in the ways of glaciers and the body at altitude. I couldn't believe it when the day arrived, a bright day seeming to illumine each snowy crystal.

"We left Base Camp at 3:00 AM. I was scared, I was thrilled and awed. Each step towards Meaning, each foothold on the shifting surface awakened my spirit's very Being: the chafing of my boots, the burning in my lungs, the heaviness of my shoulders were pungent data, In-Formations of the growing Me. We labored as One, ropes connecting us like spiritual umbilicals. I fused with this vast volcanic extrusion, this molten energy from geologic time.

"Haiku from the cold mountain drifted through me.

"But when we came to the final push, to the threshold of Summit, my bowels had filled, and comrades who'd taken care of their needs lower down turned on me; so did the guides. Time was too short: if I took care of my needs, I couldn't summit. They'd rejoin me on the way down. Total karmic bummer.

"But as I took aim at the eco-baggie, my dismay dissolved in a flood of revelation; in the glow of this infinite crystal I held myself like a baby, and merged with Me. A haiku poured out:

> Volcano apex
> A steaming pile
> I am spirit

"Lou, failing to summit was a blessing that focused me on Me —so I can be here for you. You have a mountain of worries, impurities tearing your gut—but they open the Possible!—Are you ready to work? Are you moist?"

She look my hand and drew me into the cavernous shadows of the triple-wide, pushing through black curtains she called the "velvet vulvic portal to Being," guiding me to a giant beanbag she encouraged me to form into any shape I was moved to shape, to take any position to which my body led me.

I poured out my story, finishing with my waterfront dream.

"Go with it Lou. What does the dream bring on?"

"Fear. Loathing. Disgust."

"Oh yes, Lou, oh yes."

Naming my troubles signaled my spirit to perform alchemy in the alembics of my gut, synthesizing energies to expel my pain. Soon I would experience what I already knew, embrace its Healing Love. I must take a day to myself, "a day for Lou to love his inner Lou."

"Now we stand together, Lou. Show me some head."

Our foreheads together, she droned her personal mantra, synching our bodies' wisdom. Her forehead was moist; I cherished the warm drops trickling down my nose and cheeks.

"Remember: self-time, self-time. You'll go deep into Lou, where you'll find all the answers. Go deep. It will come to you; *you* will come to you. *You* are your answer. You are moist, you are ready. Take self-time. You'll find what you need in Lou."

Eager to try, I took a few days off.

-12-

Laura rushed me into my office. Juliana had confided in her.

-13-

Entering Big Jim Jones' 40-yard-long office atop the Jesus Tower (formerly the Wells Fargo Building), you walked a gallery whose subdued lighting allowed the bright glass cases preserving "Images from Our Chronicles" to lead the way. Photos and video loops captured his rise from showroom through parking lot to glory;

the ribbon-cutting ceremonies heralding franchised mega-churches, malls, theaters and gated communities; the momentous meetings with Bill Clinton and his powerful wife, Rios Montt, George H.W. Bush and his charming wife, the Reverend Moon, Dr. Phil, Rupert Murdoch and his young wife, Mel Gibson, Robert Mugabe, Ted Haggard, Bill Gates and his intelligent wife.

Beyond the gallery loomed the stage on which Big Jim worked behind a vast mahogany desk fronting a wall of glass framing Mount Rainier. Statues carved into cedar by power-saws, formed scenes from his novels, hanging like shadows over the mahogany slab.

When Gina, Sylvio and I mounted the stage, Big Jim formed us into a prayer circle. "Brother Jesus, you've made us prosper and lifted us to these heights. May we do nothing to disturb these blessings, and always strive to thrive. Amen."

During his prayer, Big Jim's eyes darted from Gina to Sylvio. He directed us to a circle of leather chairs yielding as infants' flesh.

Like most public figures, Big Jim could not be called handsome. Had he grown his hair longer, rather than razor-cut it like a soldier, his cheeks might not have seemed so bulbous, his chins so fleshy. Were his Armani suits cut less severely, perhaps the overdevelopment of his breast would have seemed more masculine. A massive six-foot three, he marshaled his bulk to dominate meetings like an intruding bull—nauseating to imagine Juliana in his fat grasp.

" —Now, what can I do you-all for, Lou? Your girl said you'd be here to discuss some investment ideas. You know how close I am to the Nuzzle family and Nuzzle management. And I *love* the work Gina and Sylvio do for our Christian youth, but I didn't expect the pleasure."

"Reverend Jones, what can you tell us about the Special Angels, and their services to you and the Elders?"

Gina clenched her fists, and Sylvio growled, "Ha!"

"I believe we had an agenda, Lou. My time is valuable; if you're not here on business, we'll have to ask you to leave."

The room went quiet.

Big Jim rose to move behind the desk. We knew he'd summon his squadrons of bodyguards: Sylvio shadowed him, smashed his communications console with a cedar effigy. He grabbed

Big Jim by the scruff of the neck and the seat of his pants and pitched him face-first into Gina's flying dropkick, which flattened the great man's nose amidst a spray of blood and sweat. Sylvio spun him on the polished surface of his desk like a suet pinwheel, and Gina belabored his scrambled face as it spun by.

I'll never forget Sylvio's eerie falsetto intoning, "You're lucky we don't tear your balls off, dickface."

-14-

The Northwest enjoys a dramatic landscape, an abundance of beautiful waterways, lakes, rivers, and a cloudscape that makes hills and mountains resemble classic Asian scrolls. When the clouds cover us, the temperatures mellow.

On a cloudy night that June, a powerful speedboat idled in the Puyallup River basin, as five young men from the Hylebos Tribe received crates of geoducks in dry ice from silent Italians, who gestured with their pistols for Indians to do the loading.

Two Indians pulled the boat away slowly, running lights off. Reaching the limits of the brown silt from their sacred river, they steered Northwest past Brown's Point, opening the throttle gradually, to avoid cavitation under the heavy load. They could see no more than twenty yards beyond the bow, but these waters were their home, and they raced toward Seattle at 40 knots.

When they smashed through the graceful schooner at anchor, splitting it evenly between the two masts, their boat was like an axe cleaving a dry log. The halved yacht disappeared.

Charlotte and Jimmy, who had consistently refused to discuss anything to do with their parent company throughout my weeks pestering them, swore they know nothing about the accident, "But Lou, you know how we Indians love myths and legends. There's this tale that those boys were pissed about their wages, and there's this myth growing that your friend Captain Ollie was cut in half like his yacht, and two pieces of him floated ashore in Federal Way at dawn. Some even say that when he landed his head was jammed into his crotch and the crabs were feasting."

-15-

Throughout the meteoric rise of God's First Church, Brother Bob Boone's God's Only Church had festered on the fringe, occupying the glassy structure formerly housing The Bon Marché in the Tacoma Mall, where it sought vainly to attract attention from the I-5 with spotlights and religious pyrotechnics. Brother Bob's depiction of Jesus as a scourge of immigrants was more militant than Big Jim's. Fundamentalist bikers, law-enforcement professionals, and military families dominated GOF's demographic, limiting the expansion of his enterprises, stifling incubation of synergistic alliances with the downtown business establishment.

But when God's First Church was exposed as a criminal enterprise, Brother Bob embraced opportunity. A milder, kinder Brother Bob—"humbled but inspirited by what these sad events tell us of Satan's ways"— ran for mayor of Tacoma, promising to clean house, to protect Tacoma's youth from the depredations of perverts like Muslims, Catholics, and the High Elders of GFC, whose drug-and-geoduck-laced orgies with young women from the Hylebos Tribe were emblematic of everything he'd inveighed against for two decades. Nor did Mayor Bob let his resentment at Nuzzle Investments' former eschewal of his business prevent investing with us as GOC grew like a mustard seed.

Mayor Bob preached moderation in pursuit of Coach. Relieved fans renewed their beliefs and rituals.

Coach and the Little Woman adopted two toddlers orphaned by drone strikes in Yemen. The Little Woman is alone in disciplining the kids: Coach dotes on them with baby-talk that befuddles youngsters struggling with American English.

The Special Master administering God's First Church's bankruptcy forced the sale of Emerald Bay Casino Enterprises, afflicting the Hylebos with an epidemic of unemployment Jimmy and Charlotte's startups, enhanced tribal museum and marina, could not mitigate. Politicians continued to shake their verbal fists at the socialist tribal allowances.

These economic, social and political vicissitudes moved Jimmy and Charlotte to re-examine their emotional independence. Once Jimmy completed an insulated prefabricated hut in her back yard, complete with "eco-friendly turd toaster," she consented to be be his bride, and allowed him to live within her boundaries. Charlotte slapped Jimmy when he told me that, no longer needing to wink at the corruptions of his people by church and state, he could look Charlotte in the eye, not just up and down. They became afficianados of Coach's wild meat roasts, where they wrestle, so to speak, with the issue roiling Gena and Sylvio's Wrestlemania Readiness sessions at the Tribal Center: should Indian grapplers be good guys, villains, both?

By then I was blessing the accountant who browbeat me into saving all the money possible in my deferred compensation plan: when the worthless GFC paper in the Nuzzle money market fund forced it to break the buck, when its fund-of-hedge-funds swung for the fences and missed, when its real estate fund froze, my family-oriented company rolled on profitably, discarding 20% of the hourly employees innocent of these hubristic blunders, and the one managing director who warned against them—me.

(from *A Mystery's no Problem*)

Adventures In
Translation Land

George Economou

In 1728, Thomas Gordon began the preface to his translation of
Tacitus with this self-assured pronouncement: "I am going to offer
to the publick the Translation of a Work, which for wisdom and
force, is in higher fame and consideration, than almost any other that
has yet appeared amongst men; a work often translated into many
Languages, seldom well into any, into ours worst of all."

  Gordon's naked articulation of his low opinion of previous
translations of his author into English and the insinuated superiority
of his own may have had some merit, for his two-volume edition of
Tacitus enjoyed the status of 'standard translation' until the end of
the eighteenth-century, a full five decades beyond his death in 1750.
The longevity of translations, Gordon's Tacitus included, is by nature
subject to numerous unfriendly influences, from the overcrowding
effect of persistent competition——consider the piling up of Homer and
Dante translations in our own time——to the states of obsolescence
or quaintness imposed upon them by the simple fact that languages
continuously change and call for translations to keep up with them.
The response to this call is what keeps the translations coming,
fueled by what Gordon reveals as lurking in his heart and, I surmise,
in that of every self-respecting translator, the desire to produce a

work that excels in its realization of a level of performance that is comparable to that of its original, whether as an effort to surpass all previous translations or, in the absence of a competing field, to set an enduring standard.

The preceding remarks about translation as a kind of pursuit of excellence, cued as they are by the title of this address, are meant to hint at a comparison between translating and knight-errantry, to suggest, if only for a moment, that by undertaking what Walter Benjamin called, in the title of his celebrated 1921 essay, "The Task of the Translator," the translator is setting out on a kind of noble quest, albeit one that calls more for *sitzfleisch* than it does for expert equitation. It is a pursuit, I would argue, that has deeper affinities than it does differences with that of the poet, as intimated by Jorge Luis Borges' astute observation in his essay "The Homeric Versions" that "No problem is as consubstantial to literature and its modest mystery as the one posed by translation."

Like Borges, I hold a deep allegiance to the modest mystery of poetry, its translation as poetry, and to its defense against such tiresome, otiose quips as the often parroted pairing of the Italian words for "traitor" and "translator," *traditore tradutorre*, and Robert Frost's written with a stiletto, "poetry is what gets lost in translation." On the contrary, poetry may be found in translation if the adventurer knows how and where to seek it. And it is not to be sought or found in theory, whose prickling thicket, no matter how stimulating, seems better at preventing than at producing acts of poetic translation. At one point in his essay, for example, Benjamin avers that translation, having no muse of its own, is situated someplace midway between poetry and theory and brings out "the kinship of languages...far more profoundly and clearly than in the superficial and indefinable similarity of two works of literature." Despite the enrichment to one's intellectual store such observations may confer when encountered in a time of solitary detachment, along with the relentless flux of perceptions that precede and follow them, a flood of stunning, occasionally oracular insights that can muddle as well as enlighten, how would it benefit a translator to read "The Task of the Translator" just before taking on the actual task? Would the ingenious, little allegory that disappears almost as quickly as it materializes in which Benjamin situates the work of literature "in the center of the language forest" and translation on its "outside facing the wooded ridge," calling into the forest but never entering it, waiting to capture its singular echo, motivate our *chevalier-translateur* to pursue his quest with all his might or paralyze him?

Ever since Plato extended the number of muses by one in his famous testimony to Sappho in the ninth book of *The Greek Anthology*—"Nine muses, you say? Look again./ Sappho the Lesbian makes it ten!"—writers of all kinds have claimed a tenth muse as their inspiration. Not least among them have been translators, especially poet-translators, though the only title as such I have encountered is the 1980 anthology edited by Charles Doria, *The Tenth Muse: Classical Drama in Translation*, to which I contributed my translation of the satyr play "Cyclops" by Euripides, my first serious effort at translating an ancient Greek work of literature. Call this tenth muse "inspiration" or by any other name, the poet who translates should be free to invoke her, despite Benjamin's disclaimer, as he plunges twice into the forest of language, first in behalf of his author and then in behalf of himself and his audience.

To begin the adventure, then, by taking a short detour, which will directly reconnect with the main path, let's follow Thomas Gordon just a bit longer, even though he did not translate poetry, by considering his censorious observation, made later in the preface to his Tacitus, concerning the translation of the Roman historian by John Dryden, whose "poor and languid" contribution was based literally and slavishly on a French translation by Mr. Amelot de la Houssaye. It's more than likely the only intention behind this rebuke, after which Gordon went on to criticize Dryden for allowing convenience and expediency to supplant the requirements of his artistic judgment and experience, was simply to score an invidious comparison. Still, a faintly confirming echo of Gordon's complaint about Dryden's Tacitus performance might be heard two-hundred years later in Benjamin's striking remark that "Translations…prove to be untranslatable not because of any inherent difficulty but because of the looseness with which meaning attaches to them." To my knowledge, Dryden, whose well-known 1680 preface to his translation of *Ovid's Epistles* contains some discerning observations that are profitably cited to this day about the three, in his view, approaches to the translation of poetry—by metaphrase, by paraphrase, and by imitation— never addressed the issue of translating from translations; in fact, in that essay he insists that the man who would translate poetry must not only have a genius for the art but must also be a master of both his author's language and his own. Since translating Tacitus is a matter of prose, and in the making of Dryden's version a team effort as well, there is no real contradiction between what Gordon says Dryden did as translator of prose and what Dryden says he must be as translator of verse. Somewhere inside this mildly aporetic state of affairs stir the pros and cons of the issue of what has become a fairly common practice in our time, the translation of poems based by necessity, because of the would-be translator's deficiency in the language of the original, entirely on other translations. Some of these source translations, whether in the same language as the translation dependent on it or in a completely different language, are consulted as published works, some are prepared by a collaborator with linguistic expertise in the language of the original, and a few, on rare and special occasions, by the poet who made it.

When I first started translating poetry out of Modern Greek in the late 1950s, it would never have occurred to me that one day I would translate a handful of poems in languages of which I had no knowledge whatsoever. I have also, since the early 1990s, done translations of a number of poems from the Spanish of contemporary Latin American and Cuban writers with a co-translator, Luis Cortest, who, though not a poet himself, is a university professor of Spanish and Hispanic literatures, the master of the original author's language in our collaboration, a role for which he is recognized through equal credit in all of our publications. But since I am hardly a total stranger to Spanish, there is no comparing this co-translation process with that of the translations I did for two of the ground-breaking anthologies, *Technicians of the Sacred* and *A Big Jewish Book*, edited by Jerome Rothenberg and published in 1968 and 1978, respectively. The initial despair of dealing with a source text in a language from which one simply draws a blank can be suddenly supplanted by an alluring, some might argue even slightly perverse, sense of liberation. Provided with a linguistically expert literal interlinear version, supported by scholarly annotations concerning pertinent formal, stylistic and cultural details, as a launching pad, the would-be translator can be projected into a heightened state of action from which to pursue the making of a poem in terms of which accountability to his mastery of his own language greatly

outweighs that which is demanded by the author's. Precisely and
unambiguously guided thus through the language forest of the
original, he may revel in the exploration of his own—or so my
situation at that time seemed to me.

When Rothenberg was gathering work for *Technicians of the
Sacred*, he invited me to contribute translations of poems from Africa.
Relying on the foundation laid by the anthropologist D. F. v.d.
Merwe in his article "Hurutshe Poems" in the 1941 volume of *Bantu
Studies* that I came upon while wandering through the Columbia
Library stacks, I wrote this version of the praise poem "The Train,"
especially pleased that just by including it in my text I was able
to incorporate the onomatopoetic effect of the Hurutshe word for
rhinoceros, *Tshukudu*.

Iron thing coming from Pompi, from the roundhouse
where Englishmen smashed their hands on it,
It has no front it has no back.
Rhino Tshukudu going that way.
Rhino Tshukudu no, coming this way.
I'm no greenhorn, I'm a strong, skillful man.
Animal coming from Pompi, from Moretele.
It comes spinning out a spider's web under a cloud of gnats
Moved by the pulling of a teat, animal coming from
    Kgobola-diatla
Comes out of a big hole in the mountain, mother of the
    great woman,
Coming on iron cords.
I met this woman of the tracks curving her way along the
    river bank and over the river.
I thought I'd snatch her
So I said
"Out of the way, son of Mokwatsi, who stands there at the
    teat."
The stream of little red and white birds gathered up all of
    its track
Clean as a whistle.
Tshutshu over the dry plains
Rhino Tshukudu out of the high country
Animal from the south, steaming along

It comes from Pompi, the roundhouse, from Kgobola-
diatla.

Recalling as I worked on "The Train" v.d. Merwe's
comment on Hurutshe praise-poems, " A man may add a few lines
to a poem heard by somebody else, with the result that a given poem
may be the creation of two or even more persons," I felt as if I were
participating in an ongoing communal song about man's experience
of adding whatever comes into his field of vision to his real world.
This feeling has only deepened with my recent awareness that a
French translator has added his voice to the singing of "The Train"
through his translation of my translation of a translation of this
poem for the forthcoming French edition of *Techniciens du Sacré*.

Ten years after the appearance of *Technicians of the Sacred*,
Rothenberg asked me to contribute to a new anthology entitled
A Big Jewish Book, and I obliged by making translations out of
translations—Rothenberg favored the word *workings*—of several
poems by medieval Hebrew poets. My favorite among these is a work
by the thirteenth-century native of Gascony, Isaac Ben Abraham
Gorni, a self-fashioned wandering troubadour, worked from a literal
translation by Israel Zinberg in his *A History of Jewish Literature*.
Attracted to this poem because of my academic training and
profession as a medievalist, which included work on the poetry of the
troubadours of Provence, I entitled this Hebrew *congé*, or poem of
departure, "Proensa."

> In Provence Gorni's got a lot of enemies
> who put down my songs as well.
> Yet I know I am the poet,
> the only one of my generation.
> When I sing mountains dance
> valleys & forests rejoice.
> I take up my harp & happy
> Zion's daughters form a circle.
> If I want I can wake up bones
> & make stones run like the Jordan.
> ....
> When I die girls will lament me everyday
> & merchants make big deals in world-markets

for bags of dirt from my grave, out of my coffin's
planks others will carve amulets—special for barren women.
Someone will string harps & fiddles
with my hair & the tunes will come, O
lovely tunes sans strum or bow of human hand.
Even my clothes—revered—anything that's touched my skin.
 But grind my bones to dust,
 I won't promote idolatry.

  As already implied, such acts of writing occupy a small space
in the inventory of my translations, partly because for me—I would
not dare to speak for others in this respect—they impose an arbitrary
limit on my engagement with the languages of originals and, thus,
also affect the possibilities of what I might do with my own. Dealing
directly with the source language forces me to work harder to better
find my way out of it and into English. My work as a medievalist also
influenced me by confronting me with diverse poetries in several
languages, and it is from one such work, the longest I have ever
translated, that I would now like to offer an example. I trust that
you will not take it as a deliberate provocation that I start by saying
this work is a translation into English of a poem that was written in
English—more properly speaking, into twentieth-century American
English from the Southwest Midlands dialect of fourteenth-century
Middle English. The poem, *Piers Plowman*, a lifetime work by
William Langland, has survived in three versions, of which I took
on the last and longest one, usually identified as the C-Text or
Version and dated around 1380. Langland was a contemporary of
Geoffrey Chaucer's, but his Middle English dialect is considerably
more difficult for today's readers than Chaucer's London English, the
immediate ancestor of our modern English. Doing that translation
was to be in an unusual position, at times feeling as if I were
translating out of what seemed close to a foreign language and at
others as if I were actually shifting words and phrases from one kind
of English into another, a sort of "coaxing" of my contemporary
English version out of Langland's original Middle English alliterative
verse. Nonetheless, it was an enormous task—the poem is some 7,300
lines long—that took ten years from the time I started work on it to
its publication, complete with introduction and annotations, in 1996,
during a period when my academic life was at its most demanding.

A dream vision of epic scale, comparable to Dante's *Commedia*, shifting its linguistic registers through the gamut of homiletic, reflective, argumentative, invective, narrative, and descriptive modalities, *Piers Plowman* is a major literary monument of such richness and variety that no one passage can justly represent the accomplishment of the whole. My selection, the monologue of the character Glutton from the parade of confessing personified Seven Deadly Sins in Passus VI, both reveals and typifies the making power of Langland's mind and eyes and ears. Listen for the alliteration that survives in the translation, in which I chose not to observe the formal rules of alliterative verse but rather to allow its distinctive qualities to flow from Middle to Modern English verse.

Now Glutton heads for confession
And moves towards the Church, his mea culpa to say.
Fasting on a Friday he made forth his way
By the house of Betty Brewer, who bid him good morning
And where was he going that brew-wife asked.
    "To Holy Church," he said "to hear mass,
And then sit and be shriven and sin no more."
    "I have good ale, Glutton, old buddy, want to give it a try?"
    "Do you have," he asked, "any hot spices?"
    "I have pepper, peony, and a pound of garlic,
A farthing-worth of fennel seed, for fasting days I bought it."
    Then in goes Glutton and great oaths after.
Cissy the shoemaker sat on the bench,
Wat the game warden and his drunken wife,
Tim the tinker and two of his workmen,
Hick the hackney-man and Hugh the needler,
Clarice of Cock's Lane and the clerk of the church,
Sir Piers of Pridie and Purnel of Flanders,
A hayward, a hermit, the hangman of Tyburn,
Daw the ditchdigger and a dozen rascals
In the form of porters and pickpockets and bald tooth-pullers
A fiddler, a rat-catcher, a street-sweeper and his helper,
A rope-maker, a road-runner, and Rose the dish-seller,
Godfrey the garlic-man and Griffith the Welshman,
And a heap of secondhand salesmen, early in the morning
Stood Glutton with glad cheers to his first round of ale.

Clement the cobbler took off his cloak
And put it up for a game of New Fair.
Hick the hackney-man saw with his hood
And asked Bart the butcher to be on his side.
Tradesmen were chosen to appraise this bargain,
That whoso had the hood should not have the cloak,
And that the better thing, according to the arbiters,
   compensate the worse.
They got up quickly and whispered together
And appraised these items apart in private,
And there was a load of swearing, for one had to get the worse.
They could not in conscience truthfully accord
Till Robin the rope-maker they asked to arise
And named him umpire so that all arguing would stop.
   Hick the hostler got the cloak
On condition that Clement should fill the cup
And have Hick the hostler's hood and rest content;
And whoever took it back first had to get right up
And greet Sir Glutton with a gallon of ale.
   There was laughing and louring and "please pass the cup!"
Bargaining and drinking they kept starting up
And sat so till evensong, and sang from time to time,
Until Glutton had gobbled down a gallon and a gill.
His guts began to rumble like two greedy sows;
He pissed half a gallon in the time of a pater noster,
He blew his round bugle at his backbone's bottom,
So that all who heard that horn had to hold their noses
And wished it had been well plugged with a wisp of briars.
He could neither step nor stand unless he held a staff,
And then he moved like a minstrel's performing dog,
Sometimes sideways and sometimes backwards,
Like some one laying lines in order to trap birds.
   And when he reached the door, then his eyes dimmed,
And he stumbled on the threshold and fell to the ground,
And Clement the cobbler grabbed him by the waist
And in order to lift him up set him on his knees.
But Glutton was a huge boor and troubled in the lifting
And barfed up a mess into Clement's lap;
There is no hound so hungry in Hertfordshire

That he'd dare lap up that leaving, so unlovely it smacked.
　With all the woe in this world his wife and his daughter
Bore him to his bed and put him in it,
And after all this excess he had a bout of sloth;
He slept through Saturday and Sunday till sundown.
Then he awoke pale and wan and wanted a drink;
The first thing he said was "Who's got the bowl?"
His wife and his conscience reproached him for his sin;
He became ashamed, that scoundrel,
　and made quick confession
To Repentance like this: "Have pity on me," he said,
"Lord who are aloft and shape all that lives!
　To you God, I, Glutton, acknowledge my guilt
Of how I've trespassed with tongue, how often I can't tell,
Sworn 'God's soul and his sides!' and 'So help me God,
　Almighty!'
There was no need for it so many times falsely;
And overate at supper and sometime at noon
More than my system could naturally handle,
And like a dog that eats grass I began to throw up
And wasted what I might have saved—I can't speak
　for my shame
Of the depravity of my foul mouth and maw—
And on fasting days before noon I fed myself ale
Beyond all reason, among dirty jokesters, their dirty jokes
　to hear.
　For this, good God, grant me forgiveness
For my worthless living during my entire lifetime.
For I swear by the true God, despite any hunger or thirst,
Never shall on a Friday a piece of fish digest in my stomach
Till my aunt Abstinence has given me leave—
And yet I've hated her all my lifetime." (vss. 350-441)

Although working on *Piers Plowman* required an enduring
commitment, my dearest and longest lasting involvement as a
translator, reaching back to my early twenties, has been with Greek
poetry. Growing up bilingually, memorizing and reciting poems in
Greek as a child must have had its effect, though other kids in my
Montana Greek-American community shared a similar experience

without being drawn into a vocation by it. This durable calling began with the realization that I was in a position to translate Modern Greek poems as I was beginning to learn how to write my own poems in English and over time intensified into the more daunting task of translating ancient Greek poetry as well, all part of what I have written about elsewhere as a gradual life-long reclamation of my heritage of Hellenism. So I'd like now to share with you a few of my memorable adventures in the translation of poetry from that heritage, focusing on a small group of poems by what is possibly the most distinguished pair of poetic book ends in any language, the twentieth-century Alexandrian C. P. Cavafy and the seventh-century B.C.E. Sappho from Mytilene on the island of Lesbos.

Among the first of Cavafy's poems I ventured to render into English is "Half an Hour," which has appeared most recently in my book *Complete Plus, the Poems of C. P. Cavafy in English*. Because this work, written in 1917, was never published by the poet during his lifetime, presumably because of its homoerotic connotations, it has always been presented as one of his "Unpublished Poems," and even ignored by the inexcusably ignorant. Ironically, there is nothing in the original Greek, and consequently in my translation of it, that assigns a specific gender to the individual addressed.

Half an Hour

Never made it with you and don't expect
I will. Some talk, a slight move closer,
as in the bar yesterday, nothing more.
A pity, I won't deny. But we artists
now and then by pushing our minds
can—but only for a moment—create
a pleasure that seems almost physical.
That's why in the bar yesterday—with the help
of alcohol's merciful power—I had
a half-hour that was completely erotic.
I think you knew it and
stayed on purpose a little longer.
That was really necessary. Because
with all my imagination and spell of the drinks,

I just had to see your lips,
had to have your body near.

A friend in Norman, Oklahoma, printed elegant postcards of
this poem, which I thumb-tacked alongside other literary and artistic
curios on the front door of my office for the purpose of student
edification when I was teaching at the University of Oklahoma. I
lost count of the number of times I had to replace it there after it
was ripped off, carefully I trust, by passing students whose eyes were
hooked by the poem and who, I imagined, may have also perceived
it as an aid to their own amatory ambitions. May their drafting of
Cavafy as a kind of Cyrano de Bergerac into their campaigns to
achieve true bliss have resulted in greater successes than the secret
desires of either of these famous real and fictive poets ever did. Still,
if ignorance is bliss, the pettily larcenous young lovers, whether
winners or losers in their games of love, came out ahead.

The next two poems illustrate a theme that pervades much
of Cavafy's poetry, his unique perspective of the human condition
through the trifocal lens of eros, memory, and art. Many of Cavafy's
poems deal specifically with the difficulties of the artist and poet,
most notably the problem of the effects of time upon the artist's
ability to memorialize in his work a person or experience, invariably
recalled for their erotic significance, for which he cares profoundly.

Craftsman of Wine Bowls

On this wine bowl   of pure silver—
made for the house   of Herakleides,
where grand style   and good taste rule—
observe the elegant flowers,   streams and thyme,
in whose midst I set   a handsome young man,
naked, amorous,   with one leg still
dangling in the water.—   O memory, I prayed
for your best assistance   in making
the young man's face I loved   the way it was.
A great difficulty   this proved because
about fifteen years   have passed since the day
he fell, a soldier,   in the defeat at Magnesia.

In this poem from 1921, in which the personal and the political, the private and the public subtly intersect, the artist, working on a commission by a great family, has the power nonetheless to insinuate his individual celebration of his love as he simultaneously experiences the eroding effects of time upon his memory of that love. That the craftsman persona dates his loss by the critical battle fought in 190 B.C.E. that marks the onset of Roman dominance in the Hellenized East, provides an ironic historical context that may be more meaningful to the reader of this poem than to its speaker. Relative chronological proximity to the battle of Magnesia provides the speaker with poignancy, chronological distance provides the reader with ironic perspective. Perhaps the human dimensions of this context are large enough to accommodate the poet himself and us as well, revealing all of us as participants in our own private situations, full of passion and loss, and subject to historical forces that we are fated to understand only partially. Yet these pathetic, often tragic, conditions can be intermittently dignified by art's attempt to record their sincerity and intensity.

A work that represents the consummate formulation of this rich and central aspect of Cavafy's writing, "According to the Recipes of Ancient Greco-Syrian Magicians," a late poem printed in 1931 two years before his death, is itself the answer to the question it states.

"What distillate of magic herbs
can I find," said an aesthete,
"what distillate according to the recipes
of ancient Greco-Syrian magicians
that for a day (if its power
won't last longer) or for just a moment
will bring back my age of twenty-three,
my friend of twenty-two,
bring back—his beauty and his love.

"What distillate can I find according to the recipes
of ancient Greco-Syrian magicians
that, in keeping with this retrospect,
will bring back our little room."

With almost every Cavafian persona, including the autobiographical one, neatly subsumed in this undiluted common denominator of an "aesthete," Cavafy makes the essential case for poetry, for searching out the knowledge of past masters, denoted by "Greco-Syrian magicians," in order to describe as objectively as possible the quest to which he has dedicated his life in art. If the recipes to be followed can be construed as tradition and the precious distillate as the individual work of art—an interpretation I believe the discourse of the poem supports—how are we to apprehend its singular power, extracted by ancient prescriptions from "magic herbs," if not by experiencing the poem in its totality, as a work of art, as defined by Paul Valéry, "*constraining language to interest the ear directly*"? Ever since I first read this poem aloud, it has occupied a place in my private anthology of poems great with sound. So it was reassuring to learn some years later that George Seferis considered it one of the most beautiful poems in the Greek language, an observation that redeems him in my eyes for having also remarked that Cavafy's poetry is as prosaic as an "endless plain." Surely as some things can't be bought or taught (or completely carried over from one language into another), this poem's greatness resides in the highest realization of its sense through its maker's inimitable mastery of the sounds of his own special brand of Greek.

KATA TES SYNTAYES ARCHAION HELLINOSIRON MAGON

"Pió apóstagma na vrísketai apó vótana
yitévmatos," ip énas aisthitís.
"pió apóstagma katá tes syntayés
archaíon Hellinosíron mágon kamoméno
pou yia mía méra (an perisótero
then fthan' i thinamís tou), i kai yia líyin ora
ta íkosi tria mou chrónia na me féri
ksaná; ton fílon mou sta íkosi thió tou chrónia
na me féri ksaná—tin emorfiá tou, tin agápi tou.

"Pió apóstagma na vrísketai katá tes syntayés
archaíon Hellinosíron mágon kamoméno
pou, símfona me tin anadromín,

kai tin mikrí mas kámari na epanaféri."

Testimonies to Sappho such as the epigram by Plato naming
her the tenth muse and a panegyric for her by Dioskorides, one
of the more important poets in *The Greek Anthology*, in which he
writes that she is to be greeted as a god for having given the world
her "immortal daughters, her songs," only begin to indicate the
heights of esteem her poetry secured for her from her fellow Greeks.
It is one of the most remarkable cases of literary history that this
esteem has survived unscathed into posterity when all that remains
of her work is a pitifully small fraction, and most of that in a highly
fragmentary state. Of her nine books of lyric poetry known to the
ancient Greeks, only two poems—for years it was one and would
be still but for a fortuitous recent discovery— have come down to
us complete, accompanied by some 200 fragments of one word or
a phrase or two, to more substantial passages of varying length, a
count that depends upon the judgments of her editors. Thus, the
provenance of what we call "Sappho's poetry" lies, on the one hand,
in fragments of papyrus reduced to their tattered and torn condition
by the relentless accidents of time and blind bookworms, and on the
other, in medieval manuscripts of various ancient authors who cited
her lines just as often as examples pertinent to their erudite interests
in such matters as custom, grammar, spelling, and versification as for
their literary excellence. This latter body of citations, along with the
numerous testimonials by Greek and Roman writers and poets, not
only gives us an idea of Sappho's extensive renown in antiquity, it has
also preserved what had long been considered the one whole extant
poem (by Dionysius of Halicarnassus in his *On Literary Composition*)
and a number of the more coherent, if excerpted, passages of
other fuller poems. One of the most important of these (quoted by
Longinus in his *On the Sublime*), are the first four stanzas and the first
verse of a fifth, of the famous poem that begins, "He seems to me
equal to gods that man," which was translated by Catullus into an
equally famous Latin version, "Ille mi par esse deo videtur" and by
a string of poets since, including Robert Lowell and William Carlos
Williams. The papyrus fragments represent a considerable addition
to the texts and information preserved in the medieval codices, but
their transcription by the papyrologist, once aptly described as an
"artificer of fact," involves an extremely demanding and painstaking

process, a labor of scholarly creativity that is ultimately effaced in the printed pages of his edition. What these pages show are texts in a context of absences and silences, gaps and lacks, missing words and lines, and illegible letters: it is this context that translators of Sappho must negotiate, and a few of them, for all their good intentions and purposes, do so by in effect denying it is there, producing small finished poems tendentiously aimed in a direction of their own choosing by a heading or even a title.

One of the best-known of these fragments, the one about unstoppable Eros *lusimeles*, the limb-loosener, in two compact lines of verse has been recast by translators of repute into four and six line poems puffed with extraneous details. But a fragment is a fragment is a fragment, and if its first line has twelve syllables and its second eleven, why not try to translate it with that good Greek word "economy," as in this eponymously made version?

> and again Love, the limb-loosener, excites me,
> that sweet-then-bitter, invincible critter

The challenge is concentration, not attenuation, making it with twelve and eleven syllables of English for twelve and eleven syllables of Greek and resisting the temptation to explain rather than translate the brilliant second line, *glukupikron amachanon orpeton*, with an echo of its strong assonance, and finally not to say "bittersweet" for *glukupikron*, "sweetbitter," an oxymoron that more truthfully reflects the course of love in Greek than it does in English.

In the long-prized unique complete poem, which is, of course, not without a couple of words that have required editorial emendation and restoration (and thus have produced a learned disagreement or two), Sappho evokes Aphrodite to once again liberate her from the tyranny of unreciprocated love, a summons that includes the recollection of a previous encounter with the goddess in which she made assurances of justice to her, Sappho, whom Aphrodite is then made to address by name in her poem. Among all the other things she can do with imaginative agility, Sappho certainly knows how to pray.

> Throned in brilliance, deathless Aphrodite,
> wile-weaving child of Zeus, I beg you,

my queen, do not inflict me further
with heartache,
but come here, if ever before
you heard my voice from afar,
and, disposed to leave your father's
golden house, came

with chariot yoked. And beautiful, swift
sparrows, wings awhirr above the dark earth,
delivered you down from heaven
through mid-air

and quickly arrived. But you, O blessed one,
with a smile on your deathless face, asked me
so now what was the trouble and so now
why was I calling,

and what do I want more than anything
to befall my manic heart. So now whom
do I persuade to lead you back into her love?
Sappho, who's done you wrong?

For if she runs away, soon she'll give chase.
If she refuses gifts, then she'll make them.
If she does not love, soon she'll have to love,
even if unwilling.

Come to me again now, and release me
from bitter cares, and all that my heart longs
to fulfill, fulfill. And may you yourself
be my ally.

In 2004 at the University of Cologne, three fragmentary
poems by Sappho were found in a papyrus roll that had been
recycled as mummy cartonnage. Because they were copied only
about three hundred years after their original composition, they
constitute the earliest known record of her work. One from among
this group of fragments, by virtue of its being part of a poem,
another fragment of much later date of which has been known to

scholars for several decades, provides us, when the two fragments are joined together, with another instance of that great rarity, a very close to complete lyric by this poet. In the opening lines, Sappho speaks as a teacher of singing and dancing to young girls, a role some later Greek writers believed she followed professionally. Then, after the poem turns suddenly to the contrasting state of her aging condition, Sappho shifts her focus to a remarkable and deeply moving implied comparison of herself to Tithonus, the young mortal with whom the goddess Dawn fell in love and asked Zeus that he be granted immortality, but forgetting to ask that he also remain forever youthful, an omission with terrible, irreversible consequences.

> It is for you, my girls, those lovely gifts in the Muses' violet-scented laps
> to pursue in earnest, and the keen, vibrant lyre as well:
>
> but my own skin and flesh, once so pliant, old age now
> takes over, and my dark hair is turning white;
>
> so my soul grows heavy, and my knees can't hold me,
> that once matched the light-footed dance of fawns.
>
> Which things I keep lamenting, but what can one do?
> Impossible not to grow old, being only human.
>
> Didn't rosy-armed Dawn, pining with love,
> bear Tithonus away once to the end of the world?
>
> Young and handsome then he was, but hoary old age
> in time possessed him, though wedded to a deathless wife.

In a recent book review, an American poet and translator of Latin poetry, continues our literary culture's habitual submission to Robert Frost's wisecracking truism that poetry is what gets lost in translation, but then goes on to comfort us with the assurance that the poem's *prose*, not necessarily a negligible thing, at least comes through. I know this is supposed to make good self-evident sense and does so to many people, including me perhaps—but only up to the degree of its self-evident sense, which stands at a level too low for my comfort. The proposition, perhaps unintentionally, relegates translating to the perfunctory role of saving the prose and seems to overlook or minimize the summons for individual ingenuity and originality in the dynamics of being a translator of poems into poems. As my old friend, the late Paul Blackburn, poet and translator of extraordinary gifts, once said at the end of an interview, "Much depends upon the translator." And I can't help thinking once again about how fundamentally instructive Thomas Gordon's self-assurance and the confidence of his commitment to his task should be to all translators, but especially to every hand that reaches into one world of words to bring its poetic endowments back alive to another. "Much depends upon the translator." Yes, it does.

"Adventures in Translation Land" was originally written as the Nadav Vardi English Honors Lecture at Tel Aviv University, where it was delivered on May 29, 2008. It was subsequently given at the English Staff Seminar of the Hebrew University in Jerusalem on June 1, 2008, and at the Helena Festival of the Book, Holter Museum of Art, Helena, Montana, on September 26, 2009.

Incompletable Text
Eye of Witness:
A Jerome Rothenberg Reader[1]

Peter Quartermain

"My own choice has been to write from the side of a modernism that sees itself as challenging limits and changing ways of speaking / thinking / doing that have too long robbed us of the freedom to be human to the full extent of our powers and yearnings. The struggle is immediate and the objects and attitudes to be destroyed or transformed appear on every side of us." (*Symposium of the Whole*, p. xiv.) [2]

Jerome Rothenberg asked, in 1996, "Why has the poet failed us?" (385). There is of course a considerable difference between the poet failing, and the poet failing *us*, but at first glance the question still seems pretty weird, given the sheer volume, variety, and energy of Rothenberg's work, a great deal of it sampled and reordered in this absorbing book. He has written and/or edited some 80 or more books and they're pretty substantial: poetry, prose, interviews, translations, commentaries, prefaces, letters, transliterations,

---

[1] *Eye of Witness: A Jerome Rothenberg Reader.* Edited with commentaries by Jerome Rothenberg and Heriberto Yépez (Boston: Black Widow, 2013).
[2] Jerome Rothenberg. "Pre-Face." *Symposium of the Whole: A Range of Discourse Toward an Ethnopoetics.* Edited with commentaries by Jerome Rothenberg & Diane Rothenberg (Berkeley: U of California P, 1983), xiv). All quotations except those otherwise identified are from *Eye of Witness*.

anthologies, libretti, collaborations – to say nothing of his travels, recordings, collages, investigations; his explorations of ritual and theatre; his probing of discontinuities; his stratagems to open up the eye to the ear, to shift the oral onto the page, to shift the strange into let's call it the familiar or at least recognisable, and the reverse. He's a great archaeologist of the neglected and the forgotten, retrieving such treasures as "The Seven Hells of the Jigoku Zoshi," and there are some terrific essays – that on "Harold Bloom: The Critic as Exterminating Angel" should be required reading in every English course in the land. Then there's his remarkable ethnomusicology of wordless as well as worded songs; his pioneering work in ethnopoetics. He's brought the contemporary and the archaic as well as the non-alphabetic into the resources of American poetry; he's brought the aleatory as well as the formulaic into the nature and structure of the poem.

What I list doesn't even begin to cover the territory, and he has not of course worked alone: collaboration is not simply for him a means of making works, it is a means by which to listen, to learn, and to question. And all this is never-ending: "The work is in no way complete," he said in the Pre-Face to *Symposium of the Whole* (xiv). The definitive, with its intolerant authority, is anathema: *Eye of Witness* more than once quotes Richard Huelsenbeck's Dadaist call for the "liberation of the creative forces from the tutelage of the advocates of power." The notion of failure seems never to enter Rothenberg's head, any more than might caution and timidity: with his deeply entrenched opposition to the idea of completeness at the very heart of his poetics, questions of failure or success are irrelevant. "What I come to do," says a Creeley poem, "is partial, partially kept" – you can't neglect the pun there. What counts is the *doing*, and one's partiality gets in the way.

That, perhaps, accounts a bit for his great economy of energy, for the drive that produced and *still* produces (Rothenberg's in his eighties) these thousands of pages of work. Even the most cursory of readers, casting an eye through the nearly 600 pages of *Eye of Witness*, will be struck by the sheer urgency of Rothenberg's thought, and the profound sadness that stirs necessity and informs his affirmation. The first thing you see, on the book's cover, is Goya's *Asmodea* (Goya surely kin to Rothenberg); and one of the first things you might read, the epigraph to the first section of the book (29), is from William Blake, also kin, *The Marriage of Heaven and Hell*. As Rothenberg says in "Je est un autre," his short talk-piece of 1989 titled after Rimbaud, "there is a politics in this & yet there is no politics" (162). And the politics is impassioned. In 1987, on his first visit to Poland, he went to Treblinka, site of the Nazi extermination and forced labour camps at which close to a million were killed, now "only an empty field & . . . thousands of large stones," a graveyard of voices, a site of *khurbn*. *Khurbn*, a Yiddish-Hebrew word for disaster pure & simple -- what Christians call The Holocaust (implying sacrifice), and Jews call *Shoah* (a Hebrew word for catastrophe) – is what Rothenberg names "the word as prelude to the scream" (310), the word for the unspeakable, for that which is beyond witness – no sacrifice, no false ennoblement, nothing left to say beyond the word and perhaps not even that, but emptiness. To our dismay, there are other forms and occasions of the unspeakable, other empties, other roots of that "impasse in the soul" (59) Rothenberg faced at around the time he was writing *Poland / 1931*, in 1961: the sheer impossibility of witness, of bringing to speech, and the inescapable *urgent* necessity to give the dead their voice. "The poems that I first began to hear at Treblinka," he reports, "are the clearest message I have ever gotten about why I write poetry" (306).

The second volume of *Poems for the Millennium*, edited with Pierre Joris, closes with these lines from 1996 (they are also in *Eye of Witness*, 387); it all – anthologies, collaborations, essays, poems, talks, everything – makes but *one* work:

A woman's breast & honey.
She in whose mouth the murderers stuffed gravel
who will no longer speak.
The poet is the only witness to that death,
writes every line
as though the only witness.

Silence: the blank subtext which has ever since suffused our lives, which we attempt to pass over, to cover as best we can with noise and empty chatter. The very first entry for "attend" in the OED is "to turn one's ear to, to *listen*"; the word also means to *heed*, as well as to *serve*. In the graveyard of voices (the phrase is from page 38) which is the world, the eye of witness is also an ear, perhaps an ear

most of all; an eye and an ear of *attendance*, and of retrieval; by that
it is an eye and ear of discovery, revealing that which is to be found.
"The poems that I first began to hear at Treblinka" were carried by
the wind, by the stones, by the grass. By memory, and by imagining.
So the task of the poem is to conjure, to conjure the absent, the
silent, the forgotten and the lost. One early meaning of "conjure"
is *to swear together, to conspire* – Wycliffe used it that way in his
translation of the Bible – and in his time as in ours it also meant *to
call forth* angelic or demonic spirits into one's presence, *to invoke and
body forth* powers of the invisible world. It would take some three or
four hundred years, suggests the OED, for it to mean *beseech. Eye of
Witness* constitutes Rothenberg's pact with the reader, and that pact
demands conjuration in all the senses I just proposed. There can be
no idle reading of this book.

That's where the energy comes from, then; not only
Rothenberg's astonishingly productive energy that drives these
multitudes of pages, but the very energy in the writing itself. The
sheer urgency of the task is assuredly source, and that urgency
burdens the poem with its task the way a groundswell of rhythm
and tonality might carry an undersong across and through the
wordless silence of the abeyant gap between stanza and stanza,
like the unvoiced silent beat between the lines of nursery rhymes
like "Hickory Dickory Dock" or "Mary had a Little Lamb." That
urgency is *dire*: it carries through the writing and carries the writing
through; when the Muse *has* to say *some*thing, that gist may be
inescapable. But at the same time and perhaps by the same token it
may not be voicable nor even tellable; then language fails; it cannot
be sufficient. "Take the legacy of Auschwitz," Rothenberg enjoins,
"as a call to vigilance against all forms of chauvinism and racism"
(394). *Eye of Witness* is a call to arms – "Why has the poet failed
us?" indeed. Such pressures break the poem open, call for any
resource or recourse, so that aesthetics inevitably play second fiddle.
It hardly needs saying, surely, that *testimony* and a sheer necessity for
accuracy of witness sit very uneasily, to say the least, with the idea of a
masterpiece and a hunger for the beautiful – thus Rothenberg, in an
essay on the poetics of performance, talks of "a move-away from the
idea of 'masterpiece' to one of transientness and self-obsolescence of
the poem as art-work as performed." Permanence doesn't come into
it at all, for "life," as William Carlos Williams told Harriet Monroe

in 1913, "is above all things else at any moment subversive of life as it was the moment before -- always new, irregular."[2] Rothenberg takes that a step further: "The work past its moment becomes a document (mere history)." Hence "the value of a work of art isn't inherent in its formal or aesthetic characteristics . . . but in what it does," (209) and what it does includes the act of composition as well as performance as well as reading or looking, and the artist will use whatever means come to hand, *as* those means come to hand.

"Write carelessly," Williams said in Book Three of *Paterson* (129), "so that nothing that is not green will survive"; he too cared above all for the energy of the poem. Like Blake, he is a constant presence throughout *Eye of Witness*, a provocative and welcome model of urgent inventiveness – his disturbances of convention and form, his transgressions, and his deployment of what Blake in "A Descriptive Catalogue" called "the bounding line and its infinite inflexions and movements" (550) – leaping its own limits. "Write carelessly" does not mean "write without care"; it shifts priorities and *reconstitutes* the aesthetic. Some years ago Jacques Attali proposed that "subversion in musical production opposes a new syntax to the existing syntax, from the point of view of which it is noise"[3] – a comment that surely gets at the neglect of Williams for most of *his* lifetime. *Paterson* in its expansive inclusiveness crosses generic boundaries, including as it does personal letters, geological reports, newspaper clippings, lyric, laments, narrative, pastoral, dialogue, and who knows what else besides; Rothenberg may have first got permission for his genre-and-other transgressions from Williams, but in his extraordinary diversity of output and range of reading and listening he stands alone.

But despite its rich diversity, *Eye of Witness* at first glance can be a bit frustrating. For one thing, the book necessarily prints extracts as well as whole poems and essays, but it does not always give their source. If you want to follow something up, or restore a passage to its context, you can't do that at all easily. But it is, after all, "A Jerome Rothenberg *Reader*," and like any other such it makes no claim to completeness. If, like me, you want to know what book a particular poem or prose piece might be from (perhaps because

[2] William Carlos Williams. *Selected Letters*, ed. John C. Thirlwall (New York: McDowell, Obolensky, 1957) 23-24.
[3] Jacques Attali. *Noise: The Political Economy of Music*, tr. Brian Massumi (Minneapolis: U of Minnesota P, 1985) 34.

you do want to follow it up), or want to know *when* it was written,
the book frequently doesn't tell you; the relationship of one work
to another in the Rothenberg canon (which work came first, say) is
often not at all clear. A chronology, sketchily implicit as a substratum
to the book, is scrambled in deference to thematic considerations.
The seventy pages of "Gallery One: Prolegomena to a Poetics," for
instance, are followed by sixty-five pages of "A Book of Otherings"
which are followed by forty pages of "Poetry and Polemics 1:
Toward an Ethnopoetics" which in turn are followed by more than a
hundred pages of "Gallery Two: The World Turned Upside Down."
Work in any given section may be from the 1960s or the early 2000s,
you can't necessarily tell which, and it is hard to find your way
around the book even though there's an analytic Table of Contents
constructed along the lines of those in the three volumes of *Poems
For the Millennium*. There is no index of titles and first lines, there is
no bibliography, not even a checklist of the books the works come
from. Overall, this lends the book a kind of slapdash homogeneity –
write carelessly, perhaps -- but the careful organisation along other
than chronological or conventionally canonical lines suggests that
Rothenberg's work here has been carefully groomed into a unity,
and that very unity draws the reader – this reader at any rate – to
read straight through, a sequential reading of the whole book. That
grooming obeys Rothenberg's recognition, some time around the
mid-1960s, that ethnopoetics, a word he coined "circa 1967" (171), is
"a necessary part of a poetics (an idea of poetry)," and his discovery,
not made by him alone, that "ethnopoetics, once it had entered our
work, altered the nature of that work in all its aspects" (*Symposium*,
xv).

There is indeed a politics in this, the politics of a "work
intended – above all – to question and disrupt the power of
dominant European discourse" (169); it underlies the whole of *Eye
of Witness* and is a well-spring, and the rhetoric, embodying as it
does Rothenberg's persistent late twentieth-century Romanticism,
is persuasive. In October 1961 he commented on "the poetic image
struggling with the darkness. The image rescued from the lie of
the unthreatened. Not as a literary prescription, for writing better
poems or nurturing the language, but from an impasse in the soul,
in which the protective 'reality' & false emblems of the inherited past
have drawn a blank" (59). Thus *Eye of Witness* is a purpose-driven

book which eschews, utterly, the literary: it is driven by a sense of loss closely linked to its sense of the incomplete. It is that sense of the incomplete that propels the symposium of the whole, a symposium from which, ideally, nothing can be omitted. Such expansive inclusiveness is very close to Whitman's resolve, in "Eidólons," to "put first" the ever-mutable range of human activity in its entirety:

> Of every human life,
> (The units gather'd, posted, not a thought, emotion, deed left out,)
> The whole or large or small summ'd, added up,
> In its eidólon.

Whitman, another constant in this book: his encyclopaedism informs the whole of Rothenberg's activity.

So if one of Rothenberg's aims is, as he says, to "open up to voices other than our own," then it's essential that those voices not be separated out, compartmentalized off from the welter of human speech and art and music, essential that we read this book as a single work, whether that work be composition, compilation, or performance, albeit a work in progress and in process. Rothenberg's poetics demands a mingling of his voice with others – "my own words interlaced (collaged) with theirs" (391) – in an encompassing never-definitive text, unindexed and unclassifiable, always tentative, always of the moment. We are invited to view the book as a continuum, all of a piece, even while discontinuities remain and are preserved and even emphasized, and tentativeness persists. The book thus out of deep need challenges not only empty conventions and emotional and social-political habits, but also long-held and seemingly ineradicable assumptions. Those assumptions are based on a syntax and ways of seeing which determine that the world can be understood, and that such understanding can be *certain* and *true*; which is to say, immutable. But incompleteness has its own necessities.

Eye of Witness challenges deeply-inscribed patterns of belief, and works to undo those "monotheistic habits of thought" which Pound called "the curse of our time."[4] Such motives, I need

---

[4] Ezra Pound, "Studies in Contemporary Mentality . . . XIX.--? Versus Camouflage," *New Age* 22.11 (10 January 1918): 209.

hardly add, carry their own dangers, for purpose-driven writing, like thesis-driven poetry, drifts rapidly into monotone. It fosters listless reading and is not to current taste. That's the risk, but *Eye of Witness* successfully counters it through playing, or rather, *plying* a centrifugal move against a centripetal, an outward move against an inward, each folded with, against, and into the other. This is as true of the prose as it is of the poetry – and there is indeed a lot of prose here, over 200 pages of essays, letters, manifestos; much of the work reaches out to other cultures, other voices, other realms "which only a colonialist ideology could have blinded us into labelling 'primitive' or 'savage" (*Shaking*, xxi) – the archaic, the ancient, the autochthonic. At the same time many of the individual poems (the Lorca poems, say, or the Goya), though they none of them behave like a conventional lyric, are tightly focussed; they push inward, the move is centripetal. For instance, there's the quite extraordinary and lovely charge of the repeat in these lines from "The Wedding" (214-215), the opening poem of his early book, *Poland / 1931*:

> thy underwear alive with roots o poland
> poland poland poland poland poland
> how thy bells wrapped in their flowers toll

There's comedy here, but there is also great affection, and the poem is, in its psalmodic and liturgical rhythms and vocabulary, its management of long vowels and repetitions, a ritual or ceremonial lamentation whose power arises from its mildly surreal comedic elements. Whoever the speaker might be, male or female, that speaker is individual (but not by that solitary); the voice might be reflective, directing its monologue to the self; it preserves its private elements, it moves inward. The voice is personal, and its ironies largely gesture outward, as do the "poland poland" repetitions (they appear several times) especially if voiced in something approaching a cry (as Rothenberg does, in some performances). In this poem such ironies are primarily social, suggestive more of the comedy of manners than of any romantic lyric. The poem, then, calls to and invokes a more-or-less definable and familiar group, nicely balancing the life of private feeling with an implied public and social order.

In their deployment of repetition the lines I quote have discernible kinship with such radically different work as Frank

Mitchell's horse songs or Richard Johnny John's songs. Here's "A Song About A Dead Person – Or Was It A Mole?" (325), John's poem-song written *with* (rather than *by*) Rothenberg. Citing Haroldo de Campos he calls this process "transcreation" (137): outsidering the work lest we think we "understand" it. I quote the poem in full:

      YOHOHEYHEYEYHEYHAHYEYEYHAHHAH
g thru the big earth
      YOHOHEYHEYEYHEYHAHYEYEYHAHHAH
                        I went thru this b
      YOHOHEYHEYEYHEYHAHYEYEYHAHHAH
                 I was going thru the big earth
      YOHOHEYHEYEYHEYHAHYEYEYHAHHAH
                    I went thru this big earth
      YOHOHEYHEYEYHEYHAHYEYEYHAHHAH
                   I was going thru the big ea
      YOHOHEYHEYEYHEYHAHYEYEYHAHHAH
I went thru this big earth
      YOHOHEYHEYEYHEYHAHYEYEYHAHHAH
                                      I

      YOHOHEYHEYEYHEYHAHYEYEYHAHHAH

      YOHOHEYHEYEYHEYHAHYEYEYHAHHAH

      YOHOHEYHEYEYHEYHAHYEYEYHAHHAH

      YOHOHEYHEYEYHEYHAHYEYEYHAHHAH

It might be tempting to skip, but the song warrants close attention: Three blank lines of silence between the final four lines of upper-case chant; seven lines of rather bald let's-call-it-prose narrative somewhat irregularly and unevenly marching thru the block of uppercase, its claim not always completed, and indeed, without clear beginning – *in medias res*, then. With its two (or more) voices – and one if not both of them emphatically out loud – the song's ritual and ceremonial elements are much more prominent than they are in "The Wedding," and they beckon the group. The song almost irresistibly calls for performance, moving towards the shared speech of chorus. It also moves toward simultaneity, not just of voices in chorus but lines spoken/voiced together in simultaneous overlap, a public act which affirms an identity in, for, and of the group; a shift towards communitas in which that isolate "I" of the fourteenth (otherwise silent) line is *perhaps* subsumed into the group-voice of line fifteen, but equally perhaps absorbed into and thus constructing, well, constructing *what?* Maybe it reflects what Rothenberg calls "self-othering," wherein "there are many 'others' in me" (161). Where does the "big earth" come into all this? How do we account for it? I run into difficulties here because my own habits, my own cultural baggage, get in the way – my own cultural baggage rests uneasily when matters are not *explained* – but the poem folds one culture into another with that *in medias res* and that ply of narrative and chant and refuses accounting. The lines fold ear into eye into ear in quite complex play, story into chant, single voice into multiple voices, and that repeated "thru the big earth" – with its variants, and the shifts in the verb -- gestures towards, even invokes, an apperception beyond words, an apperception of a physical world and, yes, to western eyes an *imagined* experience.

The physicality of the world thus sung is crucial, in much the same way as Rothenberg's conjuration and invocation of the body and the life of the senses (not always pleasant, not always celebration) are central to his more conventional poetry. This poem, with its foldings, is in what Velimir Khlebnikov might have called a "beyondsense language." Rothenberg, quoting that phrase of Khlebnikov's in his 1990 talk on "The Poetics of the Sacred" (169), sounded a principal theme, constant throughout his poetics, that we must return to, recover, an understanding of language (and hence meaning) as motivated rather than arbitrary. This is what we have lost. An essential step in such recovery is to move outside our language, step outside our cultural norms, which all get in the way. We must somehow find a means to see our language as Other. For the last century or more, or at the very least since the publication of Ogden and Richards's *The Meaning of Meaning* in 1923 and Leonard Bloomfield's *Language* in 1933, it has been fashionable to believe that meaning is entirely a social construct: Bloomfield's pronouncement that "the connection of linguistic forms with their meanings is wholly arbitrary"[5] has more or less the status of gospel. *Any* sound, in this view, can be attached to *any* referent, and the meaning of any given

---

[5] Leonard Bloomfield. *Language* (New York: Holt, 1933), 145.

word is necessarily a matter of social convention. So, if there is nothing in a word *per se* that reveals its ineluctable meaning, then our perceptions are filtered by and through language, itself an inevitable and unavoidable screen between us and the world: language mediates; it hides the world from us. And there's a price attached, for such a view takes us at least one remove from the world of direct feeling and direct apperception, and the world in its very reality is hidden.

The alternative view is that a sign really does designate what it signifies, that words actually do mean what they say; it sees language as unmediated, what linguists call *motivated*. In this view, our experience of the world and the things in it is immediate. Words say what they mean, and the essential connection between words and things not only provides or confirms an essential and sympathetic concordance between humankind and the world of what might be called nature, but in addition makes language itself a significant agent of discovery and the word itself a thing, contemplation and investigation of which opens the hidden world to view. Whence Ferdinand de Saussure's dictum that in symbol "there is the rudiment of a natural bond between the signifier and the signified," and his work on anagrammatic composition as the basis of poetic texts.[6] In Michel Foucault's account (in Chapter Two of *The Order of Things*), words "once had an absolute, primary, initial relation to the world," and a sign once really *did* designate what it signifies, much as might those repeats of "*poland*" and *yohoheyheyeyheyhahyeyeyhahhah* (the lower-case or upper case bringing eye to bear on ear. Rothenberg's somewhat puzzled first response to Jackson Mac Low's "aleatory / chance experiments," that "something real & important was taking place" (158), points to the possibility that a "natural bond" between words and the real can be restored, Mac Low opening up even in a tentative way the world of the hidden, obscured as it is by habit and belief. The motivated and the arbitrary are not, of course, mutually exclusive; they can exist side by side in a single practice, and even in a single utterance, but it is our daily habit to linger with the arbitrary. Most English poets, at least since Blake and Wordsworth but also before, write *as if* the words they use were indissolubly linked to things, and were things in their very nature.

---

[6] Ferdinand de Saussure. *Course in General Linguistics*. Charles Bally and Albert Sechehaye, ed.; Wade Baskin, trans. (New York: Philosophical Library, 1959), 68. For his work on anagrams see Jean Starobinski. *Words Upon Words*. Olivia Emmet, trans. (New Haven: Yale UP, 1979).

The poem is a means by which to discover / recover that bond; it is *sound*, along with its rhythm, that gets you out of the arbitrary and into the motivated.

In a 1976 note, on Tristan Tzara, Rothenberg described ethnopoetics as "a positive work of recovery & return to the lost basis of human poesis" (141); he had elaborated that sense of loss fifteen years earlier, in October 1961, writing about "deep image":

> The world as it existed for the first man still exists. It taunts us & breaks into our dreams. The poet dares to face it without hope & to create from pure desire, from pure love. The world as it existed before man. The primal world, not yet hardened into the mold of law, but a new law to be imposed on it in the daily encounter. A return to the beginning. A struggle to shape the world . . .Poetry as a total & desperate act (59).

That's not far from Jack Spicer's desire, in *After Lorca*, to "make poems out of real objects . . . a real lemon like a newspaper in a collage is a real newspaper . . . . make a poem that has no sound in it but the pointing of a finger." But, perhaps unlike Spicer, Rothenberg does not succumb to a sense of loss but seeks in its place to assert and rediscover hope in a language which has a "true" connection to the "real," however that real might be construed, imagined, imaginary.

So *primal* is a favourite Rothenberg word, and you have to pay attention to what the words say: "As a way of making the poem I must still come on the source directly, as a head-on confrontation, . . . I can't build it up yet through intermediaries, but have to create it new in order to accept it" (56). But that's an impossible dream, and it derives as much from the Romantic poets as it does from Pound's *make it new*. Writing about Picasso, Gertrude Stein talked of the difference between "things, things seen, and things known," and thought "things" were unknowable, even unperceivable. Wordsworth sought to restore the immediacy of language and thought the language of ordinary men would rescue poetry from the artificiality of literary convention. It would thus open up the hidden real. Rothenberg's determination to escape "the protective 'reality' & false emblems of the inherited past" (59) and open up the hidden real leads to the great range of his sources; his strategy is encyclopaedic: the sum total cumulative mass of all human (and other?) discourse might possibly add up to an unmediated relation with the real. *Ostranenie*: each strange voice, each step, however incomplete, into another culture, makes it possible to step, no matter how briefly, outside one's own language and culture. So almost the last poem in the book, dated 30 August 2011, (it is followed by a coda) closes with:

> the book of witness
> opens   all the words we have
> are theirs & lead us
> eyeless whispering
> the years themselves
> a miracle
> over against a world of pain. (575)

Unable and Unwilling:
The Other Woman's
Love Poem for the Wife

(A Response to Joseph Donahue's "Unable")

Martha Nell Smith

With "unable" I presume to intuit Dickinson's world, to find there, in a phrase that has long been key to my understanding of poetics, "an adjoining zone."

- Joseph Donahue

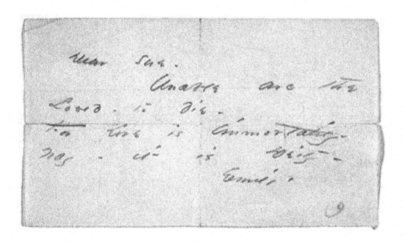

- Emily Dickinson[1]

Unable. Taking his title from a consolatory letter-poem from Emily to Susan Dickinson, Joseph Donahue's "Unable" consoles, cajoles, provokes, reflects, opens, bemuses, astonishes, excites, clarifies as he muses on declarations of love unwilling to go away, however and by whomever commanded. Musing on the scars upon Emily Dickinson's textual body, the art of a particular blacking out to make effusive expression of love for her sister-in-law Susan Dickinson impossible to read via a violently imposed illegibility, Donahue leads us into the brilliance of that darkness, or rather into his brilliance about that painstaking overwriting, those carefully formed loops designed to obscure enacting something altogether against their intention. Rather than blotting out, their overscore points attention toward and highlights.

"unable" begins noting the traces of the "Spry arms of the Wind" (FP 802)[2] "censorious," inspired by Mabel Loomis Todd's hatred in love with her friend Susan, her friend betrayed, beloved wife of her lover Austin Dickinson. This "anti-script of / pure lightlessness" is indeed Manichean, working against itself as it enacts its enraged deed, enraged in what seems perfect control, working for itself as it says "and I love her," even as it declares "no, NO, she, Emily, did not love her, not her, not Susan." Mabel's "And I love her" is for Susan, not for the dead woman whose hand-sculpted poems, flexible urns, Mabel's canceling hand worked to make legible to a late nineteenth century audience. Each obliterating loop sings "and I love her" for the muse Susan, the muse of Mabel's labors. Mabel works hard not for the dead poet, not for love of the poems, nor even for the fame, which she coveted enough, but for her beloved Susan, whose role as editor/reviewer for Emily she envied and role as volume editor she could inhabit, as she did her style of dress, her manner of speaking.[3] In love, and out of the pain of missing Emily, fleshly Emily gone, her flesh on pages left behind, reminding the beloved Susan of her absence. In love and out of the pain of missing Emily, Mabel could perform the editorial work more quickly. She did not stop, gasping, as the powerful words made powerful presence from the absence of the fleshly Emily departed. No, Susan stopped, halted, gasped with tears, with missing. Not Mabel. In love and out of the pain of missing Emily, inhabiting Susan's job, she performed those duties more quickly than "the Only Woman in the World" (OMC 182)[4] to whom she and the corpse Emily were in thrall. In love and out of the pain of missing Emily, Mabel moved with the editor's blue pencil more quickly, more efficiently, until, until. With "One Sister have I in the house" staring up from the manuscript page, the blue pencil stopped.

Gasping, gnashing her teeth, Mabel let the blue pencil fall to the floor. No, NO, you did not love her, Emily, you did not. I love her. I LOVE HER. Blind with jealousy, Mabel knocks over the inkwell, spilling the black river, Lethe shimmering, onto the desktop. Feverish, she determines to write her beloved Susan a poem, a poem scripted right over, on top of, Emily's words that surely did not mean what they say. Her poem in love with hatred will be written, she mutters to herself, in the waters of Lethe. No one will remember your love, Emily, and will remember only what I know—that you did not love her, Emily, no, you could not, you did not. So the careful loops begin to appear on the page, so very scrupulously scripted, covering each line written for Susan meticulously, precisely. All her readers, all your readers, Emily, will know only my script drawn from and drawn in the waters of Lethe. So Mabel mutters to herself, and rocking her rage into loop upon loop, painstakingly inscribes her love as that passion for Susan on Lethe's waves rides.

The other woman Mabel's love poem has no syllables. Her love for the wife Susan takes her beyond words. There is no way to say, to write, that valentine in meter and rhyme. She inhabits a bed with Austin, Susan's husband. Dresses like Susan, inhabiting her style. Inhabits Susan's role as editor because she is not weighed down by sorrow. Not weighed down by sorrow, buoyed by hatred in love, Mabel writes her love poem to Susan:

Of "One Sister have I in the house" (FP 5) and the lines "I spilt the dew / But took the morn - / I chose this single star / From out the wide night's numbers - / Sue – Forevermore!" Donahue writes, "The poem calls the universe to be around the name of the beloved." He continues, ". . .this artist has struck out. . .not just the whole poem but the entire tradition of what was once famously called love in the western world. . . . We might understand our artist to be saying that a part of Love's agony is precisely to experience within the act of desiring such a negation as the blackening out of the letter enacts." Mabel's agony was to experience, to live, her thralldom to Susan as hatred. Looking at that inking over, I understand that now. Of this textual sadism, Donahue remarked "How densely whoever it was had to scribble to blot out the original! And there's a weird beauty in the cancelled lines, shining through the attempted erasure" (posted to Facebook Thursday, November 12, 2012, at 9:31 p.m. EST).

Unable. Mabel, working by yourself on a third *Poems of Emily Dickinson*, perhaps the memory of your inability guides the editorial scissors as you transcribe "A solemn thing – it was – / I said – " (FP 307) in deep dark and in white ink. Is that right? You removed the deep dark from the well and copied the last two stanzas in white ink:

> I pondered how the bliss would
> look –
> And would it feel as big –
> When I could take it in
> my hand –
> As hovering – seen – through
> fog – glimmering
>
> And then – the size of this
> "small" life –
> The Sages – call it small –
> Swelled – like Horizons – in my
> breast – vest –
> And I sneered – softly – "small"!

You had taken great care to render them invisible, and there were those words again. Again. Pentimento on the printer's copy. The Harvard-sanctioned editor R.W. Franklin says Thomas Wentworth Higginson, your coeditor on the first two volumes *Poems by Emily Dickinson*, was "probably the one who marked out the final two stanzas" (*Editing of Emily Dickinson* 86). But Mabel, it was you, right? Weren't you enraged when you saw them there again, the violent white ink apparently having turned to blood, or some visible substance, at the printer's shop and now returned to you in type? When you saw those words, you were enraged, weren't you? Enraged by those words, again, you amputated the poem's body, removing the third and fourth limbs altogether. In "To Fill a Gap," my first article on Dickinson, I argued that you did so because a 19th century lady, the literary star you were promoting, could never, should never be imagined uttering those stanzas, would never sneer. You turned Dickinson's poem blaspheming the social order into one celebrating matrimony as holy, hallowed. In *Rowing in Eden*, my first book, I said that again. But now I wonder. Was it the "as hovering – seen through / fog – glimmering" that drove you mad because you were reminded of your love poem to Susan written over Emily's to Susan? Emily's hovering behind yours. Are you reminded that the black ink did you no good? "hovering – seen through / fog – glimmering" reminds you that you are unable, Mabel, unable to remove your beloved Susan from Emily's side. For unable are the loved to die, even under the Lethe ink of your love poem to Susan. Perhaps, you mutter to yourself, editorial scissors will do the job.

Unable. Joe, Joseph. I was unable to see Mabel's Love Poem for Susan until you showed me what I never saw. "Thank you" won't do.

> the garden is Eden
> > the garden is grief

> the garden is Eden
> > the garden is grief unbridled in joy

May you row there, in Eden, always.

[1]Images of many of Emily Dickinson's manuscripts are available via *Emily Dickinson Archive* (http://edickinson.org), *Emily Dickinson Collection* (https://acdc. amherst.edu/collection/ed), *Emily Dickinson's Correspondences: A Born-Digital Textual Inquiry* (http://rotunda.upress.virginia.edu/edc/), *Radical Scatters: Emily Dickinson's Late Fragments and Related Texts* (http://radicalscatters.unl.edu), and the *Dickinson Electronic Archives* (http://emilydickinson.org). This manuscript is housed at the Houghton Library, Harvard University, and the image is from the *Dickinson Electronic Archives* (http://archive.emilydickinson.org/working/hb18.htm).

[2]Emily Dickinson's poems are quoted from her manuscripts. For the reader's convenience, they are indicated by "FP" and the number editor R.W. Franklin assigned for Harvard University Press's most recent variorum edition. *The Poems of Emily Dickinson*. Cambridge, MA and London, England: The Belknap Press of Harvard University Press, 1998.

[3]Lyndall Gordon extensively documents Mabel's obsession with Susan, noting that "she splurged her savings on a sealskin cape like Sue's, which Mabel had long coveted," and concluding that the "danger to Susan Dickinson was Mabel's need to *be* her" in *Lives Like Loaded Guns: Emily Dickinson and Her Family's Feuds* (New York: Viking Penguin Group 2010), 238. See also 180, 202, 238, 256, 267 for more on "Mabel's desire to *be*/replace Sue."

[4]OMC refers to *Open Me Carefully: Emily Dickinson's Intimate Letters to Susan Huntington Dickinson* (Ashfield, MA: Paris Press 1998). The number indicates that assigned to the Dickinson text in this edition.

The Many Errors of our Way

On Ken Edwards'

Down With Beauty[1]

❦

Brian Marley

Uncertainty lies at the heart of many of the fictions collected in *Down With Beauty*. And bemusement. And, perhaps inevitably, a creeping sense of unease and foreboding. It can start, as it does in 'Us and Them', with one of several seemingly innocuous factors. For example: "There is excessive arm swinging while walking." Unusual, perhaps, though none too troubling. But soon something more ominous is felt, something oppressive: "The air is heavy with their breath." The title lets the reader know where the narrator's sympathies lie, so what needs to be defined is what the gulf between *us* and *them* consists of, and how great it is. And how could it not be great, given that "Their knowledge seems to them to be perfectly systematic, yet it is complete nonsense from start to finish." Like all such binary social constructs, misunderstanding and misrepresentation are key: *they*, quite obviously, are not like *us*, and as we are right in how we behave, according to well-established and respected social norms, then *they* must be wrong. And if they're wrong, as indeed they are, it surely follows that they must be punished for their wrongdoing. Unless, of course, the tribe of *them* is the dominant tribe of the two and better placed to mete out punishment. This authoritarian model of social

[1]Hastings, UK: Reality Street

division, which triggers and sustains conflict, and which flourishes in even the most advanced democratic societies, provides no solution and no obviously workable way to achieve resolution. For the writer of fiction, though, it offers an extremely rich seam of material.

In the title story, the pile-up of slanted, exaggerated observations creates an atmosphere of tense alertness, paranoia and dread. Peculiarly, the specifics of the threat aren't important. In an undisclosed country, war is imminent – or perhaps it's already begun, just over the horizon, felt as nothing more than an ominous rumble, a dusty shimmer in the air, blotting out the sun. What's feared is that at any moment the settled life of the community may be thrown into chaos. The opening paragraph sets it out perfectly:

> War is coming I'm telling you about it what is now won't last can't last and that what is coming who can say when the filth will be swept away when the language will be cleansed when our hands will shape up when the button will be pushed when the adorable scholars will prevail this is a wake-up call

The agenda suggested here is massive, the urgency of which is emphasised by the absence of punctuation. Massive: not just, as one would expect, the cleansing of the language and the filth swept away – totalitarian regimes always action this, it's their vain attempt to wipe clean the slate of history and create year zero, from which everything will be as it should be and would always have been had things been perfect from the outset. I love the notion that the "adorable scholars will prevail", running, as it does, contrary to the prevailing sentiment. Unless, of course, those scholars, though once adorable, have become compromised to such a degree that they start to work under the totalitarian thumb grumblingly, cynically or even willingly. Corrupted or cowed, they may indeed prevail. But how adorable will they then be? This is what Edwards does: present the reader with material that seems, at times, contradictory or at least hard to reconcile; he forces us to think about what we're reading and bring intelligence and judgement to bear on it. That's especially true of the novella-length 'Nostalgia for Unknown Cities' (to which I provided a sidebar in GHR Vol. 1 No. 11), which was previously published as a separate slim volume but finds its natural home in this collection.

Edwards is a fine poet, too, which is apparent in occasional surreal run-ons and odd but apt choices of word and phrase. Not only that, he's capable of introducing a big idea within the confines of a short sentence. Incongruity is his watchword. "His thoughts were collected, before being dispersed for profit," as the narrator acknowledges passingly in 'A Memoir of Our Father'. What thoughts? How much profit? Who can say. And does it really matter? He suggests that stories, no matter how rooted they are in everyday reality, become, in their retelling, increasingly fictive, and one individual's retelling will almost certainly fail to tally with that of another: "That's what they say, anyway, that's the story. It's only a story. A series of rooms, one leading off the other" ('The Story of Nobody'). Fiction at its best is a tricky enterprise, a complex of smoke and mirrors, which most writers try to ground and simplify and, in the process, often inadvertently drain of its quirks and energy. In essence, they do all the thinking they can for the reader, on the reader's behalf. That's nice of them. It's cosy. But Edwards' work is tougher, more challenging, and much more satisfying.

If it seems, from what I've written here, that his work consists of nothing but a litany of paranoia, grief and handwringing, then I'm remiss. Take, for example, 'Free Improvisation', the comic tale of a saxophonist invited to sit in at an improv workshop, of which the other participants inexplicably fail to attend. Acting in accordance with the instructions he's been given, he starts to play from the moment he arrives at the venue, expecting the others to turn up eventually and join in. His levels of puzzlement, disappointment and annoyance fluctuate, but against all the odds he turns in an ecstatic performance, surpassing by far the prior expectations he had concerning his technical ability and quality of musical invention – of which he, reflected in a mirror, is the sole witness. In a dystopian vein, though just as comic, is the promotional/instructional machine-speak of 'The Edge', in which glitches in the software of a futureworld theme park, whose principal attraction is spectacular views of the worryingly near Event Horizon, pepper the corporate bumf with jarring error messages and inappropriate instructions, leading to a total collapse of the system.

Eye on the Pose
How does a single blade of grass thank the sun?[1]
By Doretta Lau

❦

Meredith Quartermain

"God Damn, How Real Is This?" Doretta Lau asks in the title of her opening story and thus right off the bat puts the nature of fiction and reality and their relations with each other at stake, a thread that continues in many of the other stories in this notably witty debut collection. The narrator in Lau's opening piece is pursued by phone messages from her future self, like "Hey rickets breath have you taken your calcium and vitamin D supplement today?" Messages that sound an awful lot like common anxieties of people in a pampered western society. She is also pursued by messages from other people's future selves, like that of her therapist whose fees will go up if the narrator doesn't warn her to change her stock investments. The therapist doesn't have a cellphone because she's a Chronology Purist "who wants her life to play out exactly as it would have if communicative time travel hadn't been invented." Reminding this reader a lot of present day communications purists who refuse to have cellphones. Eventually the future self is diagnosed with "a touch of Münchausen by proxy" for her abusiveness.

The fiction/reality threshold is also at stake in "Sad Ghosts" where the narrator tries to convince Gene, a scientist, that

---

[1] Nightwood, 2014

supernatural beings exist. She tells a series of anecdotes challenging Gene to respond, which he does but in a surprise twist he outrages the narrator with his own anecdote.

Other stories explore photography and scripted role-playing in the production of fictions/realities. In "Days of Being Wild" the narrator suffers writer's block while writing a screenplay (the writing of screenplays being after all a good metaphor for what we all do everyday). Then she applies for a job (another form of screenplay) where she will act as what she already is, a speaker of Chinese, but her employer, ironically, is only interested in her because she has a friend who looks like a Hollywood movie star. "Rerun" involves an actress with a drinking problem being forced into the scripted lines of an arranged marriage. "The Boy Next Door" involves a photographer addicted to his iPod who is forced by his wife to search for work and ends up as a photographer at a porn studio. In "Woe is Me" the script casts the narrator in a drama involving hurling rotten produce at him "like Shakespeare"; he's a freak and a paintball target at a Coney Island attraction.

One of my favorites is a story called "Writing in Light" which includes a trip to a Jeff Wall show in New York city but also includes reflections on various pieces by Wall, particularly Wall's *Double Self Portrait*. The Wall double portrait then frames the narrator's own self portrait in the story, with Lau foregrounding the narrator's lens looking first at Wall from a setting in Vancouver and then at Wall from the perspective of a grad student writing a screenplay in New York. She makes a double portrait of Vancouver both as art object and also as site of serial killer Picton's horrendous violence. The "bones" (bulbs) in the light box behind Wall's photograph of a Stó:lō grave excavation parallel the bones of Pickton's victims as this deeply thoughtful story exposes the underpinnings of narrative and image-making.

One of the delights of this book is its nifty reframing of Vancouver and its history in provocative ways. "Sad Ghosts" alludes to the history of Vancouver General Hospital and the Burnaby Art Gallery, neatly commenting on the institutionalization and perhaps illness of art. In "Robot by the River," a poignant story of love and loneliness, a Penelope-like narrator unravels the scarf she's knitting for her faraway beau, while incorporating ghostly bits of Vancouver history into her story, such as the now destroyed Ms T's Cabaret, or Shaughnessy apartments equipped with iceboxes. Similarly, the collection's title story concerns three disgruntled teens, Riceboy, Yellow Peril and the Sick Man of Asia who cleverly challenge and own cultural stereotypes of Asians in "Lotus Land" (aka Vancouver).

I was also intrigued to explore how Lau's references to pop music in these stories commented on her narratives. Appropriately, the out-of-work photographer addicted to his iPod listens to Fugazi's album *A Steady Diet of Nothing*. He also listens to the *Destroyer* album *City of Daughters* whose lyrics one reviewer describes as "a stark town populated by hopeless eccentrics." Similarly Lau's story title "Robot by the River" comes from a Smog album and particularly the song "Ex Con" which the narrator listens to repeatedly. The song describes someone who while alone in her room feels part of the community, but out on the street feels like a robot.

Lau is intensely interested in how cultural tropes from pop music to high literature shape the lenses through which we experience life. Like a mad scientist or a Shakespeare fool, she delights in dismantling these tropes. How do they make us into robots? Her cheeky inventiveness is utterly engaging. She's a writer who always has an eye on the irony of her pose.

Cats or No Cats:
Notes on *Fancy*,
by Jeremy Davies

Hal Hlavinka

In the dark recesses of what we might be so bold as to call America's "literary underbelly"—its small presses, indie presses, micro-presses, the occasionally adventurous imprint at HarperCollins, etc.—there seems to be a growing contingent of writers willfully playing with/ in formal constraints. To be fair, they're not asking readers to decipher lipograms or metro poems or snowballs; these aren't the hyper-formal, A-meets-B-so-C-rubs-noun-7-all-over-D constraints. Neither should we make it out to be anything remotely resembling a movement—a star-spangled Oulipo, this is not. But a glance at works by Joshua Cohen, Padgett Powell, Rowland Saifi, Jenny Boully, and Jeremy M. Davies, among others, shows a complicated relationship between narrative and its formal delivery, from strictures on language (the meta-constraint at the root of Cohen's "McDonalds"; the whole of Powell's *The Interrogative Mood*) to entire structures (the maze form of Saifi's *The Minotaur's Daughter*; Boully's aptly-titled *The Book of Beginnings and Endings*). But of these form-focused writers, I would argue that Davies has been the most singularly focused on the constraint's potentially liberating function, and his work is, admirably, the strangest for it.

Speaking with Lily Hoang in a 2009 HTMLGIANT

interview, Davies riffs on the familiar Oulipian argument
for constraints: that with complete freedom in writing, "it
isn't you talking, it's the culture: we're all plugged into the same
calcified memes, cadences, and clichés." He goes on: "The only way
to circumvent the unclean spirit is to put pressure on our means of
expression...to frustrate one's compositional impulses at their root."
Without constant vigilance, a writer's well of words can become
poisoned, choking the potential life of a text with art's opposite,
cliché. Elsewhere, in an essay on Gilbert Sorrentino, Davies, with
some fury, picks up this thread again, concluding:

> Language is the enemy, because to use it for aesthetic effect is
> to tip yourself into an arena where your very human decency
> (presuming one has begun the game with any) is endangered
> by your medium: to write pabulum is to let it circulate freely in
> your thoughts and enter into your life, you plague rat. For one's
> language to be refined to the point where the "absolute falsity
> of the representation of reality" is clearly delineated is all the
> honesty, all the morality, literature can give us...and it is still not
> enough, for the glorification of this "falsity" can as easily calcify
> into a new form of cliché. Yes, art is ruthless.

What we're seeing here, developed over and over with increasing
finesse and moral weight, is an aesthetic sensibility in opposition
to the banal, the automatic, the regurgitated. To participate in our
saturated "world of letters" is to throw in one's lot among various
camps of innovators, on the one hand, or crank-turners, on the other,
and it amounts to a very real ethical decision. To welcome the lazy,
bored, and rote into a text is to yourself become lazy, bored, and
rote. And what graver sin can a writer commit, in this late stage of
American publishing, than to shovel another tired narrative onto the
pile? For Davies, constraints are then the generative force that guards
one's writing against language's cultural rot.

So we enter *Fancy*. Rumrill, an aging cat owner, invites a
young couple into his home to pet-sit his numerous cats. He begins
with instructions and, digression leading to digression, we're soon
learning of his boyhood, his sexual life, his unusual dreams, his
problem with the state of "being," and Brocklebank, an Austrian
cat fancier for whom Rumrill once pet-sat and who died under

mysterious circumstances. The constraint is apparent from the start: the words "Rumrill said" introduce an image, argument, or event and "He added" moonlights as a conclusion, augmentation, coloring, reappraisal, contradiction, etc., paragraph after paragraph through the whole of the book. The novel's momentum is then controlled less by how the story develops than by how Davies navigates the different variations of this intro-augment pattern, to coin a clunky phrase. An example:

> Rumrill said: Nor can I doubt that you're a lovely young couple, in spite of your monstrousness in my eyes. I mean that I imagine there are standards according to which you would be deemed nothing less than a lovely young couple, such a lovely young couple, without peer in our town, well known to be so poor or rich in lovely young couples.
>
> He added: Though mister smells of pickles and missus is a little popeyed.

A Rumrillian formulation if ever there was one. The text playfully teases out a tension between etiquette ("lovely young couple") and impropriety ("your monstrousness in my eyes"), between a collective sense ("standards according to which") and a personal one ("mister smells of pickles"). We could redefine this tension in a number of ways—surface and depth, superego and id, speech and perception—but the base formal symmetry remains the same.

As the narrative progresses, if that's what we can call its movement forward, Davies controls each new incursion into the story—from details on Rumrill's cat-fancying apprenticeship to his sexual liaisons in the library and on to Brocklebank's immolation—within this intro-augment pattern, slowing down and even halting the momentum that might propel a more standard plot. The only variation on this pattern—that of "Brocklebank writes," used sparingly to interject that character's own baroque cat-sitting instructions—does not disrupt the control the intro-augment constraint has on the story, but rather reinforces it. Brocklebank's notes serve as a running commentary on *Fancy*'s form: "a cat has certain constraints that have to be dealt with—you can do this but you can't do that." Like the novel's structure, his system "establishes terms and particulars for creative participation." Brocklebank is an unofficial Oulipian in spirit as in method: "Seeing myself as an adventurer, giving myself tasks without knowing how I am going to solve them." It is prohibition as a means of liberation; or trading a rotten cage for a fancier one. Certainly, there's more than a little of Davies's own aesthetic raison d'être in the recluse's words.

The chief function of Davies's intro-augment constraint is then to eliminate the various clichés of plot and character and mood and setting that tend to clot our Typical American Literature. *Fancy* is like Brocklebank, "never aiming at an accord with the basic tendencies of our time." With its generative, albeit aggressive constraint, the novel develops micro-tones of voice and theme while protesting, pinching, and prodding every strand of what might amount to a story until it unravels into strings of logic, or illogic, or fear. Oh, but if the plot were to thicken; if we were to invite the monsters, or the house guests, into our home; if something were to *happen*—that is the real terror that the novel, that new fiction, faces.

I'll add: It's a damned funny read, too.

<u>Sources</u>

Davies, Jeremy M. *Fancy*. Jackson Heights: Ellipses Press, 2014. Print.

Davies, Jeremy M. Interview by Lily Hoang. *HTMLGIANT*. HTMLGIANT, 2009. Web. 2014.

Davies, Jeremy M. "Well You Needn't, Motherfucker: Sorrentino Underground." *Hidden Agendas: Unreported Poetics*. Ed. by Louis Armand. Univerzita Karloca v Praze: 2010. Rpt in *Requited*. Requited. Web. 2014.

"me, me, me";
or, Google as Fiction

Hal Hlavinka

One had a grandmother who hid her children from falling bombs. One had a grandfather who was knifed in a car park. One had a father who recycled bars of soap. One had a mother with a colostomy bag. One almost died from drowning. One fell in love. One looked for patterns in the infinite. One sought out the sound of absolute silence. One found a magic coin. One died in a desert. One dreamed of a gray fog that could stop time. One survived a terrorist attack. One hoped her children would be good people. One lost her children in a car crash. One wandered the empty halls of a hospital. One met a time traveler. One speculated that somewhere, in some other reality, perhaps the correct one, he had actually drowned long in the past.

Chris Eaton, a Biography abounds with life. The author has collected the apparently numerous online personas bearing his namesake—stories of Chris Eatons from all over the world—and collaged them into something whole and new. The result is a novel filled with novels, a biography filled with biographies. We start at the beginning of life, one Chris Eaton's life, and soon we're on to more: other struggles, other loves, other dreams and failures, other families and tragedies, other timelines that fold into and out of our histories, other Chris Eatons. It's a book that opens itself up to let in as much light as possible, as much world as possible. In all of its horror and sadness and humor and joy, *Chris Eaton* attempts to be the story of everyone, laid flat on top of one another, told all at once. Or maybe one of the Chris Eatons, the painter, tells the stories best:

> Chris Eaton spent a year painting his own portrait, daily, always using the same canvas, just painting directly over the one from the day before. At any given moment, all you saw was one Chris Eaton. But all the rest of them were always there. As one.

I keep going back to the first sentence of the front matter: "Haven't we all been driven, at some point, to Google ourselves?" My initial reaction was that it's a lousy way to start so sophisticated and entertaining a novel, this idea that we'd need any sort of reminder to glance into the digital mirror and see down an infinite hall of reflections. We already know what we'll find. Those of us who spend enough time online know how minutes can fall away. The internet's colonization of our desire to navel-gaze is already total. The game was rigged. The battle lost, and to return to the front—as Chris Eaton did, culling the eponymous stories online— seems terrifying and banal. Yet, there's something intriguing about using fiction to slow down and creatively participate in this process of identification—this desire to gaze at ourselves and, in ourselves, our own little worlds. There's something to the idea that the novel can reclaim and recast and renew some of these digital selves that seems radical and important and perhaps even pro-social. And if *Chris Eaton* is an example of such a method—as research or sheer creative spark—then maybe there's a potentially liberating, or at least potentially generative, role that the internet's infinite halls might have for turning noise into narrative.

One sits in a park with hundreds of people all listening to a piano. One drinks wine in a bookshop. One poses in front of a Soviet statue. One outlives a grandmother. One outlives a grandfather. One hides inside a castle. One stands inside a cathedral of junk. One writes about Richard Hughes. One writes about sentence fragments. One writes about not writing. One writes about himself. *Hal Hlavinka, a Biography.*

Nocturnal Remarks
Regarding Selected Poems of Rochelle Owens: Eros Speaks from Northwest of Basra

\(\text{❦}\)

Norman Weinstein

Although poets and poetry editors of your time bandy "erotic poetry" about as if poetry readers recognize it as a charming consumable like personal lubricant, I speak this evening with an awareness that in the 21st century as few comprehend and appreciate erotic poetry as understand the identity of Eros.

I come to praise one of your most neglected contemporary poets of deep eroticism. And trace her lineage – we're only considering poetry in flavors of English since I can't trust your working knowledge of Greek, Hebrew, and Latin - in a way she herself might question – but Eros should be trusted more than the poet in this case because genius tho she is, she still comes utterly under my spell.

Surely Rochelle Owens, like the best of the experimental writers of her generation coming of age in the 1960s, must have read Gertrude Stein carefully, particularly Stein's major Eros-primers: "Lifting Belly" and "Pink Melon Joy." Owens gets inside the quivering flesh-and-spirit rhythms Stein musically celebrates: sensual slippery sibilants, wagging tongue fluttery vowels, whole buttery pelvic melt enacted in synapse-zapping lines.

And in Owens poems like "I am Very Excited. It's July the

3rd and I Am on a Destroyer" and "Lesson in Songmaking, Song of Kim," playful/strutting erotic urgency becomes shadowed by thieving Death, moving into an archetypal Eros/Thanatos tango swirl. Where Gertrude Stein feared to step (and bend), Owens advances, donning the masks of "wild-man" and "wild-woman" borrowed from Ethnopoetics, with wry Yeatsian sagacity.

And while I'm reluctant to talk of Owens' mastery in purely literary terms, surely along with Stein's influence there is Louis Zukofsky's, his Catullus transformations. Not a huge stretch of undergarment elastic to suggest that Zukofskian pidgin-comic-homophonically-bumptous ur-English transforms comic hesitations during lovemaking into stand-up comedic poetry. In Owens that Zuked-boxed sound comes out like this in "Say Old English Wishe Me":

> th th
> twease my paws. My voice her tits
> were loafs of bread just dadabeeyah

I, Eros, stammer, fucking or not, I do. Owens gets the sublime humor of Eros stammering, her contemporaries taking me entirely too seriously in the worst way-cooly ironic. Stammer also a consequence of pleasure-pain transits and transformations so quick as would make Ovid's shade blush.

And finally among her influences, let me single out Jack Spicer who instructs forcefully, exhorting Rochelle Owens to fulfill her career as poet by heeding his call in the opening of his "Poem for Ramparts": "Get those words out of your mouth and into your heart."

In your time when poetry is so reduced to games of intellectual recreation underwritten by English departments in dispirited virtual factories of "higher education," Spicer's marching orders remain as necessary, and as difficult to follow as ever. Owens decades ago refused any intellectually flyweight academic con-game because she was, and is, too smitten in her life and work by passional realities (Robert Duncan's Eros-electrifying phrase) tugging at her soul demanding poetic and dramatic expression.

These passional realities in a significant portion of Owens' poetry happen in an unlikely location: in a mirthfully imaginary

Mediterranean/Middle East, ornately seductive as Scheherazade,
and deliciously campy and kitschy – Eros in drag, Sample these lines
from Owens' "J.S. Bach's Blisters":

> why can't i have the shiksa
> wailed the queen of sheba why
> must it be the descendent of
> haile selassie & the original queen

And from "The Smell of Apples":
> the smell of apples
> by the negev
> the color of a gasp
> is the color of apple
> the rusted nail
> behind black apples
> breast-rib & nose rings
> drool of Samuel
> evil archangel

There's an ideal soundtrack for reading the Owens poems
dancing across this terrain: "The Sheik of Araby" by Fats Waller,
and two jazzy works by Raymond Scott (whose music gained fame
through becoming the musical accompaniment for the golden age
of Warner Brothers cartoons): "Dinner Music for a Pack of Hungry
Cannibals" and "Ali Baba Goes to Town."

As Eros, how can I not adore cartoony music, cartoons
where libidinous anatomy in ferocious jazz swing stretches to gigantic
proportions or is wonderlandedly miniaturized? And Owens is so
close to the impulses of jazz and cartoon, all integral to my identity,
queen of such coyly convulsive violence in such animated short takes
of buggy/Bugsy animal selves diving into freeze-frame abyss.

And more: Owens is that rare poet who knows how to write
poems critically examining other arts in depth. Never have the erotic
tensions birthing Picasso's cubist period been as joyfully called-
forth as in her "Museum Curator in a Cube," or the shimmering
transparent erotic play of glass art been illuminated as in "Never
Having Seen a Wave."

Daylight is arriving. Get back to your writing. See if your

words tumbling out of your too-bright heads can incubate in your hearts ripe for my theft. See if you can locate your poems in some Ur that while being northwest of Basra on a map is also where these Rochelle Owens poems live.

And listen for Fats Waller there too. His knowing "urs" between verses in those Rhythm King recordings between the grooves of which I spin nightly.

Rochelle Owens, Out of Ur: New & Selected Poems 1961-2012 (Shearsman Books, 2013)

Proud Men in Their Studies:
On Mark Scroggins

Robert Archambeau

Poetry, drawing away from the collective life of the court, can only withdraw into the privacy of the bourgeois study, austerely furnished, shared only with a few chosen friends, surroundings so different from the sleeping and waking publicity of court life that it rapidly revolutionizes poetic technique. Crashaw, Herrick, Herbert, Vaughn — all the poetry of this era seems written by shy, proud men writing alone in their studies... Language reflects this change. It is a learned man's poetry.

That's a passage from Christopher Caudwell's 1937 book *Illusion and Reality: A Study of the Sources of Poetry*, in which the young writer — who'd have proved a second George Orwell, had he not been gunned down in the Spanish Civil War — describes the formal changes that came about when English poetry stopped being a public game played at court and became the pursuit of solitary men among their books. No longer something for public declamation, poetry became learned, private, knotted with a kind of profound cleverness that, requiring time and erudition to appreciate, wouldn't have pleased much as a glittering gentlemanly accomplishment at court.

Certainly 21st century America has little enough in common

with England in the 17th century, but when I read Mark Scroggins'
Torture Garden: Naked City Pastorelles, Caudwell's passage on
Crashaw, Herbert, and company came immediately to mind. Why,
though? It's not as if anyone would confuse a poem like George
Herbert's "Easter Wings" with Scroggins' "Perfume of a Critic's
Burning Flesh":

> *Animus* deploys nurses exceptionally diligent
> attention finely tuned skills culture
> of detachment *unreliable deceptive* the
> law of the negative *everlasting*
> *Nay* structures of determination truth
> of the labyrinth *quasi-persons reeling*
> in customized systematic reeling pain.

But despite the very different texture, and the eschewal of reference
and discursive meaning, Scroggins' poems have a lot in common
with the English 17th century as described by Caudwell: they are
learned, private, written for the few rather than the many. And, like
the works of that greatest poet of 17th century England, John Milton,
they are angrily at odds with the dominant culture of their time.

To begin with, there are the matters of form and allusion.
All 42 poems in *Torture Garden* are seven lines long, with each
line limited to between five and seven stresses. Why? In part, I
imagine, to say "this is formed — it may look like cacophony, but it is
deliberately assembled, the product of a mind and a will." The mind
and will in question may well drive in the direction of chaos, but this
is no runaway car: the mind and will do indeed hold the wheel. In
fact, when we look to the book's principle allusions, we see that this
is very much a carefully formed entity, perhaps an obsessively formed
one. The title steers us to the avant-garde composer and musician
John Zorn who, with his band Naked City, released an album called
Torture Garden in 1990. The album's 42 tracks, for which Scroggins'
42 poems are named, are short, some just a few seconds long, and
give us an uncompromising cross-cutting of jazz, hardcore, and
noise, in which the juxtaposition of unlike elements is, in some sense,
the point — along with the evident dark humor, anger, and fetishistic
eroticism (the cover of the album, featuring a whip-wielding Japanese
dominatrix, caused much controversy). Behind Zorn, there's another
reference, to the French decadent writer Octave Mirbeau's novel

Torture Garden, which, like Zorn's album, is a pastiche of different styles, depicting terrible acts of violence as if they were works of art.

Looking back at "Perfume of a Critic's Burning Flesh," we can see a number of concerns reminiscent of Zorn and Mirbeau. Firstly, there's the speed of the thing: we scarcely see a clause gaining coherence before the language turns in another syntactic direction. Then there's the referencing of language from different sources: "animus" certainly brings to mind hatred, but it's also a word from Jungian psychology. This allows us to see the diligent nurses as both the agents of a psychological clinic, and, perhaps, as the agents of a malevolent system. The "culture of detachment" could indeed be something like medical professionalism, but is this detached professionalism *"unreliable deceptive"* in some Foucauldian way: is it merely the mask of cruel power? No sooner does this possibility establish itself than we hear of an *"everlasting / Nay"* — a phrase that resonates with the 19th century sage Thomas Carlyle's notion of the "everlasting no," the smug spirit of the debunker and eternal critic. Is debunking of the kind that would see medical professionalism as the cold mask of power just some kind of adolescent criticism for criticism's sake? Or is professionalism really something that reduces real people to *"quasi-persons"*? The poem jams these and many other interpretive possibilities together, quickly referencing many possible sources, then moving on, leaving nothing resolved and a residual sense of the world as a malevolent place where we wander in "labyrinths" of "systematic reeling pain."

There's something obsessive about Scroggins' concern with art in *Torture Garden*: the poems reference music, film, garden design, architecture, and quite frequently the tradition of the pastoral. To some degree, the idea seems to be similar to what Octave Mirbeau had in mind when, in his *Torture Garden*, he took us on a tour of aestheticized violence: Scroggins returns again and again to the notion that pastoral is a way of hiding both privilege and violence. But it's also interesting for how it reveals Scroggins' sense that poetry is, first and foremost, affiliated with other kinds of aesthetic expression. Poetry is at best secondarily a means of communicating information: it is primarily about formal effects and the construction of aesthetic experiences — a view common enough in our time, but far from prevalent in all times and places. There have been moments, some of them recent, when poetry was about speaking to a community about that community's needs and desires: think of the heyday of identity politics and the poetry associated with it. Scroggins' poetry isn't like that at all: it is for a smaller number of readers, particularly those willing to parse out the sudden turns of phrase, and able to pick up the quick, deft allusions. It's a poetry for art-gobbling, music-obsessive humanists, fingers at the ready on their keyboards to Google a particular phrase, or track down an allusion on Wikipedia.

This is not to say that *Torture Garden* takes no interest in community. In fact, many of the poems are dedicated to poets and critics of Scroggins' acquaintance: Tyrone Williams, cris cheek, Rita Felski, Gustaf Sobin, John Taggart, Forrest Gander, and the late Guy Davenport, among others. One suspects there are private jokes and references for these people embedded in the poems: in a poem dedicated to me, for example, I recognized several phrases from a scholarly paper I delivered at a conference Scroggins attended. And here we see another connection to Caudwell's 17th century poets, who wrote for "a few chosen friends."

Affection in Scroggins' poems is directed at specific individuals, who get to recognize their words transformed; but anger is generalized, almost ambient throughout the book. There's anger at the powerful, there's anger at the bureaucratization of the world, there's anger at consumerism and commodification, there's even anger at the kind of knowing, self-reflexive verse that comprises so much of *Torture Garden*. It's very different from the specific, localized anger that most of us encounter in daily life: there's nothing like simple frustration at a local drainage ordinance that leaves one's backyard waterlogged after a heavy rain. The anger of *Torture Garden* is more abstract. It is the anger we have when we sit in our studies and look coldly at the world's corruption.

I know this kind of poetry speaks to me. I know, too, there are many who will turn from it in disdain, despair, or boredom. I suppose this tells us something about the position of poets, or, at any rate, of certain kinds of poets, in our society: that they are steeped in art and erudition, alienated from the large structures of power and corruption, affectionate to their friends, and that they address, for the most part, people much like themselves: people shy and proud in their studies, or in their offices not far from the English department lounge.

Nox: Anne Carson's Scrapbook Elegy

\(e

Françoise Palleau-Papin

"An elegy is a lament. It sets out the circumstances and character of a loss. It mourns for a dead person, lists his or her virtues, and seeks consolation beyond the momentary event." Mark Strand and Eavan Boland explain that this type of poetry goes beyond private mourning and stands for "cultural grief", and that although recent elegies have tended to turn inward, the long-standing tradition of public utterance makes it "one of the forms that can be said to be co-authored by its community."[1] This reading examines the way Anne Carson turns a private elegy for her brother into a cultural elegy to the history of printing and communication, assessing the revolution of technology in her lifetime.

In the tradition of the 18th-century mourning diary[2], Anne Carson has published *Nox*, the reproduction of a scrapbook[3] she made after the death of her brother. Thematically, the book recapitulates not only elements from her brother's life, but more

---

[1] Mark Strand and Eavan Boland, *The Making of a Poem, A Norton Anthology of Poetic Forms*, New York, Norton, 2000, p. 167.

[2] For an example of such a diary, see « Un journal de deuil : Mme de Genlis, 1788 », introduced and edited by Philippe Lejeune, *Orages* n°12, *Sexes en révolution*, mars 2013, Atlande, p. 191-206.

[3] The scrapbook pages bear no page numbering, so I will reference them by the section number in which they appear, such numbers being given in the text.

importantly, the void he left in her own life and in her mother's
after he disappeared from their hometown in his youth, and led his
life abroad until his death in Europe at a mature age. The medium
in which the book is published carries the message. It comes in a
box set, and unfolds as an accordion-folded scroll. In its published
form, it recapitulates the history of publishing, from the hand-made
doodle, drawing or inscription, to the scroll, and to the codex. The
box, encapsulating the history of publishing, stands as a sarcophagus
for the dead brother, not holding his physical remains, but bearing
witness to his elusiveness. It bears the traces of his long absence, such
as the few letters he wrote over the years, that the mother passed
on to her daughter, his sister, the poet Anne Carson. The box and
the elegy for the brother contain the pain of his disappearance,
his refusal to share their lives as they were living it. It is a box of
mourning, mourning for the adult brotherhood he refused to share
with his sister, mourning for the life of both siblings that has passed
now that one is dead, and the other aging, after a life built over a
form of deprivation. The box holds the questions the poet asks of her
family life, of herself, and most of all, of her times, when she states
in the first section that "History and elegy are akin." (section 1.1)
and when she explains that etymologically both words originate in
"ask[ing] about things": "It is when you are asking about something
that you realize you yourself have survived it, and so you must carry
it, or fashion it into a thing that carries itself." (section 1.1)

The narrative voice is autobiographical in its guises. It
begins as the learned voice of a professor of classics, who tells of her
admiration for an elegy Catullus wrote on the occasion of his own
brother's death, many centuries ago. By the end of the mourning
scrapbook, Professor Carson has translated the poem from Latin
into English, a task she set herself to doing throughout her career,
she writes, revising and honing her translation to get to the version
she provides in this book. From a dead to a vernacular language,
she mourns the passing of a language as well as she revives it in
her homage. In this learned pursuit, she gradually breaks the mask
of academic discourse to reveal another voice, that of a sister who
sounds melancholy because she found it difficult to mourn the
brother who was actually alive, but dead to her. In that sense, the
box set is her mourning diary, as she describes the way she learned
about his death, how she coped, visited his widow in Copenhagen,

attended a memorial service, and learned to come to terms with his disappearance.

But this book also has a broader scope than a private mourning diary, because it encompasses general history in the process: not only the history of publishing, but also the history of languages and more generally, of cultures. Anne Carson takes the form of the elegy not only to bury her brother in a box, but also to assess the state of her culture. She takes stock of how a culture thinks through the way it leaves traces, and of how it publishes its productions, from Roman times to our contemporary times, by discreet parallelisms between life from the 1970s, and life in Antiquity.

1. Inscription, on wax or on paper as a malleable surface.

Just as in Antiquity, a stylus was used to inscribe words on a wax tablet, the narrator doodles words on paper with a point working as a dry stylus, in the way children encode secret messages in their spying games. One needs to blacken the surface to reveal the message hidden invisibly in the dry print engraved without ink on the paper surface. This early form of inscription reproduces the illusion of actual inscription in a mass-produced printed work. Nostalgically, it glorifies the gesture of the writer, just as much as it reveals the absence of the brother to play along in the game. The remaining sibling signifies the repression of her loss, and her estrangement from her brother, by inscribing it as a secret message. Thus, on the page describing her mother's bequeathing her correspondence to her on her death bead, the secret message "WHO WERE YOU" (section 2.1) comes out of the blackened page in capital script, revealing to the narrator what had escaped acknowledgment so far, what she had not dared ask out loud or in plain writing before: that one may not fully know a sibling, no matter how close one feels to a brother because of a childhood spent together. Making invisible writing legible by gentle use of a soft graphite pencil was also a traditional technique of the detective in mystery fiction—and this reflects one of the complications in ascribing a genre to *Nox*, which unravels a psychological mystery by uncovering something supposedly hidden and dragging it into the light.

The inscription of the word "WHO" in "WHO WERE

YOU" (section 2.1) is still visible on the next four pages, on the verso pages in a mirror image, and on the recto pages as on the first inscription, but getting fainter on each successive layer of paper. The facsimile edition reproduces the pages of the scrapbook so convincingly that one constantly feels the need to touch the pages, to feel the volume of the three-dimensional inscription, only to experience frustration, as the pages are flatly photographed from the original scrapbook, not actually mauled over by a hand holding a dry stylus with the energy of grief or anger, and inscribing its emotions on the page. After the four pages bearing the encrypted question "WHO ARE YOU", the core of the revelation comes four times as well in the successive four pages:

> My brother ran away in 1978, rather than go to jail. He wandered in Europe and India, seeking something, and sent us postcards or a Christmas gift, no return address. He was travelling on a false passport and living under other people's names. This isn't hard to arrange. It is irremediable. I don't know how he made his decisions in those days. The postcards were laconic. He wrote only one letter, to my mother, that winter the girl died. (section 2.2)

After four mentions of the same text, each with a slight displacement to the right on the page, another encrypted dry print reveals the following verb, in capital script as well: "DIES" (section 3.1).

This may be read as the center of pain, the utterance that required preambles and preparation, bracing for the harsh fact of death, conjugated in the present tense, inscribed in hidden writing, and revealed through pencil blackening. Finally, the last use of the wax tablet principle, or here dry stylus engraving principle, comes on a full page, with the capital script spreading large, with one word per line, three lines on the entire page, inscribing: "I HAD TO" in vertical layout. From the narrative, we may gather that the assertion was the brother's, probably during his very rare phone conversations with his sister, five over twenty-two years. For Carson, the invisible doodle in dry point thus emerges over time, from the conversation to the scrapbook composition, mimicking the emergence of ideas from preconscious to conscious, then mediated by writing, which functions as a third party between the two instances of the same consciousness, one repressed, the other acknowledged. Once the writer has moved on, from a doodle to actual writing through the blackening of the previously secret message, the text decoding the message may be passed on, from writer to reader, because the writer herself has turned into a reader of her own inscription, setting it at a distance. Surfacing script emerges from dark context, engraved from the front to the verso page, ponderous and liberating at the same time. The revealing black pencil is so thickly applied on the page that it blackens the opposite page by contact. Thus, the scrapbook bears all the traces of the deciphering hand at work in its production, cancelling the history of the printing press, reverting writing to the immediate and unmediated action of the ancient scribe, but with the memory of the loop. Other techniques reveal a similar return to the past, to ponder on the meaning of print reproduction and transmission throughout history.

2. Stencil duplication, between private and public transmission

The poem of mourning by Catullus is given on what looks like a stencil duplicator, or a spirit duplicator. This technique was used to duplicate documents in schools and colleges throughout the seventies and eighties, and was replaced by digital technology. "A stencil, a waxed sheet attached to a carbon sheet with a paper backing, held in place by a perforated strip at the top, is used especially for typing on prior to the duplicating process. Once the master stencil has been typed, it is placed on the drum of the stencil duplicator to transfer an ink image onto paper. Multiple copies can be made at a time." The process is similar in spirit duplicators, which require "a special type of carbon paper used for spirit duplicator known as Hecto sheets or spirit carbon paper."[4] What matters is that the technique is obsolete, and bears witness to the classics professor's mode of transmission to students in the past.

She provides several versions of the poem, framing her narrative scrapbook: the first opens the book in Latin. The second occurrence is a translation into English in section 7.2. The last version closes the book with the same English translation, but now made almost illegible by tears smudging the scrap of paper, which

---

[4] Duminy et al., p. 43-44.

also looks burnt around the edges, as if it was burnt by the dark background of the page it was glued onto. The translation was made in the pain of loss, of mourning, and came down to the scrapbook publication in 2010 from the past history of reproduction, which makes it look antiquated.

In section 8.5, across from the definition of the word "fraterno," the same scrap of paper is cut into vertical bands, glued together in an artistic layout that renders it illegible, but it is recognizable in its sepia tint, unmistakably a stencil reproduction dating back before the digital age.

By limiting the reading process through the fragmentation, attention is drawn to the medium as a signifying tool. This duplicating process limited mass reproduction and transmission, because each use of the master stencil held less ink than the previous one; it was therefore less contrasted, fainter and less legible with each turn of the rotor for each printing from the master copy. The transmission still mimicked the copies one could almost have drawn in longhand, as a medieval amanuensis, but not quite, because the numbers of reproduced copies were too high for human patience. In the history of technology, such means of duplication stands for a transition between the wax tablet in its uniqueness and digital mass reproduction in its unlimited outreach, via web transmission. However, it was still a direct transmission from a teacher to a limited group of students, in a hand out, passing from the teacher's hand to that of the student, with minimal machine intervention (which itself was entirely done by hand), again, directly from the teacher's hand. The stenciled poem is thus a transition between the brother's letter, addressed only to his mother, and the mass-produced paper reproduction of Anne Carson's scrapbook published by New Directions, which is widely distributed and which anyone can buy. It is the open letter of mourning that Professor Carson sent to her students during her teaching career, without making it a personal issue, but in the hope of getting them to relate to the way Catullus expressed his emotion for his deceased brother (section 7.1). The stencil copies stand in a middle ground also between the words of justification, "I HAD TO" (section 8.1) engraved on paper and recovered through blackening the page with a pencil, and the publication of that message in digital photo-reproduction.

Like previous messages discovered through graphite pencil,

"I HAD TO" is a very private message surfacing at a given time, widely differing from the later mass reproduction of the book, which may extent to later times through reprints, for example, in a more open timeframe and print life.

3. Aorist, or time unmoored.

By inscribing her brother's justification on the page, the narrator arrests time to his decision and justification, as inside a tomb time has stopped and transmission has been cancelled. The message stays on against a black background, symbolically imitating stasis and death. One may liken this text to the tense called aorist, a tense that arrests time, indeterminate between continuous and momentary, between perfect and imperfect, as in a tomb, a mummy no longer decays, being impervious to the degradation of time. Through her use of inscriptions and her insistence on the materiality of writing, as though it cancelled the history of mass reproduction it actually uses, the poet (or maker, creator etymologically) insists on the parenting act of creation, which stands outside of time. Walter Benjamin makes the point that the original work of art has its own "aura" in his essay "The Work of Art in the Age of Mechanical Reproduction": "Even the most perfect reproduction of a work of art is lacking in one element: its presence in time and space, its unique existence at the place where it happens to be." (p. 214). Parenting a work of art gives it unique existence, but the act of creation itself stands outside of time. In Carson's dictionary definitions of Latin words, which she regularly provides on the left hand page of the accordion scroll at each folding, the definition of "parentum" begins with the aorist origin of the word.

parentum
parens parentis masculine noun
[apparently old aorist participle of PARIO] a parent, father, mother, (plural) parents; (of animals); (applied to stock of trees); ancestor, progenitor; *parenti potius quam nocti obsequi* to obey one's parent rather than night; the departed spirits of parents or other dear relations; as honourific title; foster-parent; a mother country or city; the universal creative power or agency, the creator; the originator, first practitioner (of an art or science); inventor (of an instrument); founder (of a school, etc.); author

(of a book); (of abstract qualities, etc.) the origin, source, cause. (section 8.1)

Although it takes the form of a dictionary entry, this item is not as authentic as it seems. For example, the quotation given in italics has been tampered with, to fit the title of Carson's book. In Terence's comedy *Hecyra*, Pamphilus's line reads: "Nam me parenti potius, quam amori, obsequi / Oportet." (act III, scene 4, line 34), "for obedience to a parent ought to take the place of love." (p. 286-7, trans. S. Patrick): Carson has turned "amori" (love) into "nocti" (night) to suit her subject.

The fictional dictionary entry thus provides much more than translation information, and manages to be lyrical in an unexpected way through the form it takes. It connects the story of the family to the writing of the book entitled *Nox* (night in Latin), through the aorist form of the verb meaning to give birth, generate. Just as Anne Carson chose to look after her mother, "to obey one's parent rather than night" in the example given in Latin and translated in the entry, her brother chose to "obey night" by disappearing and letting their mother die without giving her any news of him. Just as the brother is the "origin, source, cause" of the loss Anne Carson writes about in *Nox*, she is the poet, the "author" and progenitor of the book upon such night as the brother chose, the book of mourning also being a creation shared with all her readers. In turn, the poet invites her readers to create through reading, to put the fragments together, to translate not only the Latin poem from the sum of its words, but to connect the pieces of information into a story thus made private, as in any reading, but more actively so when the reading material is fragmented. The aorist origin of the noun thus covers the past events, the present of the poet's creation, as well as the future creations of readers in the present of each reading. Tellingly, in this pseudo-dictionary entry, Carson uses an adverb of uncertainty to connect the noun to the aorist form of the verb, which she gives between brackets: "[apparently old aorist participle of PARIO]" (*ibid.*). The adverb "apparently" shows that she explores the ancient language, which eludes certainty, just as much as her mourning scrapbook looks for a language of expression, between English and Latin, as well as between text and image, while it pretends to define and classify the mess of experience we call life. In an essay, Carson has written a beautiful definition of the aorist, which seems to apply to her vision of "parentum" in *Nox*:

> The Greek verb system includes a tense called aorist (which means "unbounded" or "timeless") to capture that aspect of action in which, for example, a man at noon runs directly on top of his own shadow. So in fr. 13 (a) Mimnermos uses an aorist participle to describe how men move in war. Like acrobats of the psychic misdemeanor we call history, warriors qua warriors live hovering above the moment when action will stop. They are the receptacle of a charge that shoots itself toward the night side, spoor of its own explanation." (*Plainwater*, p. 16)

By extension, the last sentence also defines *Nox*, which may be read as "the receptacle of a charge that shoots itself toward the night side, spoor of its own explanation" because of the reflexivity of the creative process, the work taking form and figure as it unfolds on the band of paper before our reading eyes, like the potential messages waiting to be discovered through the graphite pencil.

4. Active reading, or parenting the fragments.

As often, and in this book more than in any other, Anne Carson presents a hermeneutic quest for her readers. She likens translating and writing "the history of a person" to a "web":

> Prowling the meanings of a word, prowling the history of a person, no use expecting a flood of light. Human words have no main switch. But all those little kidnaps in the dark. And then the luminous, big, shivering, discandied, unrepentant, barking web of them that hangs in your mind when you turn back to the page you were trying to translate. (section 7.1)

Carson does not make an explicit analogy to digital webs of information, but the metaphor of electrical circuit seems to invite the comparison. As in a web search, information is not put into a coherent whole. Likewise, in *Nox*, each Latin word is defined in succession, but the syntax is missing. To understand the poem, we must understand more than the sum of its words. Like the printing technology and the media that are presented visually but not as objects of discourse, we need to understand a process, a set of functions at work, syntax in language as well as in technology. We need to connect. In the narrator's mind, the page under translation is one in a web of words available "in the dark" that each branches off to other sets of connections, a web revealing an arborescence of connectivity rather than a linear, hermeneutic progress. The translator gropes with translation hurdles as she assembles her scrapbook on her brother. Her scrapbook, that includes her translation, suggests possible links like a web page, but unlike a web page, it freezes the possibility of the click and leaves any further connections to the reader's active reading.

Anne Carson likes to invite her readers to fill in the blanks and does not provide any hypertext, the better to stimulate our creative imagination. When she translated Sappho's fragments, she explained her use of brackets in her translation to show the missing or illegible parts of texts in an invitation to a thrill: "Brackets are exciting. Even though you are approaching Sappho in translation, that is no reason you should miss the drama of trying to read a papyrus torn in half or riddled with holes or smaller than a postage stamp—brackets imply a free space of imaginal adventure." (p. xi)[5] Her scrapbook invites to share in such a thrilling "imaginal adventure" because we too are hermeneutically gathering the fragments, engaging in uncovering the discreet changes from the standard Latin definitions, and generally participating in the mysteries of life by figuring absence. We are invited to create further text, in a metafictional experience, as Carson invited her reader of Sappho's poems: "As acts of deterrence these stories carry their own kind of thrill—at the inside edge where her words go missing, a sort of antipoem that condenses everything you ever wanted her to write—but they cannot be called texts of Sappho's and so they are not included in this translation. (xiii)

Nox emphasizes the continuity of the reading pact, from writing to reading, the latter being the reader's creation. The band of the scroll can be deployed laterally in the reader's space, unfolding its meaning in the reader's idiosyncratic syntax that puts the fragments together. We become experts in metaleptic leaps, our

---

[5] "On Marks and Lacks" (introduction) in *If Not, Winter. Fragments of Sappho*, trans. Anne Carson. New York, Alfred A. Knopf, 2002, p. xi-xiii. My warmest thanks to Clément Oudart, who suggested this connection between Carson's translation of Sappho and *Nox* at the AFEA Conference in Paris, on May 24, 2014.

exercise of syntax including deciphering text and image, recognizing recurrences and patterns, and acknowledging various disciplines such as psychology (with the explanation that the brother was isolated as a child among his friends), Latin (to read Catullus), history (to understand the criticism of Thucydides), etc.

Carson also insists on what is lacking in the information, on what impedes transmission and understanding: the lack of communication between brother and sister, or brother and mother, the stilted and rare phone conversations, the few letters, one being shown in reverse, on the retro page, as if its recto page was not enough. When the narrator learns of her brother's death, she sees the information as a flux on the waves, coming across the Atlantic, literally and metaphorically in waves of news: "While I swept my porch and bought apples and sat by the window in the evening with the radio on, his death came wandering slowly towards me across the sea." (section 6.1) The news of his death reaches her like a message in a bottle launched on the ocean. Such slow transmission of information holds the mystery of the relay between transmitter and receiver, and the hurdles in space and time, throughout the many years of separation that the information needs to overcome. The metaphor to express such problematic news is that of "wandering" in an erring way, almost without a purpose, while the radio, with its well-established technicality, stands as a counterpart to such haphazard, lackadaisical transmission. This translates the difficulty, even the impossibility, of understanding death. Such "wandering" reaches the mystery of the reader's own empathy with loss and mourning, to the point of fascination, or possibly, even fetichism. We want to put our fingers into the wounds Carson has inflicted on the page, because the excellent reproduction of the scrapbook simulates the piercing of paper by a stapler, the staple's recto or verso sides appearing on either side of the page of the scrapbook being reproduced on two consecutive pages in *Nox* (section 7.1, for example), or with a stain smudging through to another page (in simulation), as is the case of the shadow drawn in soft pencil over the photographic shadow at the end of section 1.1.

5. Figuring absence

Such passages give the uncanny impression that we are touching the unique object produced by the writer's hands, while we know that the scroll is a photographic reproduction. This provides both a comforting illusion and an unsettling sense of frustration, common to the issue of representation in art. The work offers the illusion that one may touch absence, emphasizing the gaps between the fragments, before any connective reading. Ultimately, by alluding to the history of printing from the scroll to the codex, to the stencil copy, to photography, and even to the interconnectivity of the web, *Nox* plays with the illusion that the sign could bridge the gap to the referent by the sheer cumulative power of all the reproduction modes into the same work, in a magical sense of presence that art has suggested and eschewed at the same time throughout the centuries. *Nox* is not only an elegy on the loss of her brother, but also to the modes of reproduction of our culture in art and craft. It is an elegy to the dark arts of magic, once we have lost faith in icons and do not believe they incarnate the absent figure represented as an image. In that sense, *Nox* is a process, a figuration in passing (the word is used three times in section 9.1, before a photograph of a stairway) by means of absence. Such absence is best captured in the image of the stairwell represented in several photographs, drawings or passages of prose (see sections 5.3, and 10.1, text and image alike). The stairway/ stairwell pairing, like the proverbial sides of the same coin, comes to exemplify the nexus of *Nox*, its gathering of apparent opposites, its moot point, and its method.

A stairwell under the stairway, like the regular folding of the scroll into pages that are as many steps of reading, obverse and reverse of the facsimile reproduction, one perfecting the illusion of the scrapbook, the other blank and as unreadable as absence; a stairwell under the stairway, on Carson's page (section 10.1) carrying text above and below, as in engraving a plate and its reverse image on paper both carry ink, one side and the other together during the printing moment but each invisible to the other, at all times, in the blind mirror image, like brother and sister in the final explanation of the conjunction "atque" ("and," in Latin): "*similiter atque ipse eram noctuabunda* just like him I was a negotiator with night." (section 10.1) Like the other pseudo-dictionary entries, this translation of the conjunction contains autobiographical portraying. As an author and a poet, the melancholy narrator has been "a negotiator with the night" of the sign, with its conventionally established relationship to the real, and its semiotic split from the real. Or, in T. S. Eliot's words from *The Hollow Men*, she has written about the "shadow" of obscure discrepancies and discontinuities:

> Between the idea
> And the reality
> Between the motion
> And the act
> Falls the Shadow. (p. 91-92)

In setting a greater distance from the writing hand to the reading hand and eyes, mass reproduction has made the contact between the minds more abstract. By retroactively giving figuration to the page as contact, Anne Carson bridges the gap of abstraction and reaches out broadly, in the webbing, random contact of our times, but with renewed historical sense and consciousness. She thus enables us to come, ourselves, closer to an understanding of loss, which is impossible to express directly.

Acknowledgments

The author wishes to thank Clément Oudart (Sorbonne University) and Peter Vernon (University François Rabelais, Tours) for their generous suggestions.

Bibliography

Benjamin, Walter. "The Work of Art in the Age of Mechanical Reproduction" in *Illuminations*, ed. and intr. Hannah Arendt, trans. Harry Zohn, London, Fontana Press, 1992 (1968), p. 211-244.

Carson, Anne. *Nox*. New York, New Directions, 2010.

---. *Plainwater: Essays and Poetry*. New York, Vintage, 1995.

---. "On Marks and Lacks" (introduction) in *If Not, Winter. Fragments of Sappho*, trans. Anne Carson. New York, Alfred A. Knopf, 2002, p. xi-xiii.

Duminy, P. A., A. H. MacLarty, N. Maasdorp. *Teaching Practice*. Capetown, Maskew Miller Longman, 1992, p. 43-44.

Eliot, T. S. *Collected Poems 1909-1962*. London, Faber and Faber, 1963.

Lejeune, Philippe. « Un journal de deuil : Mme de Genlis, 1788 », introduced and edited by Philippe Lejeune, *Orages* n°12, *Sexes en révolution*, March 2013, Atlande, p. 191-206.

Strand, Mark and Eavan Boland. *The Making of a Poem, A Norton Anthology of Poetic Forms*, New York, Norton, 2000.

Terence. *Hecyra*, trans. Samuel Patrick. Dublin, Gilbert and Hodges, 1810.

Notes on Contributors

Robert Archambeau's books include *The Poet Resigns* (Akron), *Laureates and Heretics* (Notre Dame), *Home and Variations* (Salt), *Word Play Place* (Ohio), and others. He has received awards from the Academy of American Poets, the Illinois Arts Council, and the Swedish Academy. He is professor of English at Lake Forest College and blogs at Samizdat Blog.

Andrea Augé is an artist and art director for film/video and print living in Seattle.

Richard Berengarten's poems in this issue are based on hexagram 22 of the I Ching, □(bi). They are excerpted from his long work *Changing*, written in homage to the *I Ching* (forthcoming 2016). Aka Richard Burns, he was born in London in 1943 into a family of musicians. In 1975, he founded the international Cambridge Poetry Festival. His books include: *Avebury, Learning to Talk, Roots/Routes, Black Light: Poems in Memory of George Seferis, Against Perfection, The Manager, Book With No Back Cover, For the Living: Selected Longer Poems 1965-2000, In a Time of Drought, The Blue Butterfly, Under Balkan Light, Manual,* and *Notness: metaphysical sonnets.*

The Critical Companion to Richard Berengarten (eds. Norman Jope, Paul Scott Derrick and Catherine E. Byfield, Salt, 2011) contains thirty-four essays from contributors in eleven countries. Berengarten is recipient of the Eric Gregory Award (1972), the Keats Memorial Prize (1974), the Duncan Lawrie Prize (1982), the Yeats Club Prize (1989), the Jewish Quarterly-Wingate Award for Poetry (1992), the international Morava Charter Prize (Serbia, 2005) and the Manada Prize (Macedonia, 2011). His book The Blue Butterfly provided the Veliki školski čas memorial-oratorio for Nazi massacre-victims in Kragujevac (Serbia, 2007). He is currently Praeceptor at Corpus Christi College, Cambridge, a Bye-Fellow at Downing College, and a Fellow of the English Association.

Laynie Browne is the author of ten collections of poetry and two novels. Her most recent collection of poems, *Lost Parkour Ps(alms)* is out in two editions, one in English, and another in French, from Presses universitaires de Rouen et du Havré (2014). She is a 2014 Pew Fellow. Forthcoming books include *Scorpyn Odes* (Kore Press) and *P R A C T I C E* (SplitLevel Texts).

Julie Carr is the author of six books of poetry, most recently *100 Notes on Violence, RAG,* and the forthcoming *Think Tank.* She is also the author of *Surface Tension: Ruptural Time and the Poetics of Desire in Late Victorian Poetry,* and the co-editor, with Jeffrey Robinson, of *Active Romanticism: The Radical Impulse in Nineteenth-Century and Contemporary Poetic Practice.* She teaches in the creative writing MFA and the Intermedia Arts Writing and Performance Ph.D. programs at the University of Colorado, Boulder. She lives in Denver where she helps to run Counterpath Press and gallery.

Joseph Donahue is the author of five full-length collections of poetry, including *Incidental Eclipse, Terra Lucida,* and *Dissolves.* With Ed Foster and Leonard Schwartz he edited *Primary Trouble: An Anthology of Innovative Poetry in Our Time.* He has lived in New York City and Seattle, where he was a member of the Subtext Collective. He now lives in Durham, North Carolina, and teaches at Duke University. The third volume of his ongoing poem *Terra Lucida,* entitled *Dark Church,* is forthcoming from Verge.

Rachel Blau DuPlessis is the author of *Drafts*, a significant contemporary Anglophone long poem. The volumes are available from Salt Publishing and Wesleyan University Press. *Interstices* (Subpress, 2014), *Graphic Novella* (Xexoxial Editions, 2015) and *Days and Works* (Ahsahta, 2016) are books of recent shorter poems published or in press. DuPlessis has written six critical books (from Cambridge, Iowa and Alabama University Presses), often on poetry, poetics and gender. She recently edited *The Oppens Remembered: Poetry, Politics and Friendship*, forthcoming from University of New Mexico Press.

Chris Eaton is from Sackville, New Brunswick, Canada. He is the author of three previous novels (*The Inactivist* (2003), *The Grammar Architect* (2005) and *Chris Eaton, a Biography* (2013)) and a retrospective book of short fiction, as well as founder of the band Rock Plaza Central. The excerpt in this edition of *Golden Handcuffs* is from a future, multi-volume project that will hopefully begin publishing in Spring 2016, the first volume focussing on the life of French composer Camille Saint-Saens, who would later become Jack the Ripper.

George Economou is the author of thirteen books of poetry and translations, the latest of which are *Complete Plus—The Poems of C. P. Cavafy* in English (Shearsman Books, 2013) recently selected for the ALTA Annual Translation Award longlist, *Ananios of Kleitor* (Shearsman Books, 2009) and *Acts of Love, Ancient Greek Poetry from Aphrodite's Garden* (Random House, 2006). His latest book, *Finishing Cavafy's Unfinished & Selected Poems and Translations*, is scheduled for publication by Shearsman later this year.

Ken Edwards still runs the small press Reality Street and plays in the band The Moors somewhere on the south coast of England. His novel Country Life is out from Unthank Books later this year. The pieces in this issue are from another book being assembled right now, provisionally (and probably finally) titled A book with no name.

Craig Foltz is the author of two books, most recently *We Used to Be Everywhere* (Ugly Duckling Presse), and his work has appeared in numerous journals. He currently lives and works close to the water table in Auckland, New Zealand, in the shadow of a dormant volcano. More info: www.craigfoltz.com

Jesse Glass: latest works: *Peter Stubbe Selections* (A Painted Book), The Knives Forks and Spoons Press; *Play for the Dead:* a Zimzalla multiple; writing in *Gargoyle* and (in Dutch) in *Ballustrada Journal.*

Hal Hlavinka is a bookseller in Brooklyn. His work has appeared (or is forthcoming) in *Knee-Jerk Magazine, The Texas Monthly Online, Three Percent, HTMLGIANT,* and *The Review of Contemporary Fiction.*

Bernard Hoepffner has lived in various European countries and entertained himself with diverse jobs, the last one being that of a translator and, very occasionally as a writer. He has translated Robert Burton, Thomas Browne, Mark Twain, Herman Melville, Gilbert Sorrrentino, Robert Coover, Toby Olson, James Joyce, Jacques Roubaud among many others, which can be found on his site: http:// wvorg.free.fr/hoepffner/.

Fanny Howe has written numerous books of fiction, essays and poetry and has won the Ruth Lilly Lifetime Achievement Award. Her most recent collection of poetry *Second Childhood*, a Finalist for the National Book Award 2014, was published by Graywolf Press.

Leslie Kaplan was born in New York in 1943, and was raised in Paris. She writes in French. After studies in philosophy, history, and psychology, involvement in the 1968 student movement in France, she turned to writing. Since 1982 she has published a number of works of poetry, prose, and theater. Her most recent novel is *Millefiuille*, published by P.O.L and Gallimard in 2012. Her website contains a number of essays and brief translations into English: www.lesleykaplan.net

Hank Lazer's eighteen books of poetry include *N24* (hand sewn handwritten chapbook in the Little Red Leaves Textile Series, 2014), *N18* (complete) from Singing Horse Press (2012), *Portions* (Lavender Ink, 2009), and *The New Spirit* (Singing Horse, 2005). Pages from the notebooks have been performed with soprano saxophonist Andrew Raffo Dewar at the University of Georgia and in Havana,

Cuba. Features on the Notebooks appear in *Talisman #42* (http://www.talismanmag.net/ and *Plume #34* (http://plumepoetry.com/2014/04/featured-selection-5/).

Brian Marley is in the slow throes of completing a book of fiction, *The Shenanigans: A Novella, Six Shorts & Six Miniatures.*

David Miller was born in Melbourne (Australia) in 1950, and has lived in London since 1972. His more recent publications include *The Waters of Marah* (Shearsman Books, 2005), *The Dorothy and Benno Stories* (Reality Street Editions, 2005), *In the Shop of Nothing: New and Selected Poems* (Harbor Mountain Press, 2007) and *Black, Grey and White: A Book of Visual Sonnets* (Veer Books, 2011). He has compiled *British Poetry Magazines 1914-2000: A History and Bibliography of 'Little Magazines'* (with Richard Price, The British Library / Oak Knoll Press, 2006) and edited *The Lariat and Other Writings* by Jaime de Angulo (Counterpoint, 2009) and *The Alchemist's Mind: a book of narrative prose by poets* (Reality Street, 2012). *Spiritual Letters* (Series 1-5) appeared from Chax Press in 2011, and a double CD recording of David Miller reading this same work came out from LARYNX in 2012. He is also a musician and a member of the Frog Peak Music collective. His *Collected Poems, Reassembling Still*, was published by Shearsman Books in 2014.

Rick Moody is the author of five novels, three collections of stories, a memoir, and volume of essays on music. His forthcoming novel (from Little, Brown and Company) is entitled *Hotels of North America.*

A former student of the École Normale Supérieure (Lyon), **Françoise Palleau-Papin** is Professor of American Literature at the University of Paris 13-Sorbonne Paris Cité, where she co-directs the research center Pléiade (EA 7338). After completing a PhD dissertation on Willa Cather, she has published a critical monograph (*This Is Not a Tragedy : the Works of David Markson*, Dalkey Archive, 2011), and edited two others (on Patricia Eakins, and on William T. Vollmann). She recently co-edited *An Introduction to Anglophone Theatre* (Presses Universitaires de Rennes, 2015), and has written numerous articles on contemporary American authors, including John Edgar Wideman, Carole Maso, Ben Fountain, and William T. Vollmann.

Jennifer Pap teaches French literature, culture, and language at the University of Denver. Her published articles and works-in-progress concern the dialogue and interart collaborations between poets and painters such as Apollinaire and Picasso or René Char and Georges Braque. For several years, she and Julie Carr have worked together on translations of French poetry by Guillaume Apollinaire and Leslie Kaplan. Selections of their translation of Apollinaire's *Alcools* have appeared in the the *Kenyon Review* and other journals, and sections of Kaplan's *L'Excès-l'usine* have come out in chapbook form with Commune Editions.

Meredith Quartermain's most recent book is *Rupert's Land: a novel* about aboriginal/settler relations in 30s dustbowl Alberta. *Recipes from the Red Planet* was a finalist for a BC Book Award, and *Vancouver Walking*, won a BC Book Award for poetry. *I, Bartleby*, a collection of stories and essays on writing, will be published in April 2015 by Talonbooks.

Peter Quartermain lives in Vancouver, BC. Earlier chapters of *Growing Dumb*, his memoir of childhood during the Second World War, appeared in earlier issues of *GHR*, along with sundry essays and book reviews. He retired in 1999 after teaching for many years at the University of British Columbia. His most recent publications are *Stubborn Poetries: Poetic Facticity and the Avant-Garde* (U of Alabama Press), and his edition, in two volumes, of *The Collected Poems and Plays of Robert Duncan* (U of California Press).

Marthe Reed is the author of five books: *Nights Reading* (Lavender Ink), *Pleth, a collaboration* with j hastain (Unlikely Books), *(em)bodied bliss* (Moria Books), *Gaze* (Black Radish Books) and *Tender Box, A Wunderkammer* (Lavender Ink). She has published chapbooks as part of the Dusie Kollektiv, as well as with above/ground press and Shirt Pocket Press. She is Co-Publisher of Black Radish and Publisher of Nous-zōt chapbooks.

Jerome Rothenberg is an internationally celebrated poet and performer with over ninety books of poetry and twelve assemblages of traditional and avant-garde poetry such as *Technicians of the Sacred and Poems for the Millennium, volumes 1-3*. Recent books of poems include *Concealments & Caprichos, A Cruel Nirvana, A Poem of Miracles,* and *Retrievals: Uncollected & New Poems 1955-2010.* His most recent big books are *Eye of Witness: A Jerome Rothenberg Reader* and *Barbaric Vast & Wild* (Poems for the Millennium, volume 5), both published by Black Widow Press. A new book of poems, *A Field on Mars: Poems 2000-2015,* is scheduled for publication by Jusqu'à (To) Publishers, Presses Universitaires de Rouen et du Havre, in joint English and French editions.

Lou Rowan neglected graduate school to participate in the independent presses, little magazines and readings flourishing in New York's Lower East Side during the late 60s. He earned his living as a teacher, and then an institutional investor – the latter taking him to the Northwest United States, where he works on his fictions, edits *GHR,* and does freelance projects. Previous books: *Your Pages are not Numbered* (New Yorker Bookshop pubs), *My Last Days* (Chiasmus), *Sweet Potatoes* (ahadada).

Susan M. Schultz is author, most recently, of three books from Singing Horse Press: *Dementia Blog* (2008), *Memory Cards: 2010-2011 Series* (2011), and *"She's Welcome to Her Disease": Dementia Blog, Volume 2* (2013). She wrote *A Poetics of Impasse in Modern and Contemporary American Poetry* (Alabama, 2004) and runs Tinfish Press out of her home in Kāne'ohe, Hawai'i, where she also blogs at tinfishditor. blogspot.com. She is a lifelong fan of the St. Louis Cardinals baseball team. These poems were included in a Vagabond Press (Australia) booklet called *Memory Cards: Dogen Series* (2004).

Mark Scroggins lives in south Florida. His books of poetry are *Anarchy* (Spuyten Duyvil, 2003), *Torture Garden: Naked City Pastorelles* (Cultural Society, 2011), and *Red Arcadia* (Shearsman, 2012). His nonfiction books are *Louis Zukofsky and the Poetry of Knowledge* (University of Alabama Press, 1998), *The Poem of a Life: A Biography of Louis Zukofsky* (Shoemaker & Hoard, 2007), and the forthcoming essay collection *Intricate Thicket: Reading Late Modernist Poetries.* He is currently writing a monograph on the British fantasist Michael Moorcock and playing electric bass in a power trio called Drööd, who have one more umlaut than Motörhead.

Maurice Scully was born in Dublin in 1952. *Several Dances,* his twelfth book of poetry, appeared from Shearsman Books, UK, in Nov 2014. In the 1980s he travelled a good deal with his young family & spent some time with the American poet Robert Lax on Patmos. Now he divides his time between Ireland and Spain.

Martha Nell Smith is Distinguished Scholar-Teacher, Professor of English, and Founding Director of the Maryland Institute for Technology in the Humanities (MITH http://www.mith.umd.edu) at the University of Maryland. Her print publications include five singly and coauthored books—*Emily Dickinson, A User's Guide* (2015); *Companion to Emily Dickinson* (Jan 2008); *Open Me Carefully: Emily Dickinson's Intimate Letters to Susan Dickinson* (1998; Choice); *Comic Power in Emily Dickinson* (1993; Choice); *Rowing in Eden: Rereading Emily Dickinson* (1992; Hans Rosenhaupt First Book Award Honorable Mention, Woodrow Wilson National Fellowship Foundation)—and scores of articles and essays in journals and collections.

Smith is also Coordinator and Executive Editor of the Dickinson Electronic Archives projects at the Institute for Advanced Technology in the Humanities (IATH) at the University of Virginia (http://emilydickinson.org). Smith co-edited *Emily Dickinson's Correspondence: A Born-Digital Textual Inquiry* (2008; http://rotunda.upress.virginia.edu/edc) published by Rotunda New Digital Scholarship, University of Virginia Press.

Philip Terry is currently Director of the Centre for Creative Writing at the University of Essex. Among his books are the lipogrammatic novel *The Book of Bachelors,* the edited story collection *Ovid Metamorphosed,* a translation of Raymond Queneau's last book of poems *Elementary Morality,* and the poetry volumes *Oulipoems, Oulipoems 2, Shakespeare's Sonnets,* and *Advanced Immorality.* His novel tapestry was shortlisted for the 2013 Goldsmith's Prize. *Dante's Inferno,* which relocates Dante's action to current day Essex , was published in 2014, and was a Poetry Book of the Year in the Independent.

Norman Weinstein is the author of six books of poetry, a book on Gertrude Stein's writing, and a book of jazz history written from an Afrocentric perspective. He often writes about architecture and design. He teaches Canadian Studies at Boise State University and English as a Second Language to high-tech engineers from Europe and Asia.

SPECIAL ISSUES

/// ELLIOTT CARTER /// A. R. AMMONS /// VERONICA FORREST-THOMSON: UNPUB-LISHED ESSAYS /// NEW ITALIAN WRIT-ING///

CHICAGO REVIEW

Out in 2015 from REALITY STREET

OUT OF EVERYWHERE 2
Edited by Emily Critchley
In 1996 Reality Street published Maggie O'Sullivan's anthology of innovative writing by women, *Out of Everywhere*. Nearly 20 years later, here is the sequel...

Peter Hughes:
QUITE FRANKLY
After Petrarch's Sonnets
Versions of all 317 of Petrarch's sonnets, often departing from the originals in radical and startling ways.

Lou Rowan:
ALPHABET OF LOVE
SERIAL
All you need to know about relationships, from A-Z, in 20 stories, by the editor of *Golden Handcuffs Review*.

Previously ... Reality Street has published books by Allen Fisher, Barbara Guest, Fanny Howe, David Miller, Maggie O'Sullivan, Denise Riley, Lisa Robertson and these recent selected highlights:

Bill Griffiths: COLLECTED POEMS & SEQUENCES (1981-91) and **COLLECTED EARLIER POEMS(1966-80)**
We're publishing all of this late, great British poet's work. These are the first two volumes.

Ken Edwards:
DOWN WITH BEAUTY
Linked dialogues, dramatic monologues and short fictions exploring exile, war, paranoia, music and nothingness. Includes *Nostalgia for Unknown Cities*, previously published separately.

Andrea Brady:
CUT FROM THE RUSHES
Philadelphia-born Andrea Brady is one of the most significant poets writing in Britain today. This is her fifth book and her first for Reality Street.

Philip Terry: TAPESTRY
Combining magic realism and Oulipian techniques, this re-telling of the 1066 story, inspired by marginal images in the Bayeux Tapestry, was shortlisted for the inaugural Goldsmith's Prize for innovative fiction.

Richard Makin:
DWELLING
Serialised monthly online (in the best Dickens tradition) over 2006-09, this massive work of "non-generic prose" (novel or art installation?) finally reaches print.

Paul Griffiths:
LET ME TELL YOU
A novel by this noted musicologist narrated entirely in the 500-word vocabulary Ophelia is allocated in *Hamlet*. "A beautiful and enthralling work" (Harry Mathews)

You can order all books from our website or from your favourite online or offline retailer. Please visit for up to date news and to go on the mailing list.

www.realitystreet.co.uk

CPSIA information can be obtained at www.ICGtesting.com
Printed in the USA
BVOW06s0601230316

441396BV00006B/31/P